BLOOMSBURY TEACHER GUIDE

MACBETH

Amy Smith
and
Conor Hanratty

BLOOMSBURY EDUCATION
LONDON OXFORD NEW YORK NEW DELHI SYDNEY

BLOOMSBURY EDUCATION
Bloomsbury Publishing Plc
50 Bedford Square, London WC1B 3DP, UK
Bloomsbury Publishing Ireland Limited
29 Earlsfort Terrace, Dublin 2, D02 AY28, Ireland

BLOOMSBURY, BLOOMSBURY EDUCATION and the Diana logo are trademarks of Bloomsbury Publishing Plc

First published in Great Britain in 2026 by Bloomsbury Publishing Plc

This edition published in Great Britain in 2026 by Bloomsbury Publishing Plc

A catalogue record for this book is available from the British Library

ISBN: PB: 978-1-80199-855-0; ePub: 978-1-80199-853-6

2 4 6 8 10 9 7 5 3 1 (paperback)

Cover design by James Fraser
Typeset by Lumina Datamatics Ltd

Printed and bound in Great Britain by TJ Books, Padstow, Cornwall

MIX
Paper | Supporting responsible forestry
FSC® C013056
FSC www.fsc.org

To find out more about our authors and books visit www.bloomsbury.com and sign up for our newsletters

For product safety related questions contact productsafety@bloomsbury.com

CONTENTS

CONTENTS

ACKNOWLEDGEMENTS

Amy

To mum, dad, Tim and all the passionate, inspirational teachers in my life.

Conor

My sincere thanks to the brilliant teachers, actors and directors who've shaped my thinking – and to the podcast listeners who inspired this book. This is dedicated to my brother, who remains my favourite English teacher of all.

FOREWORD

Whenever there is a conversation about curriculum reform there are some voices calling for an end to the compulsory study of Shakespeare at GCSE. Why study *Macbeth*? A centuries old text written in arcane language, with overly dramatic characters, excessive gore, and slightly dubious supernatural scenes which stretch the limit of disbelief. What kind of teenager could relate to that? Some people, apparently, don't appreciate the immeasurable potential of young people, nor the enduring power of literature which continues to speak as clearly today as it ever did.

With every passing year that I teach *Macbeth*, my students find new glimmers of truth. Macbeth says, 'the eye wink at the hand, yet let that be / Which the eye fears, when it is done, to see.' He is contemplating the murder of Duncan; he imagines that his eyes might blind themselves to the actions of his hands. One young man in my Y11 class said, "He's trying to break apart... like, tear his own body, Miss, right?". He attempted to articulate something profound: a man who is so tormented by his desire and his honour, that we start to see his physical and mental unravelling. His body parts, which should work together to achieve his will, are sundered from one other.

From the obscenity of Gloucester's blinding in *King Lear,* to the comedy of love blindness in *A Midsummer Night's Dream*, Shakespeare toys with appearances, power and people's ability to see the truth. In *Macbeth*, we are frequently told that blindness is what allows wickedness to flourish: 'Come, seeling night, scarf up the tender eye of pitiful day' (3.2). Macbeth seeks to disassociate his eyes from his hands so that his body might be used as an instrument for evil without conscience, a grotesque mutilation. Our students will remember: Macbeth beheads a man at the opening of the play, and is himself beheaded at the end. The metaphorical breaking of Macbeth's body is mirrored by his very real decapitation in that violent climax.

Putting aside the GCSE talking points, what stuck with this student was the simple feeling of being torn. It is the most human experience of all: what we want and what is right are often not the same thing. And this is why we still teach *Macbeth*. This play puts people in positions of intense pressure and shows us what they do. The characters and events are larger than life, but their experiences and behaviours ring true.

In this book, Amy and Conor have created an invaluable tool for teachers hoping to bring the humanity, truth and brilliance of *Macbeth* to their students.

Jennifer Webb

HOW TO USE THIS BOOK

This book is designed as a scene-by-scene teacher's guide and reference point when teaching Shakespeare's *Macbeth*. It can form the basis of an entire teaching module, or you can jump straight to a particular chapter for specific information. Our approach is designed to help you access the play at macro and micro levels as you introduce it to the next generation of Shakespeare fans.

Before delving into the detail of each scene, it is useful to provide students with an overview of the plot, either by reading a summary of the play (provided in our online resources) or watching a filmed adaptation. Selecting which adaptation to show your class can be a challenge, as there are so many possibilities. We recommend introducing students to *Macbeth* with the 2010 Rupert Goold production. The visual representation of the plot is clear and accessible for students who may not yet be comfortable with Shakespeare's language.

There are accompanying materials for each chapter, which you can download from **bloomsbury.pub/BTG-Macbeth**. These include a clear, printable copy of the play, as well as lesson resources which you can adapt to suit your learners' needs. Other resources available on this site will be flagged in this book by this icon: 🖱

This book is organised into thirty-nine chapters, offering a scene-by-scene guide to teaching *Macbeth*. Most have a dedicated chapter, but we split significant scenes across up to three chapters for more detailed exploration. As the play's pace quickens through shorter scenes in the final act, some of these require a less in-depth analysis. Each chapter follows a common framework, but some scenes require more (or less) of our analytical sections than others. Where a section is omitted, this reflects its limited relevance to that part of the play. Every chapter is clearly named with its scene number and an identifying quotation, and begins with an 'At a glance' introduction, summarising key information across the following features:

- **Plot and character development**: We summarise key events in the scene and comment on the character development of our protagonists, Macbeth and Lady Macbeth. We also introduce new characters as they enter the play.
- **Social and historical context**: Here we outline historical information that is relevant to students' understanding of the text. Students should fluently integrate context into their writing, and so we clearly explain its relevance to the analysis of characters, language or themes.

- **Vocabulary**: This section provides information about teaching Tier 2 and Tier 3 vocabulary to support students in articulating their analysis confidently, accurately and fluently. A more detailed explanation of our approach to teaching vocabulary is included below, and our online resources site contains a complete list of vocabulary and key terms.
- **Big question**: Each chapter contains a question focused on its key themes. We also provide a model answer for it, designed to spark discussion among students and stretch their conceptual understanding.
- **Themes**: Not every theme is at play in every scene of *Macbeth*. We include a list of key themes at work in each scene to support you in tracking these ideas as they recur and develop through the play. Most chapters will include a paragraph discussing these, but some will simply list the most obvious themes when no extended discussion seems necessary. **Appendix A** has a complete list of these.
- **Analysis**: Here, we explore key elements of language and staging, focusing on how Shakespeare uses recurring imagery and motifs to create and consolidate meaning (also see **Appendix B**). We also cover key elements of Shakespeare's text: verse, metre and prose.
- **Key quotation**: We choose a key quotation and provide a short summary of its meaning and language. All quotations are from the Arden Shakespeare Third Series edition of *Macbeth*, edited by Sandra Clark and Pamela Mason. A full list of key quotations is available to download from our online resources.
- **Handle with care**: *Macbeth* is full of murder and horror, and some scenes are more troubling than others. This section accompanies scenes of a particularly sensitive nature.

Reading the scene

At the heart of our approach is a belief that *Macbeth* should be heard aloud. We strongly encourage you to get the play off the page and into your students' ears. The play's excitement is woven into the rhythms of the verse, the ebb and flow of dialogue, the sudden shifts in energy and the juxtaposition of its scenes. When students hear these elements performed, even in a simple classroom reading, they access layers of meaning that silent study alone cannot reveal. This is why this 'Reading the scene' section is at the core of every chapter, following the introduction of key vocabulary. As it is such a constant, practical element of our approach, we have not listed it separately in the 'At a glance' overview for each chapter. Throughout this guide, these sections suggest practical ways to bring the play alive. We also include a basic primer to help teach iambic pentameter (see pages 28 and 29), the heartbeat of Shakespeare's language.

We will often encourage you, as the teacher, to read the most challenging part in a given scene. This will allow you to prevent the reading from dragging, as one of the most remarkable features of *Macbeth* is the fast pace with which the tragic hero spirals towards his downfall. We also stress the importance of re-reading: the first time around, students may be focused on the strangeness of words or the pronunciation of specific vocabulary. Repeated reading can improve familiarity and understanding of the text.

Vocabulary

In order to articulate their ideas, students need a secure command of a range of vocabulary: key ideas, terms and concepts. To support you in teaching this vocabulary, most chapters include a completed Frayer Model, explored further below. On some occasions we suggest an alternative graphic organiser (for example, Chapter 12 includes a synonyms activity). These alternative suggestions will give variety to your teaching, as well as providing additional scaffolding to allow students to explore the nuances of particular terms. All graphic organisers are included as an online resource.

As the text progresses and scenes become briefer, there are occasions where we do not suggest teaching new vocabulary, as instead we focus on the scene's contribution to the plot.

Frayer Models were designed by Dorothy Frayer at the University of Wisconsin. They generally include four standard headings: definition, characteristics or morphology, examples and non-examples. We recommend that you provide students with a blank copy of the Frayer Model and complete it in discussion with your class. As students become more confident, they can complete them independently or in groups.

The following example (taken from Chapter 2) introduces the concept of the tragic hero:

- Discuss what students understand by the word 'hero'. Shape this into the first part of the definition: 'a noble character of high rank'. This is an excellent opportunity for a think-pair-share or mini-whiteboard task.
- Discuss what students understand by the word 'tragic'. As the outcome of the discussion, add the remainder of the definition.
- Use the definition to create a list of characteristics.

Work with students to generate a list of examples and non-examples (these are instances that do not match the definition; identifying these allows students to avoid misconceptions). Use texts included in your curriculum to promote schema building.

Example 1: Tragic Hero

Definition:	**Characteristics:**
A noble character of high rank with a fatal flaw (*hamartia*) which leads directly to the character's downfall. *Hamartia* is a concept from ancient Greek drama. The word means to go wrong, or miss the mark.	• Begins the story as a noble, admirable or high-ranking character. • Fatal flaw: a character weakness (e.g. intense ambition, jealousy). This reflects the human condition. • Faces a downfall due to their choices. • Evokes our sympathy for their heroism in the face of this.
Examples (characters from Shakespeare's tragedies):	**Non-examples (characters from *Macbeth*):**
Macbeth Othello Romeo	Duncan The Witches Lady Macbeth

There are many variations on Frayer Models and the four standard sub-headings will not always be appropriate for the words and concepts we discuss. We therefore, throughout this book, suggest a range of variations on the standard methodology. Sometimes, exploring the morphology or etymology of words can be a powerful way of providing students with the skills and knowledge to unlock the meanings of words independently.

In the example below, the first step to writing a definition could be to deconstruct the word. Ask students what they recognise in the word 'demonology' and they will probably respond by talking about demons. The suffix -ology means 'the study of': so, you can link this to students' other subjects (biology, psychology, etc.) leading students to understand that demon-ology means the study of demons.

Example 2: Demonology

Definition:	**Morphology:**
The study of demons and evil spirits, and beliefs about them.	Root word: demon = spirit in Greek e.g. pandemonium, demonic Suffix: -ology = study in Greek e.g. Biology
Examples:	**Non-examples:**
King James VI and I's *Daemonologie* (1597): this text supported the belief in witches and the existence of demons.	Astrology: the study of how celestial objects (stars, planets, moons) may influence human affairs. Psychology: the study of the mind and behavior; focuses on human mental processes, not external evil entities.

As another variation you can incorporate images. This would particularly support students with SEND and/or multilingual students. These students also benefit from predictable routines for learning new vocabulary: routines reduce extraneous cognitive load, allowing students to focus on the information you want them to understand and remember.

Pause points

At relevant intervals, we include 'pause points' to suggest various classroom activities to aid lesson planning:

- **Retrieval**: Low-stakes quizzes or tasks to support encoding information.
- **Oracy**: Discussion tasks to improve verbal skills.
- **Writing**: Discussion tasks to improve written skills.
- **S-T-R-E-T-C-H**: Challenges for higher-achieving students. Each S-T-R-E-T-C-H point includes a model summary for your use or to share with students following their discussion.
- **Consolidation**: End-of-chapter tasks to solidify understanding.

Pause points contain direct questions in italics, as well as prompts and suggestions for students. We have also included model answers for these pause points, which you can use to supplement your own subject knowledge or to share with students. These are all included in the online resources.

Retrieval

We include a range of knowledge retrieval activities to assess students' retention of key information. These low-stakes activities require students to retrieve information from their long-term memories, thus strengthening the process of encoding. An excellent summary of research around memory, encoding and retrieval practice is provided by the Education Endowment Foundation (EEF) if you search for 'Cognitive science approaches in the classroom' on their site. It is crucial that students engage in regular retrieval practice *for all topics*, but it is even more critical when they are studying a play such as *Macbeth*. Shakespeare's layering of motifs across the text means that a strong knowledge base will encourage a richer understanding of the play.

Oracy

Our teaching strategy has a major focus on oracy. Students are far better equipped to write about something when they have been encouraged to talk about it, and so our activities are specifically designed to foster verbal communication, debate and discussion. We recommend books on oracy in the **Further reading** section at the end of the book.

Our oracy tasks are designed for groups of three, but can be adapted for pairs or larger groups. The idea of triplets aligns nicely with references to the number three in the play, but it is not only a nod to the Witches' coven. A triplet discussion can allow for the allocation of roles, as follows:

- Provide the students with a question about the text:
    - Student A responds to the question.
    - Student B provides evidence or examples from the text.
    - Student C summarises the discussion.

Some of our oracy tasks stretch students further by asking them to argue for or against an opinion:

- Provide the students with a controversial statement:
    - Student A puts forward an argument to agree with the statement.
    - Student B puts forward a counter-argument.
    - Student C summarises the discussion and finds a compromise.

Where you have multilingual learners in your class, Student C could initially be the note-taker, recording the discussion. They could then read the notes back to the group to check the accuracy of their summary.

It can be useful to provide students with sentence starters (marked in bold) for this type of structured oracy activity. For example:

'Shakespeare presents Lady Macbeth as an unquestionably powerful character'. How far do you agree?

- Student A: agrees with the statement **(I agree with the statement because... and... Evidence of this is... and... This evidence supports my opinion because...)**
- Student B: challenges the statement **(Actually, I think that she may lack power because... and... My evidence for this is... and... This shows us that...)**
- Student C: summarises the discussion **(So, we have agreed that while... on the other hand... On balance, we believe that Lady Macbeth is...)**

When allocating roles, consider the following:

- Put multilingual learners in groups with fluent speakers so that they hear accurate spoken English.
- You may wish to allocate dominant and confident speakers a summarising role (C), and challenge quieter students to take on roles A or B.
- Stretch higher achieving students by asking them to challenge statements or provide additional evidence (B).

- Change the role allocation in different lessons so that all students have the opportunity to develop a range of skills.

Another oracy activity we often use is 'read-reduce-rehearse-remember'. This is an interactive way to support students in using academic structures and vocabulary in their talk, and to practice extended and nuanced explanations of key quotations and ideas. For example:

Read this model analysis of Duncan's line 'O valiant cousin'.

Shakespeare communicates Duncan's admiration for Macbeth, who is initially presented as a patriotic warrior serving king and country. Shakespeare uses the adjective 'valiant' to underscore Duncan's celebration of Macbeth's dauntless courage, whilst the word 'cousin' tells the audience that they are relations. In this moment, Shakespeare lays the foundations of what is to come. Later in the play, Lady Macbeth insults her husband's masculinity, questioning the courage he has demonstrated so clearly in the battle against the invading forces. Shakespeare shows that it is this attack on his identity which finally propels Macbeth to the act of regicide.

Ask students to reduce the paragraph to around ten words or phrases.

E.g. admiration, patriotic, courage, relations, foundations, masculinity, questioning, identity, regicide

Then ask students to work in their triplets. They take turns to cover the original paragraph and use their word list to prompt a verbal explanation of the quotation. The remaining two students can use the paragraph to help their peer.

Signal for attention and randomly sample the class, asking students to use their word lists to give their explanations to the group. Provide feedback and address any misconceptions.

Finally, ask students to use their word lists to write the explanations. By this time, they have rehearsed the analysis several times and started to commit it to memory.

Writing

Throughout the text, we provide guidance for scaffolding students to write exploratory responses. One such suggestion is to teach students to balance language which is both tentative (**It could be argued**...) and assertive (**It is irrefutable that**...).

In addition to writing points, each oracy point could be concluded with students consolidating their learning by writing their ideas in the form of a paragraph.

S-T-R-E-T-C-H

As *Macbeth* is taught to students of all abilities, we have signposted ideas that will stretch and deepen students' conceptual understanding and analysis of Shakespeare's language.

Consolidation

Key chapters end with consolidation points that are designed to cement students' comprehension. These require students to process key knowledge, articulate concepts and make connections.

Upon the stage

This section, its title borrowed from Macbeth's Act V soliloquy, concludes each chapter with a discussion of noteworthy interpretations of *Macbeth* on stage and screen, occasionally posing thought-provoking questions to inspire further conversation.

Our chapters begin with an 'At a glance' overview and end with this snapshot of the play in performance, encouraging you to engage ever more thoroughly with the text. As our invitation to you to extend analysis beyond the page and into performance, this section is intentionally positioned outside the 'At a glance' framework. These insights insist on the play's theatricality and excitement. This is not a performance history, but a survey of interesting and provocative interpretations of each scene, chosen to encourage your students to investigate how *Macbeth* can work in performance. Where a single production is discussed in depth, it is because it offers a uniquely illuminating lens on the scene, whether through radical casting, directorial concept or historical significance. Watching the play in performance reveals the interpretive choices that keep it relevant, stimulating and thrilling. **Appendix C** gives a comprehensive list of the productions described.

INTRODUCTION

To encounter *Macbeth* is to step into a storm. From its first image – a burst of thunder and lightning heralding three mysterious figures – the play establishes a world of elemental forces and moral turbulence. It is Shakespeare's most concentrated and ferocious tragedy, a headlong rush from heroic heights to monstrous depths that has captivated and unsettled audiences for centuries. Its enduring power works not as a simple moral fable, but a shocking, intimate exploration of the corrupting potential of unchecked ambition, the fragility of the human psyche and the horrifying speed at which order can unravel into chaos. *Macbeth* is a profound inquiry into the nature of evil. Is it an external force that seduces us, or a potential that lies latent in the human heart?

William Shakespeare (1564–1616) was the defining figure of the English Renaissance, whose profound understanding of human psychology and mastery of language remain unparalleled. He wrote *Macbeth* around 1606, at the height of his creative powers, in an England fraught with political anxiety. The memory of the Gunpowder Plot of 1605 was still raw; that audacious attempt to obliterate King James I and his parliament had exposed the nation's vulnerability to treason and hidden conspiracy. Key episodes of insurrection – from Cawdor's treason to the Macbeths' regicidal plot – would have felt chillingly immediate to its first audiences, a stark warning of the consequences of political ambition unleashed. The play holds a dark mirror to the very real terrors of the state, exploring what happens when the bonds of loyalty and honour are severed.

Crucially, Shakespeare crafted the play under the direct patronage of a king deeply fascinated by the occult. James I was not merely a passive believer in witchcraft; his treatise, *Daemonologie* (1597), provided a philosophical and legal framework for the belief in witches as malevolent agents capable of prophecy, controlling the weather and consorting with demons. By opening his play with the Weird Sisters, Shakespeare played directly to his sovereign's obsessions, guaranteeing a riveted audience. The Witches are not mere theatrical cameos; they are woven from the fabric of contemporary belief, representing a genuine suspicion of supernatural influence in the world. They embody the period's anxiety about forces that could subvert both nature and the Divine Right of Kings, the belief that a monarch is God's anointed deputy on Earth; a doctrine James himself fiercely advocated.

This context of regicide and the supernatural is the essential backdrop against which *Macbeth* unfolds. The play relentlessly interrogates the Divine Right of Kings. To kill a king, therefore, was not merely a political crime but a violation of the natural order. When Macbeth murders Duncan, the world itself sickens: day becomes night, falcons are killed by owls and Duncan's own horses eat each other. The political disorder of Scotland under the usurper is mirrored by a rebellion in the natural world, illustrating the profound Renaissance belief in an interconnected Great Chain of Being, where an offence at one level could resonate through all others.

At the heart of this cosmic drama is one of literature's most compelling psychological studies. Shakespeare initially presents Macbeth as the epitome of martial virtue: 'brave Macbeth' whose sword 'smoked with bloody execution' in loyal defence of his king. The play dramatises the rapid erosion of this nobility. The engine of Macbeth's downfall is his own unchecked ambition, which, once ignited by prophetic temptation, proves too potent to control. Shakespeare masterfully charts the interior landscape of a guilty conscience; a mind 'full of scorpions.' Macbeth's hallucinations, from the air-drawn dagger to the ghost of Banquo, are not just theatrical stunts; they are the manifestations of a psyche that is becoming its own prison and torturer.

His partner in this descent, Lady Macbeth, is arguably an even more radical creation. In a society that defined women by their compassion and nurture, Shakespeare's staging of her appeal to spirits to 'unsex me here' and fill her with 'direst cruelty' is a shocking command. She is initially portrayed as possessing a remarkable clarity and resolve, embodying a ruthless ambition unburdened by her husband's moral introspection. But Shakespeare does not let her remain a simple monster. Her eventual unravelling (her sleepwalking and compulsive handwashing) represents one of the most poignant depictions of mental collapse in English literature. It reveals that the guilt she so confidently dismissed has been festering within her all along, proving a testament to the inescapable weight of conscience.

Throughout this descent, a single, pervasive theme dominates: appearance vs reality. From the Witches' foundational paradox, 'Fair is foul, and foul is fair,' to Lady Macbeth's command to 'look like the innocent flower, but be the serpent under't,' Shakespeare constructs a world where nothing is as it seems. The loyal subject is a regicide in waiting, the welcoming hostess a murderous conspirator and the crowned king a source of national blight. This relentless undermining of surface truth forces both the characters and the audience to question every face, every prophecy and every motive, pulling us into the same disorienting mist of doubt that envelops Macbeth himself.

Ultimately, *Macbeth* endures because the questions Shakespeare poses are timeless. Shakespeare interrogates the conflict between fate and free will: are Macbeth's choices his own, or is he merely playing out a destiny spun out by 'the instruments of darkness'? The play's examination of the nature of evil suggests it is not a monstrous external force, but a human potential unlocked by ambition and moral compromise. *Macbeth* is a play that holds a shadowed mirror up to humanity, reflecting our own potential for that darkness.

CHAPTER 1
FAIR IS FOUL, AND FOUL IS FAIR
ACT ONE SCENE ONE

At a glance

- **Plot and character development:** Three Witches gather and plan to meet Macbeth.
- **Social and historical context:**
  - King James and the supernatural
  - Male performers
- **Vocabulary:** Malevolent
- **Big question:** Why does Shakespeare start the play with the Witches, rather than Macbeth?
- **Themes:**
  - Conflict
  - Fate vs free will
  - Appearance vs reality
- **Analysis:**
  - Text: trochaic tetrameter
  - Image: threes
  - Language: double-talk
- **Key quotation:** 'Fair is foul, and foul is fair'

Plot and character development

This first scene is one of the most famous in all of Shakespeare: the image of three witches gathering on stage is enduringly popular and mysterious. The entrance of these 'Weird Sisters' is announced by the sound of 'thunder and lightning', immediately suggesting their ability to raise storms.

The second Witch explains that a chaotic battle – a 'hurly-burly' – is ongoing. We learn later that this conflict is due to the invasion of Norwegian forces, aided by the treacherous Macdonwald.

The three Weird Sisters plan to see each other later in the same day, once the battle is over, when they will meet with Macbeth. From the very beginning of the story, the tragic hero is associated with the powers of darkness.

The Witches are then summoned by their familiars (Greymalkin and Paddock), and exit as mysteriously as they appeared.

Social and historical context

King James and the supernatural

Shakespeare could assume that his audience knew a lot about witches, because they were a real source of fear in Britain at the time. King James I was particularly fascinated and scared by them, documenting his views in his 1597 book *Daemonologie*. The book contains many details that Shakespeare includes in *Macbeth*: witches were reputed to have the power of prophecy, to be able to control the weather, to appear and disappear at random and to fly.

By selecting these supernatural figures to begin his play, Shakespeare tapped into major concerns of the period, guaranteeing that his royal patron would be interested. James was already a fan of Shakespeare's company: he became their patron within ten days of becoming king, renaming them The King's Men.

Male performers

In Shakespeare's theatre, all roles were played by male performers. Female characters were most often played by teenage boys whose voices had not yet broken. In *Macbeth*, it is likely that the Witches were played by adult actors rather than boy players, allowing them to appear more mysterious and alarming.

PAUSE POINT

S-T-R-E-T-C-H

Shakespeare draws on contemporary anxieties about the supernatural in order to explore the question of evil.

Triplet discussion: Does evil originate from forces external to humanity (like the devil), or is it part of the human condition?

- Student A: Argue that evil is a result of external forces.
- Student B: Argue that evil is part of the human condition.
- Student C: Summarise the discussion.

Model answer:

Shakespeare's exploration of the nature of evil allows the play to resonate down the ages. As we look at the history of the twentieth century, or even at the news today, we find evidence of immoral behaviour in human society. In *Macbeth*, Shakespeare may present the Witches as a malevolent force, but the idea of killing comes from Macbeth himself. Perhaps Lady Macbeth's murderous thoughts are prompted by Macbeth's letter in Act One Scene Five, but her desire to be filled with 'direst cruelty' is her own. Even the loyal and virtuous Banquo has 'cursed thoughts' when he sleeps. Shakespeare suggests that although the Witches catalyse these treacherous thoughts and actions, evil itself is an inextricable part of the human condition.

Vocabulary | Malevolent

Teaching students to use the word malevolent can help them to articulate many ideas about the play – from Shakespeare's evocation of the Witches' malevolence, to his presentation of Lady Macbeth's appeal to the 'spirits' to fill her with malevolent 'cruelty'.

Definition:	**Morphology:**
An evil desire to cause harm to others.	Prefix: mal = bad e.g. malicious, malignant, malediction Root word: vol = wishing e.g. benevolent, volition

Examples:	**Non-examples:**
Dr Jekyll and Mr Hyde (1886): Stevenson presents Hyde as malevolent when he murders Sir Danvers Carew. *Othello* (1603): Shakespeare evokes Iago's malevolence when he poisons Othello's marriage.	*Of Mice and Men* (1937): Steinbeck does not present George's murder of Lennie as malevolent, because he does this out of care for his friend. *A Christmas Carol* (1843): By the end of the novella, Dickens presents Scrooge as a benevolent and caring man.

Reading the scene

- Introduce the full scene. You could read it aloud line by line, or show a film version from our list in Appendix C.
- Do a 'call and response' choral reading. You say a line and the students repeat it back to you. Ask students what they noticed about the feel of the rhythm and the dramatic power of chanting in unison.
- Next, divide the class into three large groups, each group playing one of the Witches.
- Read the scene again. Direct each group's reading.
- Read the scene a few times, varying speed, pitch and tone.

Big question

Why does Shakespeare start the play with the Witches, rather than Macbeth?

It is perhaps surprising that our title character does not appear in the first scene. Instead, the audience is confronted with three strange figures who plan to meet with him.

By starting the play with these Witches, Shakespeare highlights their malevolent influence over Macbeth's story. They set the play's tone and atmosphere; this is a world in which supernatural events and visions may appear. The Witches, and their mysterious connection to the weather and animals, are powerfully established in this short scene. Witchcraft operates as a motif, a powerful symbol of the play's central conflict: the violation of the natural order. Witchcraft functions as a vehicle to explore the themes of ambition, of fate vs free will and of appearance vs reality. Witchcraft, in short, is a dramatic catalyst and a gateway to the major themes of the play.

Beginning with the Witches also allows Shakespeare to build up our preconceptions of the tragic hero. The Witches pronounce his name as if he is a well-known military hero associated with violence and war. This impression will be reinforced in the next scene, where we hear a captain's report of Macbeth's valiant deeds in battle. By elevating Macbeth's reputation, Shakespeare emphasises the height from which he will fall.

Themes

Conflict

In this short scene, Shakespeare establishes several conflicts. We learn that this story is set in a war-torn landscape, where armies vie for political power. This battle for ascendency is reflected in the stormy weather, implying conflict within the natural world. Shakespeare also sets up a tension between the Witches and Macbeth. They say that they will 'meet with' the tragic hero, using a word that also means 'attack' or 'ambush'.

Fate vs free will

Shakespeare's presentation of the three Witches evokes the three Fates – personifications of destiny in Greek mythology. The three Fates controlled the lives of every individual, whose fate was represented by thread running from a spindle. One spun the thread, one measured it out and one cut it: thus, the Fates were responsible for the entire lifespan of every person. Shakespeare is posing a question that is fundamental to the play: are our actions determined by fate, or do humans have the free will to act autonomously?

Appearance vs reality

The paradoxical declaration 'Fair is foul, and foul is fair' establishes a clash between appearance and reality as one of the play's most central themes. This inversion of moral and visual logic introduces a world of deceptive surfaces, where apparent loyalty masks real treachery, and prophecy conceals manipulation. The tension between appearance and reality will feature throughout the play – and this book.

Analysis

Text: trochaic tetrameter

The Witches speak in a language and a rhythm that is very rare in Shakespeare, a kind of rolling, rhyming style that sounds like they are casting spells. Their language often rhymes, but it is definitely not blank verse. This metre is called trochaic tetrameter, with four stressed syllables per line.

When shall we three meet again
In thunder, lightning or in rain?

Fair is foul and foul is fair:
Hover through the fog and filthy air.

Shakespeare often manipulates the rhythm of – and even the number of syllables – in a line. The examples above, which begin and end the scene, all have four stressed beats, but have between seven and nine syllables. Shakespeare most often uses this particular rhythm to indicate a supernatural element (see also the Fairies in *A Midsummer Night's Dream* and Ariel in *The Tempest*). This striking rhythm immediately makes the Witches very different from the other characters in *Macbeth*.

Image: threes

Three was considered a very powerful, magical number, and Shakespeare manipulates it throughout the play. The Witches' rhymes, incantations and even the visions they present will all come in threes. (Think of other famous groups of three women and the influence they have!)

Language: double talk

From this very first scene, we get a sense that the Witches play with language and truth. Their final couplet proclaims that 'fair is foul, and foul is fair' – this paradox introduces how they will communicate in the play. What appears good may not necessarily be worth trusting, and as Macbeth will say later, 'nothing is but what is not'. This trickery in language will recur frequently throughout the play. It will combine neatly with antithesis and equivocation, which we explore in Chapter 15.

Key quotation | 'Fair is foul, and foul is fair'

This line is the unsettling, paradoxical foundation upon which the entire play is built. It establishes a world where appearances are deceptive and moral order is inverted. This principle immediately implicates Macbeth (who will echo it in his very first line) and it governs the play's core events: a seemingly loyal hero commits regicide, a welcoming hostess plots murder and a crowned king brings chaos. This line is the essential dramatic mechanism that propels the plot and corrupts the protagonist's perception of reality. This theme of appearance vs reality is integral to the entire play, and this line sums it up.

PAUSE POINT

CONSOLIDATION

Read-reduce-rehearse-remember (see 'How to use this book' page XIII). See online resources for a video demo of this activity.

In this scene, Shakespeare conveys the Witches' power; they are a malevolent and mysterious force, who use their supernatural abilities to throw Macbeth into chaos. Shakespeare's choice to include the Witches is a nod to King James I, who wrote a book entitled *Daemonologie* and supported witch-hunting. Shakespeare presents the Witches as a catalyst of Macbeth's downfall as well as key players in the battle between good and evil, fate and free will.

Upon the stage

The opening image of the Witches is a directorial signature, setting the tone for the entire production:

- Orson Welles (1948) presented the Witches as actively malevolent forces, moulding a clay doll of Macbeth and crowning it.
- Trevor Nunn's intimate, studio production (first staged in 1976 and filmed for television in 1979) began by juxtaposing the ceremonial, masculine order of Duncan's court with the unsettling presence of the Witches, making disquieting noise as they communed. On a nearly bare stage, the sudden thunder and lightning came as shocking disruptions, making the supernatural feel immediate and psychologically threatening.
- Eve Best (2014) opened her production at Shakespeare's Globe with the full company on stage, drumming and moving to bagpipes. The Witches emerged from this 'hurly-burly,' suggesting that evil and disorder can erupt from the heart of society itself, especially in times of war.
- In a contemporary twist, Max Webster used binaural sound at the Donmar Warehouse (2023). Through headphones, the audience heard the Witches as disembodied, whispering voices all around them. By making them heard but never seen, the production activated the audience's own imagination and implicated them directly in the play's 'sound and fury'.

Consider these different stagings of the scene: are the Witches more disturbing if we only hear them, rather than seeing them at work?

CHAPTER 2
WHAT HE HATH LOST, NOBLE MACBETH HATH WON
ACT ONE SCENE TWO

At a glance

- **Plot and character development:** Duncan, Malcolm and attendants listen to reports from a wounded sergeant and then from the Thane of Ross. There have been two separate successes on the battlefield. Macbeth has prevailed and won victory for Duncan.
- **Social and historical context:** The Gunpowder Plot
- **Vocabulary:** Tragic hero
- **Big question:** Why does Shakespeare give us such a violent first impression of Macbeth?
- **Themes:**
  - Conflict
  - Violence and masculinity
  - Loyalty vs treason
- **Analysis:**
  - Staging: reports from the battlefield
  - Dramatic irony
  - Verse: rhyming couplets
- **Key quotation:** 'What he hath lost, noble Macbeth hath won'
- **Handle with care:** This scene has descriptions of particularly shocking violence.

PAUSE POINT

RETRIEVAL

Ask students to complete a blank copy of the Frayer Model for the word malevolent. This will allow you to assess students' memory of the previous lesson and address any gaps in knowledge or misconceptions.

Plot and character development

The scene introduces King Duncan among his men, as reports arrive from the battlefield. The news is good: victory for Scotland on all sides. An injured sergeant gives Duncan and his men a battle report, in which he describes Macbeth's violent victory over the traitor Macdonwald. Macbeth has ripped open Macdonwald's torso, before decapitating him and displaying his head as a warning of the dire consequences of betraying Scotland.

Ross, the play's messenger, brings news of a separate conflict. He explains that even though the Thane of Cawdor has betrayed Scotland, the king of Norway (Sweno) and his men have been defeated. The leader of this second Scottish force is not named (he is referred to as 'Bellona's bridegroom'), but it is likely that this is Macduff. Duncan orders the execution of the Thane of Cawdor.

Duncan is respected and protected by patriotic subjects. Shakespeare emphasises Duncan's goodness when he decides to reward his most valiant fighter, 'noble' Macbeth, with the now vacant title 'Thane of Cawdor'.

Social and historical context

The Gunpowder Plot

This war council introduces an anxiety which would have been much discussed by England's nobility in the Renaissance period: treason. King James I had recently survived the infamous Gunpowder Plot of November 1605. Its Catholic plotters were opposed to James' staunch Protestantism and the restrictions he placed on Catholic worship. The terrorists' plan was to obliterate the king and his government by blowing up the Houses of Parliament. Shakespeare evokes the brutal torture and public execution of the conspirators in the descriptions of the death of Macdonwald and the execution of the Thane of Cawdor.

PAUSE POINT

S-T-R-E-T-C-H

In Renaissance England, public executions were a visual spectacle designed to warn the watching crowds against betraying the crown.

Triplet discussion: How does Shakespeare use the opening of Macbeth *to warn the Renaissance audience against treason?*

- Student A: Respond to the question.
- Student B: Provide evidence and examples from the text.
- Student C: Summarise the discussion.

Model answer:

By announcing the deaths of not just one, but two, traitors at the start of the play, Shakespeare emphasises the consequences of treason: conspirators will be defeated and executed so that the legitimate monarch can prevail.

Vocabulary | Tragic hero

In crafting the character of Macbeth, Shakespeare creates a strong military leader whose ambition makes him vulnerable to seduction by the Witches. Challenge students to explain why the non-examples do not fit the definition.

Definition:	**Characteristics:**
A noble character of high rank with a fatal flaw (*hamartia*), which leads directly to the character's downfall. *Hamartia* is a concept from ancient Greek drama. The word means to go wrong, or miss the mark.	• Begins the story as noble, admirable, or with a high rank. • Has a fatal flaw (*hamartia*). For example, intense ambition or jealousy. This reflects the flawed nature of the human condition. • Makes a choice which leads to their downfall. • Evokes our sympathy as the character demonstrates heroism in the face of destruction.
Examples (characters from Shakespeare's tragedies):	**Non-examples (characters from *Macbeth*):**
Macbeth Othello Romeo	Duncan The Witches Lady Macbeth

PAUSE POINT

S-T-R-E-T-C-H

Triplet discussion: Shakespeare creates tragic heroes who are admirable, but also deeply flawed. This makes them more realistic. Why might this be important for the audience?

- Student A: Respond to the question.
- Student B: Provide a reason to support Student A's response.
- Student C: Summarise the discussion.

Model answer:

It is important for the audience to feel pathos for the tragic hero. Rather than dismissing Macbeth (as Malcolm does) as a 'butcher', we need to understand the psychological conflict that has led him to the point of murder.

Reading the scene

This fast-paced scene contains a lot of plot information, which can be confusing for students. Watch out for the common misconception that Macdonwald and the Thane of Cawdor are the same person.

Start by introducing students to the cast of characters:

On stage	Offstage
Duncan (king of Scotland)	Macbeth (the tragic hero)
Malcolm (Duncan's son)	Banquo (Macbeth's friend)
The Sergeant, wounded in battle	Macdonwald (a traitor)
The Thanes of Ross and Lennox (noblemen)	The Thane of Cawdor (another traitor)

Then signpost the key phrases to students before they read the scene. Students can work in pairs to match the key phrases to their meanings:

Phrase	Meaning
1. 'the merciless Macdonwald'	A. Macbeth decapitates Macdonwald, displaying the head as a warning against treachery.
2. 'brave Macbeth'	B. Macbeth and Banquo are compared to brave, powerful animals.
3. 'fixed his head upon our battlements'	C. Like Macdonwald, the Thane of Cawdor is a traitor.
4. 'eagles' and 'lions'	D. Macdonwald is a violent and ruthless traitor.

5. 'disloyal traitor / The Thane of Cawdor'	E. Duncan gives the title Thane of Cawdor to Macbeth.
6. 'What he hath lost, noble Macbeth hath won.'	F. Macbeth is respected for his courage in battle.

Answers: 1D, 2F, 3A, 4B, 5C, 6E

Shakespeare emphasises the speed of this scene by splitting many lines between characters. Consequently, it should be read with pace and energy.

- Divide the roles among the class: Take the role of the Sergeant yourself, and then switch to Ross. This will enable you to emphasise most of the phrases explored in the pre-reading task. (Use the full text included in our online resources, which is laid out clearly to help with this kind of reading.)
- Explain the importance of pace: Even as one person is finishing their line, the next person should start to speak to eliminate gaps in the dialogue.
- Read the extract once, then rehearse particular sections if necessary.
- Read the extract again. This time, the students who are listening should write down three words which summarise their impressions of each character. For example: Macbeth is heroic, violent and respected.

Big question

Why does Shakespeare give us such a violent first impression of Macbeth?

Shakespeare is building our anticipation for the arrival of Macbeth, the play's title character. The Witches mention their plan to meet him before sunset, and now we hear of his gruesome feats on the battlefield. In contrast to the hidden treachery of the Thane of Cawdor, Macbeth's violence is very clear – he carves, unseams, decapitates.

Macbeth is clearly a hero. He is praised by the king, who rewards him for his violent success with a new title – Thane of Cawdor. But appearance and reality are already key motifs in the play. Duncan calls Macbeth 'noble' – but is this really the case, or is there a more ominous side to the tragic hero's brutality on the battlefield? Macbeth is presented as a valiant warrior, but there is also his possible connection to evil and witchcraft. As the witches intone, 'Fair is foul, and foul is fair' – we do not know yet what to think of Macbeth.

The fates of Macdonwald and the Thane of Cawdor both await Macbeth, but for now he is Duncan's greatest warrior. Hearing reports of how violent Macbeth is in battle gives a context for everything Macbeth will do throughout the play.

Themes

Conflict

This scene brings us to the heart of the battle that the Witches mentioned in the previous scene. Scotland is embroiled in a literal conflict as Duncan faces two opposing forces: Macdonwald's insurrection and the attack from the Thane of Cawdor and his Norwegian allies. Shakespeare introduces this conflict with descriptions of great violence, highlighting that conflict is an important thread running through the fabric of life in this Scotland.

Violence and masculinity

Although the play's opening scene depicts anxieties about powerful and malevolent women, this second scene celebrates a particular type of masculinity. Male characters are lauded for their ability to destroy their foes through physical force. First, Duncan acknowledges the 'bloody' sergeant, whom Malcolm describes as a 'good and hardy soldier'. This character's wounds 'become' him, meaning they suit him. The sergeant and Duncan then celebrate Macbeth's violence in the battle: his sword (a symbol of his masculinity and loyalty to Scotland) smoked with bloody execution'. Banquo and 'Bellona's bridegroom' (probably Macduff) are also praised for their courage.

Shakespeare is establishing a world in which masculinity is connected to military heroism, preparing us for Lady Macbeth's later accusations that her husband is 'too full of the milk of human kindness'.

Note that even though the 'merciless' Macdonwald displays a similar level of ferocity and courage, he is not a positive symbol of masculinity. This is because within the play's military context, violence should only be used in loyal service of Scotland's king.

Loyalty vs treason

The Thane of Cawdor has betrayed Duncan and joined forces with the Norwegians, against his own country. This is treason, and Cawdor will be punished for it. The choice between loyalty to the crown, versus loyalty to one's own interests (which can lead to betrayal and treason, as in Cawdor's case) is essential to this play. As a theme, it informs Macbeth's entire journey through the play.

Analysis

Staging: reports from battle

We do not know who anyone in the story is yet, so it would be very confusing if Shakespeare began the play with a battle scene. The logistics of staging violent conflict onstage are also very challenging: instead, we often see Shakespeare create inventive ways to show the tension and urgency of battle. Here, he sets the scene at Duncan's camp, and we hear back-to-back reports from various messengers. To make the scene more dramatically tense, the first report is given by a wounded man: his injuries make speaking more difficult and immediately the dramatic stakes are raised.

Dramatic irony

No technique is more central to the architecture of *Macbeth* than dramatic irony. Again and again, Shakespeare places the audience in a position of superior knowledge: we hear the Witches' prophecies before Macbeth does, we know Lady Macbeth's plans before her husband enters, and we recognise the ambiguity of 'none of woman born' long before its meaning becomes clear to the tragic hero. This gap between what we know and what the characters know is not merely decorative; it is structural. It generates suspense, certainly, but also something more unsettling: the sense that Macbeth moves toward a fate already visible to everyone except himself.

To introduce this concept, give students a blank copy of the Frayer Model and complete it as a class, drawing on their knowledge of the play to generate definitions, characteristics, examples and non-examples. Once the model is established, direct their attention to the play's strategic revelations. Why does Shakespeare disclose information to the audience before Macbeth enters? Does this build tension, or does it convey instead the grim inevitability of his descent? The question is worth dwelling on: dramatic irony will reappear under these Analysis headings throughout the book. In *Macbeth* it is never just a matter of waiting for characters to catch up. Dramatic irony is the means by which Shakespeare transforms suspense into tragic recognition.

Dramatic irony

Definition:	**Characteristics:**
The audience knows something that a character on stage does not.	• Audience awareness. • Character ignorance. • Heightened tension or suspense. • Can build a sense of inevitability.
Examples:	**Non-examples:**
An Inspector Calls (1946): Mr Birling declares that the Titanic is 'absolutely unsinkable', whereas the audience knows it sank in 1912. *Macbeth* (1606): The audience knows that Macbeth has been made Thane of Cawdor before Macbeth does.	*Macbeth* (1606): The audience and Duncan know the same information about the battle with the Norwegians. *A Christmas Carol* (1843): Scrooge learns information about the Cratchit family at the same time as the reader finds out about them.

Duncan believes that Macbeth is noble and that the Thane of Cawdor is a traitor. Ironically, he makes Macbeth the new Thane of Cawdor, foreshadowing Macbeth's later treachery.

The audience is also aware that the Witches are planning to meet with Macbeth, and so the ostensibly honourable soldier is already connected to the forces of evil. The line 'fair is foul' resonates throughout this scene, making the audience wonder whether the warrior who sounds so 'fair' is actually 'foul'.

Verse: rhyming couplets

English drama before Shakespeare was often written entirely in rhyming couplets of iambic pentameter. Shakespeare sometimes uses these throughout a scene, but he most often uses a rhyming couplet to end a scene. At the end of this scene, Duncan's last words 'hath won' rhyme with the end of Ross's line 'I'll see it done'. This highlights Duncan's celebration of Macbeth's actions, and also gives a rhythmic finality that ends the scene. The battle is complete, rewards have been allocated and the country can now start to recover: order has been restored.

Key quotation | 'What he hath lost, noble Macbeth hath won'

With this line, Shakespeare confirms that the treacherous Thane of Cawdor has lost his title and his life; Macbeth will replace him as a reward for his courage and patriotism in battle. The new title that Macbeth's bravery has 'won' will give him additional land and power: this is an important promotion for Duncan's 'valiant cousin'.

Shakespeare's use of the epithet 'noble' emphasises Duncan's admiration, respect and trust for Macbeth. The dramatic irony lays the foundations for what is to come, as it quickly becomes clear that Duncan is too trusting of those close to him. His generosity of spirit will leave him open to assassination.

These words also echo the Witches' line 'when the battle's lost and won.' This undermines Duncan's optimistic conclusions. Now another threat will appear: Macbeth's ambition, fuelled by his promotion by Duncan and his manipulation by the Witches.

PAUSE POINT

CONSOLIDATION

Triplet discussion: 'Shakespeare presents Macbeth as a loyal soldier.' With reference to Act One Scene Two, how far do you agree?

- Student A: Argue that Macbeth is presented as loyal.
- Student B: Argue that Macbeth is potentially disloyal.
- Student C: Summarise the discussion.

Model answer:

In this scene Shakespeare shows Duncan's celebration of Macbeth's courage, heroism, loyalty and violence. He considers Macbeth a loyal servant of Scotland, who uses his skill in battle to defend king and country.

In many ways, Shakespeare aligns loyal Macbeth with the traitor Macdonwald. They are so evenly matched that the outcome of their fight is 'doubtful', and it could be argued that they are both 'merciless'. Shakespeare includes descriptions of Macbeth committing several gruesome acts of violence, carving his 'passage' through the enemy forces and almost bathing in blood from 'reeking wounds'. But we cannot forget the Witches' earlier words: 'fair is foul'. Shakespeare is inviting us to imagine that Macbeth will replace Macdonwald, and the Thane of Cawdor, as a threat to Duncan's crown.

Upon the stage

Despite Shakespeare's startling descriptions, some productions choose to stage the conflict rather than reporting it:

- Kenneth Branagh's 2013 production (co-directed by Rob Ashford) began with a dynamic battle, staged in a muddy pit that ran the length of a deconsecrated church.
- Rufus Norris' production at the National Theatre in 2018 began even more violently, with the decapitation of Macdonwald.

These choices may heighten the visceral drama at the start of the play, but they can obscure a key element of Shakespeare's text: the establishment of Macbeth's valour and nobility through report. These reports are what heighten his status as a tragic hero and thus emphasise the scale of his subsequent downfall. Seeing the violence is an engaging start, but it diminishes the efficacy of our hearing about Macbeth before we meet him.

CHAPTER 3
I'LL DRAIN HIM DRY AS HAY
ACT ONE SCENE THREE (LINES 1 TO 37)

At a glance

- **Plot and character development:** The three Witches reconvene and cast a spell against a sailor's wife who they think has wronged them.
- **Social and historical context:** The voyage of *The Tiger* and King James' troubles at sea
- **Vocabulary:** Vengeful
- **Big question:** Why does Shakespeare show us the Witches casting spells?
- **Themes:**
  - Fate vs free will
  - Disorder and the unnatural
- **Analysis:**
  - Staging: witchcraft
- **Key quotation:** 'I'll drain him dry as hay'

PAUSE POINT

RETRIEVAL

In the opening two scenes, Shakespeare builds our anticipation for meeting Macbeth by giving us descriptions of his courage.

Give your students a copy of the following table, without the answers in the second column (available online). Ask them to complete the table from memory.

Character	What have they told us about Macbeth?
The Witches	The Weird Sisters connect Macbeth's name with the fierce 'hurly-burly'. Macbeth seems to be a violent and well-known warrior.
The injured sergeant	He describes Macbeth as a mighty and respected warrior, who has 'carved' his way through enemy forces to 'unseam' the traitor Macdonwald.
Duncan	The king celebrates Macbeth's military successes, rewarding him with the title 'Thane of Cawdor'. He also tells the audience that he is related to Macbeth.

Plot and character development

There are three Witches in this scene, but they do not have especially distinct characters. Some productions try to define specific elements of each: a leader, a prophetess or a particularly violent witch. However, Shakespeare doesn't even give the Witches names, so they remain mysterious. Instead, he deliberately includes several notorious characteristics of witches in order to excite his audience and play with their preconceptions about witchcraft. He also gives a nod to James I's witch-hunting manual, *Daemonologie* (1597).

The first Witch relates an encounter with a sailor's wife who has refused to share some chestnuts. In revenge, the Witch wants to curse the woman's husband, currently sailing to Aleppo on a ship called *The Tiger*. The other Witches offer their help.

The Witches then sense that Macbeth is arriving and complete their charm.

Social and historical context

The voyage of *The Tiger* and King James' troubles at sea

As discussed in Chapter 1, James's obsession with witchcraft was well-known; here, Shakespeare alludes to specific voyages thought to have been disrupted by witchcraft.

There was a real ship called *The Tiger*, which travelled to Aleppo and had a horrendous journey back to London. Amazingly, it was at sea for exactly the same amount of time the Witches mention – 567 days, or nine times nine, times seven – arriving back to London in 1606, right around the time Shakespeare wrote this play.

In 1589 James himself was sailing to Norway to collect his fiancée, Anne of Denmark, but the voyage was disastrous. The fleet was battered by storms and the king was convinced that witches were to blame. When he arrived back in Scotland, James ordered a notorious witch-hunt in North Berwick to prosecute those he felt were responsible. This trial also led him to write his *Daemonologie*.

PAUSE POINT

S-T-R-E-T-C-H

When teaching historical context, it is crucial that students embed this seamlessly into their understanding of the play.

Triplet discussion: Why does Shakespeare include the Witches claiming responsibility for real historical events?

- Student A: Respond to the question by providing a reason.
- Student B: Add another reason.
- Student C: Summarise the discussion.

Model answer:

Shakespeare may have interwoven references to real events in order to cement the audience's belief in supernatural power. This is crucial for our understanding of Macbeth's character; while a modern audience might be sceptical of the Witches, Macbeth is immediately convinced that their prophecies are true.

Shakespeare also uses these historical allusions to amplify our sense of the Witches' malevolence. Once Macbeth chooses to trust these 'instruments of darkness', his downfall will be inevitable.

Vocabulary | Vengeful

Once you have taught a word – particularly one which might appear in a variety of forms (vengeance, vengeful, revenge) – give students an opportunity to experiment with using it in a variety of sentences.

Definition:	Use it in a sentence:
Wanting to harm someone because they have done you wrong.	The first Witch is vengeful because she believes the sailor's wife has insulted her and refused to give her the chestnuts. The vengeful first Witch calls on her fellow 'Weird Sisters' for aid.

Examples (from *Macbeth*):	**Non-examples (from *Macbeth*):**
The first Witch desires vengeance because the sailor's wife has insulted her.	King Duncan is not vengeful; instead he celebrates Macbeth's successes on the battlefield.
Macduff becomes vengeful when Macbeth orders the slaughter of his family.	Malcolm is not vengeful; he does not seek vengeance against those who held him in captivity.

Reading the scene

Give parts to three readers, making sure they know that 'All' means they need to speak in unison. For this, ensure that they can connect with their fellow readers.

Read the scene once through.

Give the remainder of the class bingo cards, marked with a variety of Renaissance beliefs about witches (an example is below, and the remaining cards can be downloaded from the online resources) 🖱. Students should cross off a belief when they hear it referenced. Re-read the scene.

Provide additional support by highlighting key words on the bingo cards. For a faster activity, reduce the bingo cards to six preconceptions.

Witches can sail in a **sieve**.	Witches are agents of the **devil**.	Witches use **human body parts** in their spells.
Witches are known for **killing animals**.	Witches can **transform into rats** without tails.	Witches can **travel quickly** across sea and land.
Witches can **control the wind**.	Witches are associated with the number **three**.	Witches cast **spells**.

Big question

Why does Shakespeare show us the Witches casting spells?

Shakespeare shows the Witches going from conversation to a physical spell, their language full of disturbing details to entertain an audience fascinated by witches. At one point, they add a 'pilot's thumb' to their potion. Owning or stealing body parts for the purposes of witchcraft was a capital offence in Shakespeare's time; presenting this on stage further highlights the Witches' transgressive behaviour and their malevolence. This establishes their power, helping the audience see why Macbeth believes their prophecies and aligns himself with darkness.

The spell also raises the fundamental question of free will vs external control: does Shakespeare present Macbeth as an autonomous agent rejecting morality, or merely a pawn of fate? The tension between fate and free will was much debated in Shakespeare's time. Within religious circles, some believed that although God was omniscient, he had given humankind free will to choose their path in life. Others (such as John Calvin) argued for predestination, the belief that God predestines people to heaven or hell, and that we cannot choose our fate.

The sisters may seem 'weird' in the modern sense, but Shakespeare was actually drawing on the Old English 'wyrd,' meaning 'fate.' So, when they call themselves 'the Weird Sisters', they are acknowledging their connection to fate, and expressly to the theme of fate vs free will.

Analysis

Staging: witchcraft

Our analysis divides *Macbeth's* key ideas into themes and motifs. Perhaps fittingly, witchcraft does not really align with either of these headings. It is not a central theme or recurring motif, but a powerful dramatic device. It serves as a catalyst, designed to engage a Jacobean audience fascinated by the supernatural. The Witches' prophecies do not explore witchcraft itself; they target Macbeth's latent ambition, setting his tragic downfall in motion and allowing the play to explore its range of very human themes.

Key quotation | 'I'll drain him dry as hay'

Here, the first Witch explains that she will get her revenge on the sailor's wife by torturing her husband. This description foreshadows what the Witches will do to Macbeth, who will be comparably 'drain[ed] dry' as guilt, fear and nihilism overcome him.

PAUSE POINT

CONSOLIDATION

Read-reduce-rehearse-remember (see 'How to use this book' page XIII).

This scene is significant for two reasons. First, Shakespeare emphasises the Witches' malevolence, presenting them as vengeful agents of evil who wreak chaos. Secondly, their plan to 'drain' the captain 'dry as hay' foreshadows their manipulation of Macbeth. After meeting the Witches, Macbeth will lose the ability to sleep and pray, be tormented by guilt, become isolated from Lady Macbeth, haunted by Banquo's ghost and face his downfall.

Upon the stage

Although most productions cast three performers, Joel Coen's film (2021) subverted this by having a single actor, Kathryn Hunter, embody all three Witches. Her extraordinary voice shifted registers between the three Witches across different lines. When she produced the pilot's thumb, she didn't simply hold it; she seemed to grow it from her own body, her spine contorting as the digit appeared between her clenched toes. The performance refused stable gender categories: her body was at once maternal, senile, feral and mechanical. She was withered and wild in her attire, with chappy fingers and skinny lips, of questionable gender, just as the text itself suggests. Coen's digital doubling didn't just create three figures; it made Hunter at times a swarm, a collective, an entity that could split and reunite at will. The result is a modern, unsettling interpretation that gives new insight into the Witches' magic, gender expression and malevolence.

CHAPTER 4
ALL HAIL, MACBETH
ACT ONE SCENE THREE (LINES 38 TO 89)

At a glance

- **Plot and character development:** Macbeth and Banquo enter and the Witches give them tantalising information about their respective futures.
- **Social and historical context:** Banquo as an ancestor of King James I
- **Vocabulary:** Manipulative
- **Big question:** Why does Shakespeare include the Witches' prophecy that Macbeth will be king?
- **Themes:**
  - Ambition and power
  - Fate vs free will
  - Appearance vs reality
- **Analysis:**
  - Language: repetition
  - Staging: visible witches
  - Text: iambic pentameter
- **Key quotation:** 'All hail, Macbeth'

PAUSE POINT

RETRIEVAL

Revisit the start of Act One Scene Three by asking students to recall the explanation from the consolidation task at the end of Chapter 3.

Prompt students by providing a list of key words.

Plot and character development

Macbeth and Banquo finally enter, encountering these strange creatures. Banquo comments on their weird appearance: they 'look not like the inhabitants of the earth' and have 'beards', which makes their gender ambiguous.

Banquo and Macbeth ask the Witches what they are, but their only answer is to salute both soldiers with predictions about their future. They hail Macbeth as Thane of Glamis, of Cawdor, and king-to-be, and tell Banquo that his children shall be kings. The Witches then vanish into the air, leaving Macbeth and Banquo stunned and unsettled.

Social and historical context

Banquo as an ancestor of King James I

Banquo speaks more than Macbeth in this scene, so that we can focus on Macbeth's 'rapt' reaction to what the Witches tell him. Perhaps Shakespeare shrewdly gives Banquo so many lines in order to flatter King James I, who believed he was related to this medieval warrior. The prophecy that Banquo's children will become kings echoes throughout the play, reaching a climax when the Witches show Macbeth a vision of Banquo and his heirs in Act Four Scene One. The last heir holds up a 'glass' (a mirror), which might well have reflected the image of King James, sitting in the audience.

PAUSE POINT

S-T-R-E-T-C-H

Shakespeare presents Macbeth and Banquo similarly at the start of the play. In Act One Scene Two, both are described as powerful, patriotic warriors. In this scene, they both receive incredible prophecies.

Triplet discussion: Shakespeare shows that Macbeth and Banquo make different decisions in response to the prophecies. Macbeth chooses to respond with violence, while Banquo waits. Why does Shakespeare include the subplot involving Banquo, instead of simply focusing on Macbeth?

- Student A: Respond to the question by providing a reason.
- Student B: Add another reason.
- Student C: Summarise the discussion.

Model answer:

Shakespeare includes Banquo as a character foil for Macbeth, in order to highlight his journey to immorality and despair. Banquo could easily have plotted against his friend, but he maintains his integrity – at the cost of his life. Banquo becomes a symbol of honour and nobility, which would have flattered King James.

Vocabulary | Manipulative

When introducing new words, ensure you signpost links to other texts you are studying. This will help to build students' schemas, as well as their understanding of the nuances of words which can be used in a variety of contexts.

Definition:	**Characteristics:**
Controlling or influencing someone else's decisions or behaviour.	• Regularly lying. • Flattery. • Withholding information. • Creating dependency.
Examples (from *Macbeth*):	**Non-examples (from *Macbeth*):**
The Witches manipulate Macbeth by withholding information (he will become king, but this will lead to his downfall). Later, Lady Macbeth manipulates her husband by making him feel guilty for lacking masculine courage.	Banquo's behaviour is always honest. Duncan rewards his followers for their loyalty.

Reading the scene

Select your readers for this section and take the part of Banquo for yourself. Ask the rest of the class to circle or highlight the Witches' prophecies.

Discuss the prophecies with the class, ensuring that they understand:

- Macbeth became Thane of Glamis when his father died.
- In Act One Scene Two, Duncan ordered the execution of the Thane of Cawdor and gave this title to Macbeth – but Macbeth doesn't know this yet.
- The Witches do not suggest murder; this comes from Macbeth's own mind.

Prepare to re-read this scene. This time, ask students to underline Macbeth and Banquo's responses to the Witches. Discuss these responses with the class, checking their understanding of:

- Banquo's emphasis on the Witches' unnatural appearance.
- Macbeth's ('rapt') entrancement.
- Banquo's eagerness to receive a prophecy.
- Macbeth's desire for further explanation.

N.B. In Macbeth's title, Glamis is pronounced Glahmz (rhymes with palms).

Big question

Why does Shakespeare include the Witches' prophecy that Macbeth will be king?

When the Weird Sisters wish to manipulate a person, they identify their biggest weakness – as is suggested by their revenge against the sailor's wife. They enjoy spreading suffering and chaos, and so they create plots which will lead to torment and disorder. (A handful of chestnuts led to 567 nights of torture at sea!) For the 'rump-fed runnion', this weakness is her husband – and so the Witches place him in mortal danger. As for Macbeth, we quickly learn that his weakness – his fatal flaw – is his ambition. When the Witches ignite this, alongside Macbeth's propensity for violence, the combination is explosive.

Analysis

Language: repetition

Shakespeare uses Macbeth's first line to tie him inextricably to the Witches. He says 'so foul and fair a day I have not seen,' echoing 'fair is foul and foul is fair'. The word 'foul' will resonate throughout the play, repeated six times by different characters. With each repetition the foulness grows – as the Witches infect Macbeth's mind – and he spreads horror, violence and fear throughout Scotland.

Staging: visible witches

Unlike other apparitions that will appear in the play, the Witches are here visible to both Macbeth and Banquo. Shakespeare plays with the theatrical convention of all-male acting companies here, by acknowledging that while the Witches 'should' be women, they have masculine aspects to their appearance also. Whatever they look like, they do not say much, keeping a mysterious distance from the two men. Heightening this mystery, the Witches continue their equivocating speech: everything has two sides and nothing is definite. This invites immediate suspicion because no details are disclosed.

Text: iambic pentameter

The rhythmic heartbeat of Shakespeare's language is iambic pentameter. An iamb is a metrical foot consisting of an unstressed syllable followed by a stressed one (da-DUM), much like the rhythm of a human heartbeat. Pentameter is a kind of verse that has five feet per line. So, iambic pentameter has five iambs per line, creating a ten-syllable pattern:

da-DUM da-DUM da-DUM da-DUM da-DUM

Iambic pentameter is the standard rhythm in which Shakespeare writes. When it is unrhymed, it is also known as blank verse. Shakespeare uses this regular rhythm to mirror natural spoken speech. Take the time to familiarise your students with this rhythm. Encourage them to make up sentences with it:

'I think I'll go and have a cup of tea.'
'Our teacher never said this would be fun.'

Teaching students to hear this rhythm is key to unlocking the emotional and thematic subtext of the play. The more familiar your students are with this rhythm, the better they will be able to spot how and when Shakespeare adapts and manipulates it for dramatic effect.

Key quotation | 'All hail Macbeth'

The Witches greet Macbeth with respect and praise, repeating the phrase 'all hail' before each prophecy. There is intense dramatic irony at this point, because we have just seen the Witches plot a man's downfall and seal their charm. The audience knows not to trust them, but Macbeth is taken in by their flattering words. Perhaps it had never crossed Macbeth's mind to become king of Scotland. He inherited his title, Thane of Glamis, from his father, Sinel, but to be king 'stands not within the prospect of belief'. But does this 'all hail' signal that fate has bigger plans for him?

We can read 'hail' as an allusion to the Bible. In the Gospel of Luke, an angel appears to Mary to tell her that she is highly favoured, and will be the mother of Jesus. The angel greets Mary with 'hail' – and the prayer is still said thus today. Later, in the Gospel of Matthew, Judas greets Jesus with 'hail' and then betrays him with a kiss. These Biblical echoes, suggesting an annunciation and then a betrayal from the Witches, make the scene all the more disturbing.

Finally, it is notable that the Witches only say 'hail' to Banquo. This aligns with their prophecy that Banquo will be 'lesser than Macbeth, and greater'. The two men are equals until this moment, and the Witches are the ones who plant the seeds of what will follow.

PAUSE POINT

CONSOLIDATION

Use a blank version of the graphic organiser (found in the online resources) below to support students in exploring the word 'hail' in depth.

"Hail" ➡	Respect ➡	Praise ➡	The Witches flatter Macbeth ➡	The Witches entice Macbeth into their web ➡	The Witches cannot be trusted

Upon the stage

Polly Findlay's (2018) modern dress production featured young girls in pink tracksuits as the Witches. These girl-witches were particularly chilling in a play that has so much to say about children and death. The wide-eyed manner in which they greeted Macbeth, as though thinking up his future on the spot, was a surprising and unsettling take on this familiar scene.

Findlay's choice is just one in a long and varied history of casting these roles. Shakespeare may have used boy players or adult male performers. Ninagawa's famous (1980) Japanese production used skilled female impersonators from kabuki theatre to play the Witches. Women of all ages, from children to senior citizens, have brought much to these roles.

What does each casting choice reveal about the Witches' nature and power?

CHAPTER 5

CHANCE MAY CROWN ME

ACT ONE SCENE THREE (LINES 90 TO END)

At a glance

- **Plot and character development:** Ross and Angus enter, with news of Macbeth's promotion to Thane of Cawdor.
- **Social and historical context:** Regicide and the Divine Right of Kings
- **Vocabulary:** Soliloquy
- **Big question:** Does Shakespeare present the Witches as inspiring or revealing Macbeth's ambition?
- **Themes:**
  - Ambition and power
  - The Divine Right of Kings
- **Analysis:**
  - Dramatic irony
  - Soliloquy
  - Motif: clothing
- **Key quotation:** 'If chance will have me king, why, chance may crown me / Without my stir'

PAUSE POINT

RETRIEVAL

Revisit the key vocabulary so far (malevolent, tragic hero, dramatic irony, vengeful, manipulative).

Test students' knowledge of the definitions and then check they can use the words in full sentences.

Plot and character development

As Macbeth and Banquo recover from hearing the prophecies, Ross, the play's messenger and another thane, Angus, arrive. They tell Macbeth and Banquo about the defeat of the Thane of Cawdor, and how Duncan has rewarded Macbeth with the title. This news immediately prompts Macbeth to have 'horrible imaginings': if the Witches were right about him being Thane of Glamis, and Cawdor, perhaps he will become king of Scotland. And if this is the case, then there is an obvious, if disturbing way to make that happen.

The characters leave the stage on their way to see Duncan.

Social and historical context

Regicide and the Divine Right of Kings

As noted in Chapter 2, the recent memory of the Gunpowder Plot meant that regicide was a realistic threat. Regicide was not just a crime but a terrible sin, since, according to the Divine Right of Kings, royalty was anointed by God. As a new ruler, James I was a fierce advocate for this doctrine, and wrote extensively to promote it.

Vocabulary | Soliloquy

Remember to check understanding of all students when you introduce new vocabulary. The 'true or false' questions in the table below will help you to do this.

Definition:	**Morphology:**
A solo speech where a character reveals private thoughts to the audience.	Root word: sol = alone e.g. solitary, desolate
Characteristics:	**True or false?**
• Other characters do not hear this speech. • Substantially longer than an aside. • Reveals private thoughts or information. • Gives the audience insight into the character.	1. All the characters on stage hear a soliloquy. 2. Asides and soliloquies are the same. 3. Shakespeare uses soliloquies to give the audience an insight into the character's mind and thinking.

Answers to 'True or false?': 1. False 2. False (an aside is shorter) 3. True

PAUSE POINT

S-T-R-E-T-C-H

Triplet discussion: How would the play be different if Shakespeare didn't include Macbeth's soliloquies?

- Student A: Respond to the question by providing an idea.
- Student B: Add another idea.
- Student C: Summarise the discussion.

Model answer:

If the soliloquies were not included, we would have a significantly diminished understanding of Macbeth's character. He would appear to be a stock villain who butchers those around him without consideration of the consequences.

However, the beauty of Shakespeare's play is that he uses soliloquies to give us an insight into Macbeth's mind. Shakespeare presents Macbeth as a psychologically complex character who considers his choices in detail before acting, and who cannot escape his guilt once the deed is done. Although we do not face the same choices, many of us experience the uncertainty, confusion and despair that Macbeth articulates. This is one reason why the play still speaks to audiences today.

Reading the scene

Read this section of Act One Scene Three, taking the part of Macbeth yourself. To demonstrate the impact of the soliloquy, choose readers in one area of the room and then move between them and the other side of the classroom.

Revisit the key terms dramatic irony and soliloquy and ensure students can identify how Shakespeare uses these devices in this scene.

Key questions for discussion:

- What do we learn about Banquo?
- How do the prophecies make Macbeth feel?
- How does Macbeth feel about the possibility of killing a king?
- What is Macbeth's final conclusion on the topic of murder?

Big question

Does Shakespeare present the Witches as inspiring or revealing Macbeth's ambition?

The Witches tell Macbeth that he will become king of Scotland, but they give no further details and do not mention murder. The first hint of regicide is when Macbeth mentions the 'horrid image that doth unfix my hair'. In this soliloquy, Shakespeare shows that Macbeth cannot even admit to himself the precise nature of this image – but he recognises that it is 'against the use of nature'. This phrase implies that he is considering a heinous deed that would challenge the very fabric of society. The Witches do not articulate it, but their prophecy does seem to awaken an idea that was already somewhere deep in Macbeth's heart.

PAUSE POINT

WRITING

Stretch your students by introducing tentative and assertive language.

Tentative language: used to suggest an idea

- Modal verbs (Shakespeare might… could…)
- Phrases (It could be argued that Shakespeare… One might suggest…)
- Janus-faced sentences (While on the one hand, Shakespeare… on the other hand…)

Assertive language: used to confidently argue an idea

- It is irrefutable that Shakespeare…
- Unquestionably, Shakespeare…

Ask your students to use tentative and assertive language to write their own response to this chapter's big question.

Themes

Ambition and power

Shakespeare shows the precise moment Macbeth's ambition shifts from passive hope to active imagining. His aside ('If chance will have me king, why, chance may crown me / Without my stir') is the last gasp of patient ambition. It is immediately answered by the 'horrid image' of regicide, which his mind supplies, unprompted. The Witches have not mentioned murder; Macbeth's ambition, once ignited, volunteered the idea. Shakespeare shows that the fatal flaw is not ambition itself, but ambition's fertility: it can generate terrifying ideas all on its own.

The Divine Right of Kings

In Shakespeare's time the king was considered to have been anointed by God, and therefore it was a terrible crime (and sin) to attack him. Here Macbeth is appalled even at the thought of killing Duncan: he describes how the 'horrid image' feels totally unnatural. The sanctity of the crown and the Divine Right of Kings appear as a theme throughout the play.

Analysis

Dramatic irony

This device is found throughout Act I, heightened here by the announcement that Macbeth is now the Thane of Cawdor. Unbeknownst to Ross and Angus, Macbeth has just heard the Witches predict that he will receive this honour. The frequent use of dramatic irony suggests that not everything is as it seems.

Soliloquy

Macbeth's soliloquy highlights how captivated and 'rapt' Macbeth becomes, now that his fertile imagination is overcome with thoughts of murder. The soliloquy also reveals a shift in Macbeth's character, as he now starts to conceal his true intentions from Banquo.

Motif: clothing

Clothing recurs throughout the play as a motif representing characters' identities. When Macbeth receives the news that he is Thane of Cawdor, he asks 'why do you dress me / In borrowed robes?' The image of ill-fitting clothing suggests that he is taking a role or identity that he cannot live up to, or that is not his to take. You can see more about clothing imagery in Appendix B.

Key quotation | 'If chance will have me king, why, chance may crown me / Without my stir'

In this aside, Macbeth wonders if fate might make him king without his taking any action. Shakespeare presents Macbeth as searching for an alternative to the 'horrible imaginings' that are taking over his mind: he believes that he might be able to trust in fate, rather than taking control of his future himself. If his fate is to become king, then fate may crown him without his having to do anything terrible.

However, the balance of modal verbs in this quotation indicates a shift from certainty to uncertainty. The shift from 'will' to 'may' suggests that while Macbeth already believes that what the Witches have said will all come true, he wonders how much he will have to do to ensure that it does.

PAUSE POINT

CONSOLIDATION

Triplet discussion: 'In Act One Scene Three, Shakespeare shows Macbeth's character begin to change.' How far do you agree?

- Student A: Respond to the question by identifying two changes in Macbeth's character.
- Student B: Provide evidence to support Student A's ideas.
- Student C: Summarise the discussion.

Model answer:

In Act One Scene Two, Shakespeare tells us what other characters think of Macbeth. He is described as a hero, a 'valiant' warrior who courageously leads Duncan's army into battle. Shakespeare reveals how Macbeth confirms his loyalty to the crown by killing the traitor Macdonwald, and is to be rewarded for his valour in battle. When he first enters Macbeth is conversational, and then shares his reaction to the prophecies with his good friend Banquo.

However, by the end of the scene, Shakespeare depicts Macbeth as withdrawn and secretive. When he hears that he is to become Thane of Cawdor Macbeth retreats into soliloquies and asides, concealing his plans and anxieties from Banquo and allowing thoughts of regicide to develop.

Upon the stage

Eve Best's staging of this scene (Shakespeare's Globe, 2014) gives an important sense of how soliloquies work, in a replica of Shakespeare's own theatre. With the audience so close to the stage, Joseph Millson made Macbeth's soliloquy feel like a real-time series of reactions to what is happening. He engaged with the entire audience, addressing his speech to all sides and levels, even though Banquo and his colleagues did not hear what he was talking about.

On screen, Sir Ian McKellen and Denzel Washington had very different approaches. McKellen (dir. Trevor Nunn, 1979) stared directly into the camera for this soliloquy, while Washington (dir. Joel Coen, 2021) seemed pensive and almost too ashamed to look us, the audience, in the eye.

These examples present some of the challenges of performing a soliloquy: should an actor speak directly to the audience, acknowledging their presence? Or are these speeches more effective if they are private, as though we in the audience are just overhearing them?

CHAPTER 6
BLACK AND DEEP DESIRES
ACT ONE SCENE FOUR

At a glance

- **Plot and character development:** Macbeth and Banquo arrive at Duncan's court. Duncan praises them. Duncan announces Malcolm as his heir and says he will visit Macbeth's castle. Macbeth wonders what he will have to do to become king himself.
- **Social and historical context:** Succession and primogeniture
- **Vocabulary:**
  - Regicide
- **Big question:** Why is it significant that Shakespeare shows Duncan calling Macbeth 'My worthy Cawdor'?
- **Themes:**
  - Appearance vs reality
  - Kingship
- **Analysis:**
  - Staging: heightening tension
  - Language: foreshadowing
  - Motif: darkness and light
  - Motif: natural imagery
- **Key quotation:** 'Let not light see my black and deep desires'

PAUSE POINT

RETRIEVAL

Ask students to think-pair-share what they know about Shakespeare's presentation of Malcolm, whom we met in Act One Scene Two and who is about to become prince of Cumberland.

Students could consider how Shakespeare presents:

- Malcolm as Duncan's oldest son.
- The reference to Malcolm's capture in battle – and subsequent 'liberation' by the Sergeant.
- Malcolm as a character who says little, but as one who speaks with authority.
- Malcolm in the camp waiting for news, rather than leading the army to victory.

Stretch students by asking them to respond to this question with tentative and assertive language: Does Shakespeare present Malcolm as a strong leader?

Plot and character development

The scene opens with a description of the Thane of Cawdor's execution, reminding the audience that this title is associated with treachery. Macbeth enters just after this report, linking him immediately with the previous Cawdor. Duncan praises Macbeth – and Banquo – for their success and promises to reward them.

Duncan has decided to name his heir (the prince of Cumberland): Malcolm. This choice is a problem for Macbeth: someone else is ahead of him in line for the throne, so he will have to imagine alternative steps to the crown. Macbeth's moral decline accelerates: in the previous scene he was shocked at the thought of regicide, now he is thinking about it quite methodically.

Social and historical context

Succession and primogeniture

Succession was a major concern in Shakespeare's England, especially after the unmarried Queen Elizabeth I died without naming an heir. Although the crowning of King James I went smoothly, his accession had not been guaranteed and could have risked civil war. In *Macbeth*, Duncan's nomination of his own son as heir is unsurprising, though Scotland did not practice primogeniture at this time. Duncan could legitimately have chosen the heroic Macbeth as his successor instead of Malcolm – but then there would be no play. This scene is very dramatic, since it was a provocative choice to stage a character contemplating the murder of a benevolent king so soon after the Gunpowder Plot.

Vocabulary | Regicide

You could use a Frayer Model to teach this new word, but here are some other suggestions that you might want to explore. These strategies are particularly designed for lower prior attaining, multilingual and/or students with SEND.

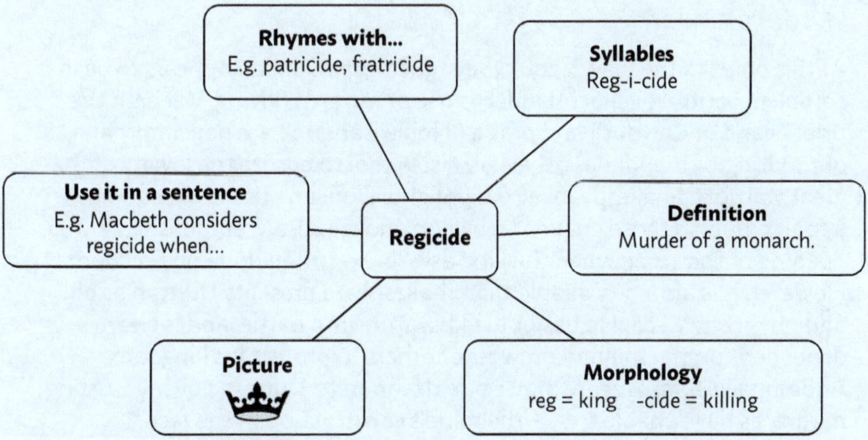

Reading the scene

The staging of this scene is crucial to understanding characterisation in the play. Therefore, instead of reading this scene, watch one of the versions we recommend in Appendix C and ask students to initially pay attention to the visual cues suggested in the table below. (We have included teacher notes in this table.)

Setting:	**Sound effects:**
The scene is Duncan's palace at Forres. It instantly communicates Duncan's power and authority. This contrasts with the heath where the Witches met Macbeth in Act One Scene Three: chaos is juxtaposed with order.	The scene is bookended by trumpet flourishes. Shakespeare consolidates our impression of Duncan's authority and rightful kingship, which Macbeth will destroy.
Entrances and exits:	**Soliloquy:**
Macbeth enters immediately after Duncan says that he placed his 'absolute trust' in the previous Cawdor. The dramatic irony here is intense. Shakespeare connects the executed Thane's betrayal and the new Thane's 'black and deep desires'.	The soliloquy heightens our sense that Macbeth is plotting against Duncan and that he absolutely believes the Witches' prophecies.

PAUSE POINT

S-T-R-E-T-C-H

Triplet discussion: 'At the start of the play, Shakespeare emphasises Duncan's total control over Scotland.' How far do you agree?

- Student A: Argue that Duncan is in total control.
- Student B: Argue that Duncan is not in total control.
- Student C: Summarise the discussion.

Model answer:

At this point in the play, it could be argued that Duncan appears to be in complete control over Scotland. His use of rewards (giving Macbeth the title 'Thane of Cawdor') and praise ('Noble Banquo') are not simply an outpouring of friendliness; they are also a tool to ensure the loyalty of these great warriors. Shakespeare also highlights Duncan's use of execution as a tool to punish those guilty of rebellion and treachery, emphasised at the opening of the scene when the king asks 'is execution done on Cawdor?' However, it is also inescapable that Shakespeare presents Duncan as old and physically weak. He has not led his army into battle, and is clearly dependent on the military prowess of others to protect his kingdom. Additionally, Shakespeare draws our attention to Duncan's overly trusting nature, as he is unable to see 'the mind's construction in the face'.

Big question

Why is it significant that Shakespeare shows Duncan calling Macbeth 'My worthy Cawdor'?

Shakespeare uses this line to heighten the dramatic irony in this scene. Duncan has admitted that he does not know the 'art / To find the mind's construction in the face' – and now he proves it by praising the very man whose face is hiding 'black and deep desires'.

Themes

Appearance vs reality

In this scene, Duncan describes how 'there's no art / To find the mind's construction in the face'. Shakespeare highlights how Duncan does not have the skill to identify traitors. He admits that he was deceived by the original Thane of Cawdor, and so mistakenly 'built / An absolute trust' in him. Just as Duncan finishes this line, Macbeth enters and the king praises his noble warrior.

Kingship

Duncan is presented as a good and popular king, but acknowledges his own weaknesses. Shakespeare will show the audience several different kinds of kingship, running as a thematic thread throughout, beginning with Duncan's humble and sanctified reign. Duncan is so good that Macbeth will later worry that his virtues themselves might plead against his murder.

Analysis

Staging: heightening tension

Duncan praises Macbeth before his court (calling him his 'worthiest cousin') but ironically the king does not know what Macbeth is contemplating. However, Shakespeare uses asides and a soliloquy to show the audience Macbeth's 'black and deep desires' – so we get to see the dramatic difference between Macbeth's public image and his private thoughts.

Language: foreshadowing

Shakespeare uses a lot of foreshadowing in this scene: Malcolm describes how the Thane of Cawdor died: he was noble, but appeared to care very little about his own death. This anticipates Macbeth's disillusionment at the end of the play. Macbeth's line 'stars, hide your fires' likewise foreshadows his feelings through the play, calling for darkness all the way as far as 'out, out, brief candle' when he contemplates his own death.

Motif: darkness and light

Shakespeare portrays Macbeth's hopes that he can hide his murderous thoughts and maintain his façade of loyalty. He uses imagery of darkness to describe Macbeth's 'black' desires and hope that the stars will 'hide' their light. In contrast, Shakespeare aligns Duncan with imagery of virtue and light ('signs of nobleness, like stars, shall shine...').

Motif: natural imagery

Shakespeare also connects Duncan with natural imagery; he says that he has 'begun to plant' Macbeth and 'will labour / To make thee full of growing'. Malcolm will echo these words in the play's final speech. This use of natural imagery not only contrasts with Macbeth's 'horrible imaginings' 'against the use of nature' (Act One Scene Three), but it also echoes Jeremiah's words in the Bible. In Jeremiah 12, the prophet writes about the 'wicked' whom God has 'planted'. Jeremiah says that these people speak about God, but the lord is 'far from their hearts'.

Key quotation | 'Let not light see my black and deep desires'

Here, Shakespeare juxtaposes light and dark. The former is associated with Duncan in this scene, suggesting his virtue and goodness, while the latter emphasises Macbeth's growing malevolence. Macbeth wishes to be overcome by darkness, which can hide his murderous desires and conceal his actions. Macbeth has just told the stars to hide their fires: concealment and hiding will be essential imagery in the lead-up to Duncan's murder.

PAUSE POINT

CONSOLIDATION

Shakespeare creates dramatic irony in this scene by juxtaposing Duncan's honesty and Macbeth's deception. Use the table below to contrast the two characters.

	Duncan:	**Macbeth (aside):**
Quotation	'There's no art / To find the mind's construction in the face: / He was a gentleman on whom I **built** / An absolute trust. Enter Macbeth...'	**'Stars**, hide your fires! / Let not **light** see my **black** and deep desires.'
What does the quotation mean?		
What does the underlined imagery suggest?		
What does the quotation tell us about the character?		

Upon the stage

In a clever piece of staging, Polly Findlay (2018) had Christopher Eccleston step forward at line 37, physically demonstrating Macbeth's conviction that he, not Malcolm, would be proclaimed Prince of Cumberland. This made his previously unspoken ambition physical, eliciting audience empathy for his newly-awakened and immediately thwarted aspirations. The cringe we feel is eminently relatable, even if the king does not notice the gaffe. Duncan's choice of Malcolm becomes a turning point, wherein we witness the real-time transformation of Macbeth's ambition into resolve.

CHAPTER 7
THE MILK OF HUMAN KINDNESS
ACT ONE SCENE FIVE (LINES 1 TO 38)

At a glance

- **Plot and character development:** Lady Macbeth enters, reading a letter from her husband, describing the encounter with the Witches and all that they have promised. Lady Macbeth resolves to see these prophecies fulfilled. A messenger brings the news that Duncan is coming to stay at the Macbeths' home tonight.
- **Social and historical context:** Women in medieval Scotland
- **Vocabulary:** Resolute
- **Big question:** Why does Macbeth write a letter, when he is already on his way home?
- **Themes:**
  - Ambition and power
  - Violence and masculinity
- **Analysis:**
  - Image: the crown
  - Soliloquy
- **Key quotation:** 'Too full of the milk of human kindness / To catch the nearest way'
- **Handle with care:** In this scene Lady Macbeth rejects her gender and the traditional associations of womanhood. The language is both sexual and anatomical.

PAUSE POINT

RETRIEVAL

What is a soliloquy, and why does Shakespeare use them?

Lady Macbeth's soliloquy is an opportunity to remind your class that Shakespeare uses soliloquies to provide insights into a character's thinking. Here, Shakespeare reveals that Lady Macbeth is ambitious and pragmatic. She knows what she must do to counteract the weakness of her husband's good nature.

Plot and character development

Shakespeare introduces Lady Macbeth in stages: first she reads her husband's words, recounting details we already know. The letter recaps the story we have seen and heard so far, but it also shows us Macbeth's response to it. He believes the Witches, and now imagines that he could become king. Lady Macbeth also responds to the prophecies. She likewise believes the Witches immediately, and has no qualms about taking action to guarantee that Macbeth becomes 'what thou art promised'. Importantly, Macbeth calls his wife 'my dearest partner of greatness.'

This epithet rings true: Lady Macbeth is introduced as a powerful, determined woman. Shakespeare often writes aggressive, dramatically dominant women, like Tamora, Margaret, Regan and Goneril. Lady Macbeth cements her place as the most extraordinary from her first appearance in this scene: unlike her husband, she does not worry about moral consequences. She knows what she wants and is determined to achieve it.

Next comes a chilling soliloquy in which Lady Macbeth determines that yes, they will become king and queen. The Messenger's entry heightens the tension by adding an immediate time limit. Duncan is coming: Lady Macbeth must make her castle ready to welcome the king tonight. This is also a dramatic opportunity for murder.

Social and historical context

Women in medieval Scotland

Medieval Scottish women were subject to patriarchal expectations of obedient submissiveness as wives and mothers. However, some wealthy women, like Lady Macbeth, would have managed estates and wielded significant power, especially when their husbands were away fighting. Therefore, her ruthless ambition, while unconventional, would not have been entirely unknown. (See Rackin, *Shakespeare and Women* [2005] for a re-evaluation of gender in Shakespeare's plays.)

The real Lady Macbeth was called Gruoch, and had been married to the Mormaer of Moray before she married Macbeth. Her son from her first marriage, Lulach, eventually became king of Scotland, but was assassinated by Malcolm III.

PAUSE POINT

ORACY

Consolidate your students' knowledge of gender stereotypes by asking them to think-pair-share information about stereotypes of masculinity and femininity.

Stretch students further by introducing the following terms: domestic sphere; conventional/unconventional; subvert and transgression.

Vocabulary | Resolute

Teaching this word provides an opportunity for revising not just *Macbeth*, but other texts your students are studying; challenge your class to write down an example or non-example for each character.

Definition:	**Characteristics:**
Determined and focused, particularly when faced with challenges.	• Focus. • Having a clear goal. • Displaying resilience. • Self-discipline.
Examples:	**Non-examples:**
An Inspector Calls (1946): Inspector Goole is resolute when he interrogates Mr Birling. *A Christmas Carol* (1843): Scrooge is initially resolute in his refusal to help those in financial need.	*Macbeth* (1606): In Act One Scene Seven, Macbeth dithers between killing and not killing Duncan.

Reading the scene

Prepare to read the scene aloud, taking Lady Macbeth's part yourself and delegating the stage directions and the role of the Messenger.

Tell the class to listen actively, considering the question: what do we learn about Lady Macbeth's character? Pause after every full stop, and each time you do so, prompt the students to bullet point their ideas.

Students could be further supported by introducing the class to key lines before reading the scene.

Quotation from Act One Scene Five	What do you think this means?
In a letter, Macbeth calls Lady Macbeth 'my dearest partner in greatness'.	Macbeth sees his wife as an equal.
Lady Macbeth says her husband's 'nature' 'is too full of the milk of human kindness / To catch the nearest way'.	Lady Macbeth recognises that Macbeth is too weak to commit regicide to get the crown.
Lady Macbeth wants Macbeth to return, so that she can 'pour [her] spirits in [his] ear'.	Lady Macbeth wants to manipulate Macbeth into killing Duncan by talking to him persuasively.
Lady Macbeth wants to help Macbeth achieve 'the golden round'.	This refers to the great value and prestige of the crown of Scotland.

PAUSE POINT

S-T-R-E-T-C-H

Triplet discussion: 'In Act One Scene Five, Shakespeare presents Lady Macbeth as a powerful woman with ambitions for her own success.' How far do you agree?

- Student A: Argue that Lady Macbeth is powerful.
- Student B: Argue that there are cracks in Lady Macbeth's façade of power.
- Student C: Summarise the discussion.

Model answer:

Shakespeare presents Lady Macbeth as her husband's 'dearest partner in greatness,' an equal who shares his ambition. We can immediately see her authority, confidence and high status. Shakespeare highlights that Lady Macbeth also believes she can exert power over her husband, manipulating him to do her will. But we must consider the fact that although Lady Macbeth is determined to help her husband to 'the golden round', she does not explicitly mention her own success. Her focus remains on ensuring that her husband 'shalt be / What thou art [he is] promised'.

Big question

Why does Macbeth write a letter, when he is already on his way home?

The letter allows Shakespeare to demonstrate the passionate and genuine love between this couple. Even though Macbeth arrives just minutes later, his affection and his need for Lady Macbeth's support drives him to tell her about the Witches as soon as possible. He also has to tell her that Duncan and his entourage are coming: she will need time to supervise preparations.

Structurally, the letter also means Shakespeare can reveal Lady Macbeth's reaction to the prophecies while she is alone. The Witches have not mentioned violence, but just like her husband, Lady Macbeth instantly considers regicide (euphemistically described as 'the nearest way' to the position that Macbeth has been 'promised'). This is also an opportunity for Shakespeare to highlight another side to Macbeth's character: he might be a ruthless 'lion' on the battlefield, but his wife is concerned that he is not quite bloodthirsty enough.

Themes

Ambition and power

A key idea in the play is that unchecked ambition and lust for power is a corrupting force. Once the couple's desire to achieve 'the golden round' has been ignited, the darker side of human nature comes to the fore.

Violence and masculinity

In stark contrast to the violent description of Macbeth in Act One Scene Two, here Lady Macbeth says that he is too soft, too 'full of the milk of human kindness' and without 'illness'. This is a surprising challenge to Macbeth's masculinity and the violence we have already heard described; her ability to challenge and inspire her husband to violence will be essential to the murderous events ahead.

Analysis

Image: the crown

The crown symbolises ultimate power and authority. Lady Macbeth's description of the crown as the 'golden round' suggests its allure; as well as political power, it represents wealth and elevated social status. The word 'round' hints at perfection and continuity – both of which Macbeth will disrupt when he takes the crown by force.

Soliloquy

The power of this soliloquy comes from Lady Macbeth's shocking subversion of gender and maternal norms. Unlike her husband, when she hears the prophecies she immediately resolves to act. She worries that Macbeth is weak and too good-natured. He has enough ambition, but lacks 'the illness should attend it'. (Illness here means evil rather than sickness.) Her invocation 'unsex me here' is a plea to be stripped of feminine compassion, replacing it with 'direst cruelty.' The speech establishes her as a driving, terrifying force, presenting ambition not just as political desire but as a fundamental violation of nature itself. She calls on Macbeth to hurry home, so that she can inspire him with her valour, echoing beautifully his description as 'Valour's minion' in Act One Scene Two.

Key quotation | 'Too full of the milk of human kindness / To catch the nearest way'

Shakespeare reveals that Lady Macbeth is troubled by her husband's compassion and humanity, concerned he will be unable to kill in cold blood. She knows him well: we also saw his scrupulous side when the 'horrid image' of murder first occurred to him in Act One Scene Three, and his 'seated heart [began] to knock at his ribs / Against the use of nature'. The image of milk contrasts with the many references to blood in the play. Blood is associated with brutal violence, but milk symbolises maternal nourishment and care. There is an inversion of gender stereotypes here: Macbeth is too full of milk, while Lady Macbeth is about to reject hers, hoping to have it replaced with gall.

Perhaps Shakespeare also hints at Lady Macbeth's own weaker side here too. Like her husband, she seems unable to name the act of regicide; instead, she calls the murder the 'nearest way'. Throughout the play, the Macbeths use euphemisms such as 'bloody business' and 'the deed', avoiding more direct terms. This might hint at a certain level of denial of the heinous nature of the crime they are going to commit.

PAUSE POINT

CONSOLIDATION

Ask students to write a summary of today's extract.

Challenge students further by reminding them to include tentative and assertive language.

Upon the stage

Simon Godwin (2024) had Indira Varma read the letter with remarkable intelligence and each new piece of information moved her. Varma went from wry surprise to murderous intent over the course of these few lines and the transformation was extraordinary. By contrast, Judi Dench seemed quite terrified of the powers she called on in the (1979) Trevor Nunn production, but she screwed her own courage to the sticking place by the end of her shocking prayer.

Show students clips of these two actors performing the same role: which interpretation do your students prefer, and why?

CHAPTER 8
LOOK LIKE THE INNOCENT FLOWER, / BUT BE THE SERPENT UNDER'T
ACT ONE SCENE FIVE (LINES 39 TO END)

At a glance

- **Plot and character development:** After the Messenger exits, Lady Macbeth invokes the help of evil spirits to help her plan. Macbeth arrives, and they resolve to kill Duncan.
- **Social and historical context:** Witchcraft
- **Vocabulary:** Façade
- **Big question:** Why does Shakespeare present Lady Macbeth's desire for Macbeth to be king?
- **Themes:**
  - Ambition and power
  - Appearance vs reality
  - Disorder and the unnatural
- **Analysis:**
  - Lady Macbeth's soliloquy
  - Text: imperative verbs
  - Staging: balance of speech
- **Key quotation:** 'Look like the innocent flower, / But be the serpent under't'

PAUSE POINT

RETRIEVAL

Start with a quick quiz, asking students to define each word. Then give students 3 minutes to write a summary of what they know about Lady Macbeth so far, using as many of the words as they can.

E.g. malevolent, tragic hero, dramatic irony, vengeful, manipulative, soliloquy, resolute.

As you discuss the scene, prompt students to use these words in their verbal and written responses.

Plot and character development

A Messenger tells Lady Macbeth that Duncan is on his way. He exits and Lady Macbeth gives an unsettling speech: she calls on evil spirits to take away everything feminine about her, so that no softness, compassion or other stereotypically 'feminine' aspects get in her way. She wants to feel no remorse, but instead to be full of 'direst cruelty'. Like her husband did earlier, she calls on night to shield her actions, so that she can operate in darkness.

Right as her prayer ends, Macbeth appears. We see the dynamic between the couple: they are well-matched, love each other and listen to each other. Although they are excited by the prospect of becoming king and queen, Macbeth is hesitant. Lady Macbeth adopts the dominant role, reassuring her husband and promising to organise everything.

Social and historical context

Witchcraft

In Jacobean England, where witches were both feared and hated, Lady Macbeth's invocation of dark forces would have been unsettling. Although she is not literally a witch, her blasphemous prayer constitutes a radical rejection of divine and natural order: she renounces her gender, plots regicide and pleads for the removal of her own conscience.

Vocabulary | Façade

It can be powerful to use an image to support the teaching of new vocabulary. This can particularly be the case when teaching students with SEND or who are multilingual.

Definition:	**Images:**
Deception, pretending to be something that you are not.	
Examples: *An Inspector Calls* (1946): Gerald puts on a façade of gentlemanliness, when his behaviour towards women is actually exploitative. *Animal Farm* (1945): Napoleon presents the façade of being a selfless leader, when in reality he is exploiting the other animals.	**Non-examples:** *Macbeth* (1606): Banquo does not have a façade – he is honest and trustworthy. *A Christmas Carol* (1843): Fred does not have a façade – his jolliness is a sincere reflection of the joy he feels in his heart.

Reading the scene

As we proceed further into the play, Shakespeare's complex interweaving of motifs and symbols becomes more apparent.

Take the role of Lady Macbeth yourself and allocate the roles of Macbeth and the stage directions to strong readers. Read the scene once through.

Read the scene for a second time, asking students to identify motifs and symbols they have already encountered. Support students in need of additional help by providing a list of symbols to look out for (see Appendix B):

- crown
- blood
- milk
- darkness.

Students might also notice the flower and the serpent, which are introduced in this scene.

PAUSE POINT

S-T-R-E-T-C-H

In this section of the play, Shakespeare presents Lady Macbeth as dominating her husband, planning the regicide and attempting to assuage her husband's anxieties.

Ask students to contrast these two key quotations from the extract.

	Lady Macbeth	Macbeth
Quotation	'I **feel** now / The future in the instant'	'We **will** speak further.'
What does the line mean?		
What do we learn about the character?		
What do you notice about Shakespeare's verb choices?		

Big question

Why does Shakespeare present Lady Macbeth's desire for Macbeth to be king?

One could argue that Shakespeare presents Lady Macbeth as simply hungry for power, revelling in her role as a murderous mastermind. But alternatively she could be portrayed as an unconventional woman who is desperate for the agency denied her in a largely patriarchal society. She rejects her own femininity ('unsex me here') and imagines herself committing a violent act ('my keen knife'), just as the men have done on the battlefield. Towards the end of this scene, she talks about the crown as if she will be able to share in its power: 'all our nights and days to come / Give solely sovereign sway and masterdom'.

Furthermore, by securing the crown for Macbeth, she offers an alternative legacy, substituting royal power for a hereditary line – even if his legacy cannot be passed down to the next generation.

Themes

Ambition and power

Lady Macbeth's ambition is distinguished not by its intensity but by its foresight. She understands, before the deed is even committed, exactly what it will cost her: her femininity, her compassion, her membership in civil society. Her appeal to the spirits is not an ambitious gamble but a calculated transaction. She will give up 'remorse', maternal feeling, her own 'milk' of human kindness and in exchange she will receive power. Shakespeare presents an ambition so clear-eyed that it can name its own price. The tragedy is that Lady Macbeth will pay it, and the crown will not be worth the 'doubtful joy' it brings.

Appearance vs reality

This theme was introduced in Act One Scene Four, as Duncan mused about the challenge of finding 'the mind's construction in the face', while Macbeth tried to hide his 'black and deep desires'. Here, Lady Macbeth recommends that Macbeth look like the 'flower' even as he behaves like a 'serpent'. The Macbeths will end this first act with a determination that 'false face must hide what the false heart doth know'.

Disorder and the unnatural

Lady Macbeth deliberately perverts the natural order in this scene. She prays to dark spirits to compromise the natural workings of her body, to make her cruel, remorseless and ready to kill. The murder of Duncan will unleash a variety of unnatural events and occurrences; this disorder is what Lady Macbeth knows must happen for her husband to become king.

Analysis

Lady Macbeth's soliloquy

This soliloquy opens with a reference to the 'raven', a carrion bird that acts as an ill omen announcing Duncan's arrival and imminent death. Yet Shakespeare reveals that Lady Macbeth mistrusts herself and her gender, calling on 'spirits' to 'unsex' her, eliminating stereotypically feminine traits of compassion and kindness, and replacing them with the kind of 'cruelty' Macbeth showed on the battlefield. She wants to be completely transformed, from the 'crown to the toe' – it can be no accident that Shakespeare repeats this symbol of power here. A simple reference to the top of Lady Macbeth's head is an opportunity to remind the audience of what is at stake: absolute power over Scotland.

As she warms to her theme, Lady Macbeth asks the spirits to 'make thick my blood'. It was believed that blood was one of the four humours, responsible for carrying emotions through the body. Shakespeare suggests that Lady Macbeth wants her blood to thicken so that no remorse can shake her from her intentions, and no 'compunctious visitings of nature [from] / Shake [her] fell purpose'. Here, Shakespeare emphasises that regicide is an unnatural act, which challenges the Divine Right of Kings and overturns earthly order.

In an echo of her first soliloquy, Lady Macbeth calls on these 'murdering ministers' to take her 'milk for gall' – replacing feminine compassion with bitter poison and preventing her from fulfilling a maternal role. Gall, or yellow bile, was another of the humours thought to govern the human body; it was associated with audacity and aggression. Lady Macbeth wants to replace what is maternal in her with something more brazen and violent. Shakespeare highlights how she is determined to do anything to achieve her desires.

Towards the end, Shakespeare introduces the motif of light and darkness. Like her husband in Act One Scene Four ('let not light see my black and deep desires'), Lady Macbeth calls for 'night', 'hell' and 'dark' to prevent 'heaven' from seeing and preventing the act of murder. The speech builds so much in intensity that Lady Macbeth has to end with the word 'hold!' – as if trying to stop herself from what she has unleashed.

Macbeth enters as this speech reaches its climax, prompting Lady Macbeth to cry 'Great Glamis, worthy Cawdor' echoing both the witches' prophecies and Duncan's praise. Macbeth's two titles remind us that the first two prophecies have come true – suggesting that it is now inevitable that Macbeth will become king.

Text: imperative verbs

Shakespeare uses many imperative verbs in this scene. These appear in Lady Macbeth's appeals to the spirits ('come') and also as she speaks to her husband ('look...be...'). These verbs reveal her ability to control and dominate.

Staging: balance of speech

Note that even when Macbeth enters, Lady Macbeth is given the most lines. Her dominance is starkly juxtaposed with Macbeth's reticence ('We will speak further').

Key quotation | 'Look like the innocent flower, / But be the serpent under't'

Lady Macbeth commands her husband to put on a façade of honesty – just like the previous Thane of Cawdor had. The image of the 'innocent flower' suggests peace and gentleness. It is also an image from nature, contrasting directly with the developing motif of unnatural events (see Appendix B). By contrast, the symbol of the serpent has a long history as a representation of evil. It is primarily a Biblical allusion to the devil, who takes the form of a serpent in the Book of Genesis, tempting Eve to eat from the Tree of Knowledge. Just as Eve convinces her husband to eat the apple, Lady Macbeth's words will persuade Macbeth to unleash hell on Scotland.

The image of the flower and the serpent is also a direct visual reference to the Gunpowder Plot discussed earlier. King James commissioned a Dutch company to create a medallion bearing the image of a snake hiding amongst flowers to commemorate the foiling of the plot (Hawkins, 1885). This pairing of images directly referenced the recent plot - a contemporary instance of betrayal, treason and ambition.

PAUSE POINT

CONSOLIDATION

This is a 60 second activity to help students to recap what they have just learned.

Students work in pairs: one chooses the flower, and the other the serpent.

The students take turns in saying a connotation linked to their chosen symbol. The first student to 'drop the ball' loses the game.

You could support students in need of further help by discussing this table before you start the game.

Flower	Serpent
Innocence	Deception
Nature	Betrayal
Beauty	Manipulation
Loyalty	Biblical allusion
Integrity	Gunpowder plot

Upon the stage

This scene relies on a magnetic chemistry between husband and wife, yet it is often staged as a public conspiracy. The Donmar production (2024), allowed for an unusual level of secrecy between David Tennant and Cush Jumbo. They performed the scene in hushed, cautious whispers, their voices amplified directly into each audience member's ears. This technology transformed their conspiracy into a private, domestic secret, making the audience complicit in their plotting.

Does this intimate, whispered approach make the Macbeths' decision more or less shocking than a more overtly passionate or confrontational staging?

CHAPTER 9
OUR HONOURED HOSTESS
ACT ONE SCENE SIX

At a glance

- **Plot and character development:** Duncan and his entourage arrive at Macbeth's castle, and they are greeted formally by Lady Macbeth.
- **Social and historical context:** Hospitality
- **Themes:**
  - Appearance vs reality
  - The Divine Right of Kings
- **Analysis:**
  - Language: formal speech
- **Key quotation:** 'Our honoured hostess'

PAUSE POINT

RETRIEVAL

In this scene, Shakespeare heightens the dramatic irony and tension as the appearance of hospitality is undermined by the reality of impending murder.

This is an opportunity to revisit quotations from earlier in the play. Students could annotate the quotations, or write a short explanation of the meaning of each one.

1. Witches: 'fair is foul, and foul is fair'.
2. Duncan: 'there's no art / To find the mind's construction in the face'.
3. Lady Macbeth: 'look like the innocent flower, / But be the serpent under't'.
4. Macbeth: 'false face must hide what the false heart doth know'.

Plot and character development

Lady Macbeth told her husband to 'look like the innocent flower, / But be the serpent under't': in this scene she gives a chilling demonstration of how to do so. As he and his men arrive at the castle, Duncan speaks warmly about how pleasant the castle feels and even Banquo points out that the location is 'delicate'. Shakespeare emphasises Duncan's kindliness and warmth. When Lady Macbeth greets him, Duncan is very gracious and makes it clear that he has a particular affection for Macbeth. The scene is deeply ironic since we know that Lady Macbeth is eager for Duncan to be murdered under her battlements.

Social and historical context

Hospitality

Throughout history there have been moral codes of hospitality: it is a host's duty to protect their guest and ensure the guest's safety in their home. Scottish Highland hospitality was legendary. For Shakespeare to stage a scene where a Scottish king – God's anointed – naively walks into a trap set by his own hosts would have been deeply provocative; always bear in mind that the then king of England was from Scotland.

Reading the scene

The language in this scene is deliberately complex and elevated, as it reflects the courtly nature of Duncan's formal arrival at the Macbeths' castle. You will therefore need to read it through at least twice, or show an adaptation instead to ensure that students hear correct and fluent pronunciation of the lines.

When re-reading, ask students to find repeated words within the extract.

These are:

- 'thanks'
- 'honour(ed)'
- 'hostess'.

Prompt students to consider why Shakespeare repeated these words; they are there to amplify our sense of Duncan's kindness and overly trusting nature and to heighten our awareness of Lady Macbeth's deception.

PAUSE POINT

S-T-R-E-T-C-H

Discuss Shakespeare's use of bird imagery in the play so far (see Appendix B).

Themes

Appearance vs reality

This scene shows Duncan's affable personality and Lady Macbeth's extraordinary ability to dissemble. The king's speech is full of pleasantness and 'heaven's breath', in direct contrast with the hellish prayers we have just seen Lady Macbeth utter. Lady Macbeth states that she will serve the king, and that she and her husband are 'your servants ever'.

The Divine Right of Kings

Lady Macbeth's ironically polite words to Duncan shows the appropriate level of respect to a divinely-anointed king entering her home. Even though she is planning his murder, she still performs the appropriate duty of welcoming the king. Shakespeare establishes Duncan both as a kindly man and a noble king, all the better to shock the audience with his forthcoming murder.

Analysis

Language: formal speech

Shakespeare gives Lady Macbeth intricate, even excessively formal language to show how hard she's working in this scene. Hers is a performance of hospitality, and so her language is complicated and overdone. This contrasts with the rather more relaxed language of Duncan's verse, which is as pleasant as it is unsuspecting.

Key quotation | 'Our honoured hostess'

Duncan's use of the royal plural emphasises his status as king, and his generous praise shows his readiness to reward loyal subjects. Having already promoted Macbeth to Thane of Cawdor and promised to make him 'full of growing', and later sending Lady Macbeth a diamond, his benevolence deepens the audience's sympathy, making his betrayal by the Macbeths all the more shocking.

PAUSE POINT

CONSOLIDATION

Triplet discussion: Where does Shakespeare use dramatic irony, and why?

- Student A: Identify where Shakespeare uses dramatic irony, providing precise evidence.
- Student B: Explain why Shakespeare uses dramatic irony.
- Student C: Summarise the discussion.

Model answer:

Shakespeare uses dramatic irony in Act One Scene Three. In the previous scene, Duncan granted the title of Thane of Cawdor to Macbeth. Yet Macbeth does not discover this until after the Witches give their prophecies. Shakespeare organises the events in this order to emphasise how the Witches manipulate the truth, presenting elements of it rather than revealing everything. [We will explore the Witches' use of equivocation further in Chapter 15.]

Shakespeare includes another example of dramatic irony in Act One Scene Four, when Duncan explains the challenge of finding the 'mind's construction' in the face. Ironically, Shakespeare's emphasis on Duncan's enthusiastic welcome of his 'worthiest cousin' confirms this, as Macbeth's façade of loyalty is already concealing his 'black and deep desires'. Here, the dramatic irony highlights the theme of appearance and reality and acts as a warning against being overly trusting.

Upon the stage

In Eve Best's (2014) Globe production, Duncan's large entourage entered through the audience before they arrived onto the stage. As Banquo pointed out the martlets, the audience and onstage company heard birdsong, which distracted from the entrance of Lady Macbeth (played by Samantha Spiro). She then had to laugh to get Duncan's attention. This delicate moment contrasted sharply with Spiro's performance in the previous scene, and saw her change very convincingly into a 'delicate flower'. In the (2021) Joel Coen film, the castle courtyard was likewise filled with birds and soft light as Duncan (Brendan Gleeson) arrived, but these disappeared as soon as Lady Macbeth (Frances McDormand) appeared.

What does each directorial choice symbolise? The birdsong represents the 'heaven's breath' Duncan feels, while its cessation (or the birds fleeing) subtly represents the darkness that enters with Lady Macbeth.

CHAPTER 10
VAULTING AMBITION
ACT ONE SCENE SEVEN (LINES 1 TO 28)

At a glance

- **Plot and character development:** Macbeth is reluctant to kill Duncan.
- **Vocabulary:** Euphemism
- **Big question:** Why does Shakespeare dramatise Macbeth's doubts in this scene?
- **Themes:**
  - Ambition and power
  - Guilt and conscience
- **Analysis:**
  - Macbeth's soliloquy
- **Key quotation:** 'Vaulting ambition'

PAUSE POINT

RETRIEVAL

As we reach the end of Act I, formatively assess your students' knowledge so far. A full list of motifs, key quotations and vocabulary can be found in our online resources; use these to create your knowledge check.

Plot and character development

Macbeth leaves the offstage feast to speak to us about his doubts. His soliloquy explains his moral turmoil: he lists all the reasons that he should not kill Duncan – his cousin, his guest and his king. Macbeth is tormented by the fear of consequences: if the murder was the be all and end all, that would make it easier. But there are too many extenuating circumstances and Macbeth resolves not to proceed with the planned regicide.

Vocabulary | Euphemism

Macbeth and Lady Macbeth frequently use euphemisms for murder to avoid admitting the brutal reality of regicide.

Definition:	**Morphology:**
An indirect way of referring to a harsh or unpleasant truth.	Prefix: eu = good e.g. euphoric, eulogy Root: phēmē = speech
Examples:	**Non-examples:**
An Inspector Calls (1945): Mr Birling refers to the 'nasty mess' of Eva's death. *Macbeth* (1606): The words 'it', 'deed', 'business' and others are used to refer to regicide.	*Macbeth* (1606): Macduff announces the 'murder' of Duncan in Act Two Scene Three. *Macbeth* (1606): Macbeth finally uses the word 'murder' in Act Three Scene One when he starts to face up to the horror of what he has done.

Reading the scene

Macbeth's soliloquy

This scene starts with a complex soliloquy in which Macbeth lists the reasons why he shouldn't commit regicide. Read the scene twice through and then explore the reasons why Macbeth is reluctant to proceed with the plan. Provide students with a blank copy of the table below with the second column left blank (see the online resources for a template) and ask them to fill it in.

Quotation	What does it mean?
'If th'assassination / Could trammel up the consequence.'	Macbeth wants to avoid the consequences of regicide.
'The life to come'	These consequences are in the afterlife.
'Judgement here'	And in this life.
'We teach / Bloody instructions, which being taught, return / To plague th'inventor.'	Macbeth is concerned that if he commits regicide, he will set a precedent that others might emulate.
'I am his kinsman'	Macbeth is related to Duncan.
'and his subject'	Macbeth should be loyal to his king.
'as his host'	Macbeth should protect his guests.
'Duncan [...] hath been / So clear in his great office.'	Duncan is a good king.

PAUSE POINT

S-T-R-E-T-C-H

Triplet discussion: Shakespeare presents Macbeth considering a range of reasons for not committing murder, but he does not mention the horror of brutally stabbing his cousin and king. Why do you think this is?

- Student A: Respond to the question.
- Student B: Provide evidence to support Student A's response.
- Student C: Summarise the discussion.

Model answer:

In this soliloquy, Shakespeare presents Macbeth as focused on the moral, spiritual and practical consequences of regicide. He is aware that killing the king will lead to his moral downfall, as well as punishment in 'the life to come'. As if that wasn't enough, he knows that the bloody deed will result in his actions returning to 'plague' him – if Macbeth sets a precedent for regicide, he could be the next victim. Shakespeare's lack of reference to the violence of the act itself may be due to Macbeth's extensive experience on the battlefield.

Big question

Why does Shakespeare dramatise Macbeth's doubts in this scene?

At the end of Act One Scene Five, the Macbeths discussed the potential murder and Lady Macbeth was certain that they were going to proceed with the plot – telling her husband to 'leave all the rest to me'. In Act One Scene Seven, all is proceeding to plan; Duncan feasts at the castle, completely unaware of the Macbeths' deception. In Act Two Scene One, Macbeth will see the 'air-drawn dagger' leading him to Duncan's bedchamber.

Instead of going directly from Duncan's arrival to his murder, Shakespeare interposes Act One Scene Seven to heighten the tension and explore Macbeth's moral quandary. Macbeth is not a stock villain who kills without remorse: he is a complex, human character caught between his ambition, conscience, fear of failure and external pressures. This is Shakespeare's great skill: he delves into the complexity of human emotion, building pathos for a character that the audience should probably perceive as a villain. The horror of Act Two Scenes One and Two is not just that a king is killed, but also that a previously heroic, admirable character crosses a moral line and damns himself.

Analysis

Macbeth's soliloquy

In Macbeth's second soliloquy, Shakespeare reveals his troubled conscience as he weighs ambition against morality.

Macbeth continues to avoid naming the crime: 'if it were done, when 'tis done, then 'twere well / It were done quickly'. The repeated use of euphemisms for murder reveals the Macbeths' desire to diminish and ignore the seriousness of the act they are going to commit. Lady Macbeth will echo these lines later in the play when she says 'what's done cannot be undone'.

Shakespeare reveals Macbeth's belief that he could commit the murder if 'the assassination / Could trammel up the consequence' – if the murder was self-contained and no further consequences came with it. He seems less concerned with the regicide than its repercussions on earth and in the afterlife. But there is no 'jump[ing] the life to come' or evading 'judgement here' on earth. Instead, the 'bloody instructions' will 'plague' the murderer. Shakespeare is foreshadowing Macbeth's psychological disintegration, echoing Biblical language to suggest a punishment from God. There is another religious reference in the phrase 'poisoned chalice', which could refer to the communion cup. Taken together, these religious terms remind the audience that Macbeth is not simply killing another person (which is bad enough) – he is also preparing to challenge the god-ordained Divine Right of Kings.

Shakespeare includes many other factors in this lengthy, uncertain speech. Listing more reasons why he should abandon the plan, Macbeth acknowledges that Duncan is his 'kinsman' (just as Duncan called him 'cousin'). He states that he is Duncan's 'subject' and his 'host', both social roles which demand loyalty rather than murder. Finally, Macbeth understands that Duncan's 'virtues / Will plead like angels... against / The deep damnation of his taking off'. Duncan is a good and honourable king and killing him will lead to outcry. Macbeth worries that Duncan will be pitied: he has a fantasy of pity being like a vulnerable newborn baby, or the angels of heaven, riding the wind and blowing the news of Duncan's murder in the faces of all humanity so that 'tears would drown the wind.' Macbeth is prone to extraordinary and poetic exaggeration; this is the first instance of many.

The soliloquy concludes with an equestrian image, as Macbeth longs for a 'spur / To prick the sides of my intent'. His 'vaulting ambition' is not enough to motivate him.

PAUSE POINT

WRITING

Give students time to process their understanding of this lengthy soliloquy.

Ask your class to write a summary of the soliloquy, using tentative and assertive language where appropriate.

Stretch students further by asking them to think conceptually: encourage them to discuss how Shakespeare reveals Macbeth's mental torment in order to explore the psychological consequences of acting on unchecked ambition.

Key quotation | 'Vaulting ambition'

Macbeth concludes his soliloquy by reflecting on his motivation for killing Duncan:

I have no spur
To prick the sides of my intent, but only
Vaulting ambition, which o'erleaps itself
And falls on th' other –

Using an equestrian image, Shakespeare highlights Macbeth's realisation that there is no reason ('spur') propelling him to commit murder – other than his ambition. And this ambition is 'vaulting', meaning that although it will elevate him for a short time, he will eventually 'fall'. These lines reveal that Macbeth is aware of the very real consequences that he could face. At the end of the soliloquy, he decides that ambition is not sufficient to overcome the arguments against the murder.

PAUSE POINT

CONSOLIDATION

At the end of this soliloquy, Macbeth decides that he 'will proceed no further in this business'.

Ask students to use their knowledge of Lady Macbeth to make predictions about how she will react to this news.

Upon the stage

This soliloquy is a tentpole in any actor's interpretation of the play:

- Ralph Fiennes (Coen, 2024) was rational and even charming in his argument, seemingly determined to proceed no further.
- By contrast, Ian McKellen (Nunn, 1979) was considerably less innocent – he seemed more convinced towards murder, almost enjoying wrestling against his own scruples.
- A very compelling version came from Rory Kinnear (Norris, 2018), who seemed genuinely horrified even to be considering a crime so terrible. Kinnear allows Macbeth to stay good, or innocent, for longer than most.

Ask your students if they are convinced by this soliloquy; has Macbeth made up his mind yet?

CHAPTER 11

SCREW YOUR COURAGE TO THE STICKING PLACE, / AND WE'LL NOT FAIL

ACT ONE SCENE SEVEN (LINES 29 TO END)

At a glance

- **Plot and character development:** Macbeth announces his decision not to kill Duncan, but Lady Macbeth manipulates him, questioning his loyalty and masculinity. They make a plan of action.
- **Vocabulary:** Imperative verbs
- **Big question:** Why does Shakespeare show Lady Macbeth using the image of a murdered child to manipulate her husband?
- **Themes:**
  - Ambition and power
  - Violence and masculinity
  - Appearance vs reality
- **Analysis:**
  - Staging: argument
  - Violent imagery
  - Dramatic irony
- **Key quotation:** 'Screw your courage to the sticking place, / And we'll not fail'
- **Handle with care:** This scene involves a brutal description of the suggested murder of a baby. If you think any students in your class will be affected by this, speak to their pastoral team for advice.

PAUSE POINT

RETRIEVAL

Shakespeare presents Lady Macbeth attacking her husband's masculinity in this scene. Ask students to think-pair-share relevant references to this theme in the text so far.

Students could consider how Shakespeare presents:

- Macbeth's masculine courage and patriotism in Act One Scene Two.
- The rewards Macbeth receives for his masculine courage.
- Lady Macbeth's concerns about her husband's ability to kill in cold blood.

Plot and character development

Right when Macbeth wishes he had some inspiration to goad him into action, Lady Macbeth appears. However, Macbeth initially insists that he will not proceed with the murder, igniting his wife's fury and frustration.

The subsequent argument sharpens the contrast between the protagonists. Macbeth hesitates, concerned with the national and moral consequences of this murder. Lady Macbeth is more concerned with the immediate, the imminent, the practical. She shows no doubt and is ruthless in her determination. Macbeth finally complies and they plan their next steps.

Vocabulary | Imperative verbs

Shakespeare uses imperative verbs to dramatise the debate between Macbeth and Lady Macbeth.

Imperative verb: a command verb e.g. do your homework; stand behind your desk; pack your bags.

Whiteboard task: identify the imperative verb(s) in these quotations (answers are underlined):

1. Duncan – '<u>Go</u>, get him surgeons'
2. Duncan – '<u>Pronounce</u> his present death, / And with his former title <u>greet</u> Macbeth'
3. Macbeth – '<u>Speak</u> if you can'
4. Macbeth – '<u>Stay</u>, you imperfect speakers, <u>tell</u> me more'
5. Lady Macbeth – '<u>Look</u> like the innocent flower, / But <u>be</u> the serpent under't.'

What is the purpose of imperative verbs?

They demonstrate power and authority.

Return to the five quotations above with your class and ask them who holds the power. (Note: in three and four, the Witches do not follow Macbeth's instructions. They therefore demonstrate their independence and Macbeth's lack of power over them.)

Reading the scene

The argument

There are many shared lines in this scene. Macbeth and Lady Macbeth's lines almost cut across one another, heightening the emotional intensity of the scene.

Before reading the scene as a class, ask students to rehearse these lines in pairs. Even as one 'Lady Macbeth' starts to say her final word, 'Macbeth' should start speaking.

Lady Macbeth

He hath almost supped.

Why have you left the chamber?

Macbeth

Hath he ask'd for me?

Lady Macbeth

Know you not he has?

Then read the scene as a class. Read the role of Lady Macbeth yourself, so that you can emphasise her vehemence as she forces Macbeth to proceed with the murder.

PAUSE POINT

S-T-R-E-T-C-H

Triplet discussion: 'In Act One Scene Seven, Shakespeare presents Macbeth and Lady Macbeth as equally powerful characters.' How far do you agree?

- Student A: Argue that Macbeth and Lady Macbeth are equally powerful.

- Student B: Argue that Lady Macbeth is actually more powerful.
- Student C: Summarise the discussion.

Model answer:

At the start of the scene, Shakespeare shows Macbeth worrying about the consequences of regicide. This hesitant figure is very different from the powerful warrior we heard 'carved his passage' through the enemy in Act One Scene Two. Shakespeare presents Macbeth attempting to assert his authority when Lady Macbeth enters: his line 'we will proceed no further in this business' is suitably dominant and certain. But Lady Macbeth challenges his hard-won self-assurance; her impassioned accusations and mentions of children unsettle Macbeth and undermine his masculinity. By the end of the scene, Shakespeare highlights how convincing Lady Macbeth is that regicide is the only way, and Macbeth agrees to it.

Big question

Why does Shakespeare show Lady Macbeth using the image of a murdered child to manipulate her husband?

Of all the acts that Lady Macbeth could have used as an example, she chooses the most horrific: infanticide. Shakespeare uses this image to reveal her absolute ruthlessness: she is prepared to cross all moral lines. The image of the child also hints at what Macbeth wants most: his ambition is not just to be king, but to father an heir to the throne. The image of the baby must surely remind him of this desire.

Themes

Ambition and power

Both Macbeth and Lady Macbeth have already spoken about their lust for power, but here Shakespeare presents Lady Macbeth taking it a step further by insisting that she would do whatever it takes to get the throne. She states that if she had sworn an oath the way Macbeth has, she would, without hesitation, kill a baby to fulfil her promise. We have already heard Lady Macbeth renouncing her femininity ('unsex me here'), and now this speech shows her utter ruthlessness. She is telling Macbeth that her commitment exceeds his and that his hesitation is therefore a failure of love as well as courage. Shakespeare reveals that the corruption of ambition is not just the willingness to commit violence, but the willingness to *use* the most intimate human bonds as weapons in an argument.

Violence and masculinity

In Act One Scene Five, Lady Macbeth suggested that her husband was 'too full of the milk of human kindness'. She elaborates now, telling her husband that he must be 'afeard' and a 'coward'. Shakespeare has already shown us that Macbeth's reputation and character are built on his military prowess; by insulting him in this way, Lady Macbeth knows that she will force him to react. Macbeth insists that he 'dare do all that may become a man', but she responds that 'when you durst do it, then you were a man'. She challenges her husband to prove his masculine courage and daring nature by committing a further act of violence – one that she will set up.

Appearance vs reality

Earlier Lady Macbeth cautioned Macbeth to 'look like the innocent flower', but here it is Macbeth who ends the scene with the determination that he must put on a 'false face' to hide his 'false heart'. The echoes of the witches' line 'fair is foul' continue to ripple through the play.

Analysis

Staging: argument

Just when Macbeth acknowledges that he needs more of a 'spur', Lady Macbeth enters and berates him for overthinking. Shakespeare portrays her as ruthlessly practical, in deliberate contrast to Macbeth's exaggerated, apocalyptic worries. The juxtaposition of ponderous monologue with aggressive dialogue dramatises their argument.

Lady Macbeth has an answer – and a plan – for every one of her husband's concerns, and it is she that drives forward their plan for murder.

Violent imagery

Shakespeare's use of language and imagery in this scene is particularly shocking. Lady Macbeth questions Macbeth's manhood while negating her own feminine identity: she says that she would murder her own child if she had sworn herself to action the way Macbeth has. These lines are particularly visceral, as the image of the 'smiling' breast-feeding baby is quickly followed by the monstrous phrase 'dashed the brains out'. Again, Shakespeare juxtaposes maternal 'milk' (connoting care and love) and masculine violence, in a description that is both fair and foul.

Dramatic irony

Macbeth is so impressed by Lady Macbeth's determination that he comments she should 'bring forth men-children only'. He does not know that she has already cursed herself with sterility for the sake of their advancement.

Key quotation | 'Screw your courage to the sticking place, / and we'll not fail'

Amid Macbeth's worries about the consequences of regicide, his biggest fear and final defence against Lady Macbeth's arguments is failure. Lady Macbeth's powerful rebuttal refers to the tightening of a crossbow for firing. The mechanism and the string are tightened until the weapon is ready to launch.

Lady Macbeth uses the plural first person here. Both Macbeths use 'we' throughout the first act, solidifying their partnership. After the murder Shakespeare shows this sense of togetherness crumbling as Macbeth isolates himself from his wife, but for now they are united. Lady Macbeth's use of 'we'll' answers Macbeth's speech earlier in the scene ('we will proceed no further in this business'). Macbeth's determination is quashed, and she prevails.

PAUSE POINT

CONSOLIDATION

This is a turning point in the play, as Lady Macbeth finally overcomes her husband's final qualms.

Ask students to make a list of what changes during the course of this scene. Challenge them to include quotations to support their ideas. Alternatively, you could provide them with the ideas listed below and ask them to find the evidence, or give students the evidence and ask them to explain what has changed.

- Shakespeare presents Macbeth as changing his mind and agreeing to murder Duncan ('We will proceed no further in this business' to 'I am settled').
- Shakespeare reveals how Macbeth is isolated at the start of the scene, but united with Lady Macbeth by the end. ('Why have you left the chamber?' to 'we'll not fail').
- Shakespeare demonstrates how Lady Macbeth grows in brutality. ('Was the hope drunk' to 'dashed the brains out').

Upon the stage

This scene's power dynamic has been staged in many compelling ways:

- Trevor Nunn (1979): Judi Dench and Ian McKellen were extraordinary, wrestling verbally and physically between hesitation and decision.
- Joel Coen (2021): Frances McDormand and Denzel Washington presented a more sober, quietly menacing couple.

- Simon Godwin (2024): Ralph Fiennes was calm and thoughtful, his diffident answers to Indira Varma's provocations culminating in the intimate, charged gesture of saying 'bring forth men children only' with his head against her stomach.
- Polly Findlay (2018): For sheer passion, Niamh Cusack's performance remains one of the most compelling.

Show your students a range of these: ask which couple they found most convincing. Do they side with Macbeth, or Lady Macbeth?

CHAPTER 12
THE HEAT-OPPRESSED BRAIN
ACT TWO SCENE ONE

At a glance

- **Plot and character development:** Banquo and Fleance talk before bed. Macbeth arrives and he agrees to talk to Banquo at some point about the prophecies. Banquo and Fleance leave and Macbeth sees a vision of a dagger leading him to Duncan's bedchamber.
- **Social and historical context:** Banquo and Fleance's Relation to James I
- **Vocabulary:** Synonyms for nervous
- **Big question:** Does Shakespeare present the dagger as a supernatural temptation or a projection of Macbeth's own guilt?
- **Themes:**
  - Ambition and power
  - Appearance vs reality
  - Disorder and the unnatural
- **Analysis:**
  - Motif: darkness and light
  - Macbeth's soliloquy
  - Text: feminine endings
  - Motif: blood
- **Key quotation:** 'The heat-oppressed brain'
- **Handle with care:** Some of the images and references in Macbeth's soliloquy are to extreme violence, predation and rape. Consider how much detail you wish to go into with your students.

PAUSE POINT

RETRIEVAL

Quiz students on their knowledge of these key terms:

- tragic hero
- soliloquy
- malevolent
- regicide
- Divine Right of Kings.

Ask students to work in triplets. Select a student to begin. Give them 30 seconds to explain how Shakespeare presents Macbeth, using all five terms; remind them not to simply list the words, but to use 'because' to explain their thinking. Signal for silence and sample several students to give their explanation to the whole group. Then repeat so that all three students in the group have had the opportunity to practice.

Added bonus: after rehearsal, ask students to write their explanation in their books.

Plot and character development

Banquo discusses his dark dreams with his son, Fleance, and he wishes to rid himself of the 'cursed thoughts' he has when asleep. Macbeth enters and Banquo talks about Duncan's generosity; not only has the king given Macbeth 'great largess', but he has also sent a diamond to Lady Macbeth. When the conversation turns to the Witches, Banquo says that they have shown Macbeth 'some truth'. In contrast, Macbeth lies that he hasn't thought of them.

After Banquo and Fleance leave, Macbeth hallucinates a dagger pointing him towards Duncan's quarters, leading him to murder. Macbeth interrogates his fears and moral concerns, but eventually decides to go through with the regicide. When he hears the agreed-upon signal from Lady Macbeth, he exits the stage to kill the king.

Social and historical context

Banquo and Fleance's relation to James I

An entirely fictional genealogy appears in Shakespeare's primary source, Holinshed's *Chronicles* (1587). Holinshed suggested that after his escape from Scotland, Fleance settled in Wales and that his son Walter FitzAlan returned to Scotland and founded the Stuart dynasty. It appears in the play as a small piece of royal flattery, since King James considered himself a descendant of Banquo and Fleance.

Vocabulary | Synonyms for nervous

As we progress towards the heart of the play, Macbeth grows more apprehensive. His 'heat-oppressed brain' is fired up by pressure from the Witches, Lady Macbeth and his own 'vaulting ambition'. Students will need to use a variety of adjectives accurately to describe Macbeth's state of mind.

First, ask students to think-pair-share synonyms for the word nervous. Then organise them on the scale below (suggestions are provided). Discuss how and when to use each word.

Concerned → Overwrought	
Concerned	Unsettled
	Uneasy
	Apprehensive
	Worried
	Tense
	Agitated
	Upset
	Distraught
Overwrought	Tormented

Reading the scene

As with many scenes in the play, Act Two Scene One includes significant shifts in tone. It begins with an uneasy conversation between father and son, before a sudden rush of anxiety as Banquo is startled by an unknown visitor in line 10. This settles slightly to a tense discussion between Banquo and Macbeth, before Macbeth is left alone on stage to give an agitated soliloquy. These shifts can be tricky to capture in the classroom.

Ask your readers for Banquo and Fleance to take their seats to the front of the classroom. They begin seated and relatively relaxed. Instruct Banquo and Fleance to stand when Macbeth enters, reflecting the sharp rise in tension. Banquo and Fleance should then walk to the back of the classroom to leave Macbeth alone on 'stage'. Download the sound of a bell ringing for the end of Macbeth's speech.

Display images of the following objects on the board to guide students' understanding of the soliloquy. You might want to discuss these objects before starting to read.

- Dagger (violence, regicide).
- Brain (Macbeth's brain is 'heat-oppressed' due to his anxiety about committing regicide).
- Marshal (e.g. at a football stadium) (Macbeth is guided towards Duncan's room).

- Blood (the brutality of regicide).
- Dead leaves (the unnaturalness of breaking the Divine Right of Kings).
- Wolf (a harbinger of danger).
- Bell (the signal that it is time to commit the murder).

PAUSE POINT

S-T-R-E-T-C-H

Triplet discussion: 'Lady Macbeth is not on stage, but Shakespeare still presents her as being very much in charge.' How far do you agree?

- Student A: Argue that Lady Macbeth remains in charge.
- Student B: Argue that Lady Macbeth is not actually in charge.
- Student C: Summarise the discussion.

Model answer:

After the heightened tension of the argument between Macbeth and Lady Macbeth in Act One Scene Seven, it is almost a surprise to see the tragic hero preparing for the murder without his wife onstage to guide him. However, Shakespeare includes several reminders of Lady Macbeth's control in this scene. Just before his soliloquy, Macbeth sends a thinly-disguised message to Lady Macbeth to ring the bell when the time for murder has arrived. The die has been cast; the tension builds while Macbeth waits and ruminates. When the bell rings, Macbeth obeys the signal and describes it as a 'knell' announcing death.

Big question

Does Shakespeare present the dagger as a supernatural temptation or a projection of Macbeth's own guilt?

The dagger is most compellingly interpreted as a projection of Macbeth's own guilt, a physical manifestation of his tortured conscience. While the Witches initially tempt him with the idea of kingship, they never suggest regicide. This vision occurs in isolation, after Macbeth has consciously committed to Duncan's assassination, at his wife's encouraging. Furthermore, the dagger's appearance – first clean, then bloody – charts the progression of his own 'horrible imaginings'. Even though the supernatural pervades the play, this moment is intensely psychological. Shakespeare uses the air-drawn dagger not to show an external force controlling Macbeth, but to dramatise the moment his ambition overpowers his morality, making the guilt he feels before the deed itself terrifyingly visible.

PAUSE POINT

ORACY

Triplet discussion: Work together to make a list of the different references to blood in the play. Then consider the symbolic meaning of blood.

- Student A: List examples of legitimate bloodshed.
- Student B: List examples of illegitimate bloodshed.
- Student C: Summarise discussion and consider symbolic meanings.

Model answer:

See Analysis 'Motif: blood' (page 78).

Analysis

Motif: darkness and light

In the opening section of the scene, the 'torch' immediately signals that this conversation takes place at nighttime. Shakespeare uses Banquo's conversation with Fleance to emphasise this; they are unsure of the exact time, but their mention of 'husbandry in heaven' means that the stars are out. Husbandry suggests thriftiness: the stars are like candles, not to be wasted. In fact, it is so dark that Banquo is on edge and, when Macbeth enters moments later, he seizes his sword.

The literal darkness onstage mirrors the moral darkness unleashed by the Witches. A restless Banquo appeals to 'merciful powers' to restrain his 'cursed thoughts,' suggesting that he is not immune to Witches' temptation. Shakespeare immediately contrasts him with Macbeth, who is actively preparing for murder. Banquo may be tempted, but he refuses to act, vowing to keep his 'bosom franchised and allegiance clear.' This declaration underscores his refusal to compromise his loyalty for ambition.

Macbeth's soliloquy

As the time appointed for the murder approaches, Shakespeare shows Macbeth's mind unravelling, beginning with his hallucination of a dagger. Macbeth is so unnerved by what he is about to do that he struggles to tell the difference between visions and reality. He attempts to 'clutch' the dagger, before realising that it might be 'a dagger of the mind'. This dagger stands in stark contrast to the patriotic sword he wielded in battle; it is a symbol of betrayal, a meaning grimly confirmed when 'gouts of blood' manifest upon it.

Macbeth's disturbed psyche then expands to encompass the world. He observes how 'o'er the one half-world / Nature seems dead.' This is both a literal description of the sleeping castle and a metaphor for the moral void his deed will create, where 'wicked dreams abuse / The curtain'd sleep.' The cosmic scale of Macbeth's dark twisted fantasy mirrors his distorted ambition: his crime isn't just murder, but an attack on the natural order itself.

As the soliloquy proceeds, the imagery becomes ever more expansive and extravagant, further evoking a sense of vast, mythic evil. Shakespeare includes an allusion to Tarquin, a notorious Roman prince who raped Lucrece (the subject of Shakespeare's long poem *The Rape of Lucrece* (1594)) and Hecate, goddess of witchcraft. These figures are synonymous with evil, violence and dark magic.

In a deft shift of focus, Shakespeare brings the soliloquy back to concrete and practical considerations: Macbeth hopes that no one can hear his footsteps on the 'stones'. The bell rings and the simplicity of Macbeth's statement that 'I go, and it is done' indicates that he has made his decision. This sense of finality is amplified by the use of a rhyming couplet to end the soliloquy.

Text: feminine endings

In iambic pentameter, a typical line has ten syllables. A feminine ending occurs when an extra unstressed syllable is added at the end of a line, disrupting the metre's regularity. For example, the first line 'Is this a dagger which I see before me' ends weakly with an extra syllable ('me').

Shakespeare uses this technique to convey hesitation, instability, or psychological tension: in this soliloquy, it is a combination of all three! By breaking the iambic pattern, Shakespeare subtly signals Macbeth's unraveling mind: the smooth, controlled rhythm gives way to erratic speech, foreshadowing his moral collapse. The feminine endings heighten the scene's dramatic unease, but as Macbeth resolves to murder Duncan, his thinking – and therefore his verse – become clearer, tighter and more metrical.

Motif: blood

Blood is a motif throughout the play and is presented in two ways. First, in Act Once Scene Two the legitimate spilling of blood is celebrated by those who are loyal to the king. Shakespeare now contrasts this with illegitimate bloodshed. As Macbeth approaches Duncan's bedchamber, he considers the 'bloody business' of murdering the king, not protecting him. Macbeth imagines drops of blood glistening on the dagger he hallucinates, leaving him in no doubt of the horror of his crime.

Key quotation | 'The heat-oppressed brain'

As Shakespeare shows Macbeth approaching the point of no return, he emphasises the growing psychological pressure and turmoil. Macbeth feels under pressure from both external (the Witches and Lady Macbeth) and internal forces (his own *hubris* and ambition). In these circumstances, his rational and logical thinking suffers and he is plunged into a period of hallucination and wildly metaphorical thinking.

PAUSE POINT

CONSOLIDATION

Triplet discussion: Shakespeare presents Act Two Scene One as the point of no return. What evidence is there to support this view?

- Student A: List two pieces of evidence to support this view.
- Student B: List two additional pieces of evidence to support this view.
- Student C: Summarise the discussion.

Model answer:

This scene marks a significant point of no return for Macbeth, as the darkness which started to encroach upon Scotland in Act One Scene One now seems to be all-encompassing. Banquo's comment that there is 'husbandry in heaven' sets the scene for literal darkness, whilst Macbeth's line 'nature seems dead' and his consideration of 'Tarquin's ravishing strides' indicate a metaphorical interpretation: Macbeth's mind has succumbed to the darkness of immorality. This sense of inevitability is amplified by Shakespeare's use of blood imagery, as the imaginary dagger is smeared with 'gouts of blood' that foreshadow the regicide to come. By concluding the soliloquy with rhyming couplets, Shakespeare creates a sense of finality: the decision has been made and the disastrous consequences will ensue.

Upon the stage

The central directorial decision required in this scene is whether the dagger is visible onstage. Is it more dramatically exciting if we see a dagger, or if it is all in Macbeth's imagination, and 'his heat-oppressed brain'? What if one of the Witches appears onstage, holding it and pointing with it?

All of these options have been used in performance, and many others besides. At the Donmar (2023), David Tennant grappled with empty air, creating a compelling portrait of internal stress and madness. No dagger was shown, locating the horror entirely within his mind. In the (2021) Coen film, the dagger was the actual handle on the door to Duncan's chamber. Branagh (2013) projected the shape of a huge dagger along the length of the playing space, before a real dagger appeared suspended in the air above Macbeth's head.

Should the dagger frighten Macbeth, or inspire him?

CHAPTER 13
I LAID THEIR DAGGERS READY
ACT TWO SCENE TWO (LINES 1 TO 14)

At a glance

- **Plot and character development:** Lady Macbeth waits for Macbeth to return from killing Duncan.
- **Social and historical context:** Censorship laws and staging regicide
- **Vocabulary:** Ambiguous
- **Big question:** Why does Shakespeare humanise Lady Macbeth in this scene?
- **Themes:**
  - Ambition and power
  - Guilt and conscience
  - Appearance vs reality
- **Analysis:**
  - Staging: sounds
  - Staging: recognitions
- **Key quotation:** 'I laid their daggers ready'

PAUSE POINT

RETRIEVAL

Many deaths have been reported in the play thus far, but Shakespeare presents the killing of Duncan as being completely different.

Ask students to think-pair-share what they know about the deaths of Macdonwald and the Thane of Cawdor.

Then explore the differences between how Shakespeare presents these deaths and Duncan's murder. Consider:

- Legitimate and illegitimate bloodshed.
- Killing on the battlefield and cold-blooded murder.
- Killing an armed soldier and a sleeping elderly man.
- Fighting to protect one's country and murdering for personal gain.

Plot and character development

As Lady Macbeth waits for her husband to murder Duncan, she reveals new details about herself. She has carefully planned the murder, opening the doors, preparing the narcotics and drugging the guards and even leaving the daggers ready for Macbeth. The only reason she does not kill Duncan herself is that he looks too much like her father. At the end of this section, she hears Macbeth returning from Duncan's bedchamber.

Social and historical context

Censorship laws and staging regicide

Due to strict censorship laws, Shakespeare could not stage Duncan's murder. Presenting the murder of a rightful monarch onstage – a direct challenge to the Divine Right of Kings – would have been considered not only offensive and blasphemous, but potentially seditious. A production of *Richard II* had caused havoc late in the reign of Elizabeth I, and the censors would never have allowed an onstage presentation of regicide so soon after the Gunpowder Plot. Instead, Shakespeare generates dramatic tension by not showing the murder and allowing us to wait for it with the character most invested in its success.

Vocabulary | Ambiguous

Shakespeare presents Lady Macbeth in an ambiguous way in this scene. On the one hand, she is excited about the murder as her imagined future as queen is soon to become true. However, on the other hand Shakespeare hints at Lady Macbeth's vulnerability: she is startled by noises and was unable to commit the murder herself.

Definition:	**Morphology:**
Having more than one interpretation.	Prefix: ambi = both e.g. ambidextrous, ambivalent
Examples:	**Non-examples:**
Macbeth (1606): The Witches' gender is ambiguous because they appear to be female but also have beards. *An Inspector Calls* (1946): Inspector Goole's identity is ambiguous: is he a ghost or a personification of justice?	*A Christmas Carol* (1843): Scrooge's transformation is not ambiguous: he is more benevolent at the end of the novella. *Dr Jekyll and Mr Hyde* (1886): It is clear that Hyde is completely evil.

Reading the scene

Capturing the nuanced twists and turns of Lady Macbeth's monologue is key to understanding the scene. She is both elated and intoxicated yet acutely agitated and watchful. To help students grasp this complex characterisation, we recommend a supported reading. After reading the text aloud, screen this scene from the Rupert Goold production (2010). Kate Fleetwood masterfully balances excitement with paranoia, providing a clear model of the character's volatile state. This can show students how an actor physicalises the text's ambiguity as well as its dramatic tension.

PAUSE POINT

WRITING

While it is important to teach students to write structured responses to examination questions, sometimes this can limit their expression. Free writing loosens the shackles. Set a five-minute timer and explain that there is no paragraph structure for this task: the focus is on students developing their own critical voice. Tell them to write about how Shakespeare presents Lady Macbeth as the ideas come to them.

Some students may still require support: if that is the case, provide loose sentence starters (e.g. At the start of the play, Shakespeare presents Lady Macbeth as...).

Once the timer goes, ask students to highlight their best three ideas. Discuss these as a class.

PAUSE POINT

S-T-R-E-T-C-H

Until now, we have considered how Shakespeare emphasises Lady Macbeth's unconventional dominance in her marriage. However, in this scene, Shakespeare starts to introduce cracks in her indomitable façade.

Triplet discussion: 'Shakespeare dramatises the weaknesses in Lady Macbeth's character.' How far do you agree?

- Student A: Argue that Lady Macbeth has some weaknesses in this scene.
- Student B: Argue that Lady Macbeth maintains her strength in this scene.
- Student C: Summarise the discussion.

Model answer:

It could be argued that Lady Macbeth maintains her strength here, but it is more likely that Shakespeare employs this scene as an opportunity to dramatise her weaknesses. Lady Macbeth's use of alcohol to bolster her courage ('made me bold') and her sensitivity to sounds ('hark!') reveal her underlying anxiety about the regicide. Lady Macbeth herself explains why she could not commit the murder: Duncan 'resembled / [Her] father as he slept'. This emotional connection to a family member is surprising, given Lady Macbeth's insistence that she would commit infanticide if she had sworn to do so. Finally, as Macbeth enters, Lady Macbeth calls 'my husband' for the first and only time in the play. Shakespeare might include this to reveal Lady Macbeth's need for emotional support. Or, alternatively, perhaps Shakespeare is showing that this is the first time she sees him as the man she wants him to be: he durst do it, so now he is a man?

Big question

Why does Shakespeare humanise Lady Macbeth in this scene?

Shakespeare deliberately avoids presenting Lady Macbeth as a one-dimensional villain. In this scene, her steely resolve – evident in her meticulous planning and her eagerness for Macbeth to become king – is complicated by a startling moment of humanity. Emboldened by alcohol, she confesses she could not murder Duncan because he looked too much like her father. This surprising admission contradicts her earlier declarations of violence, such as wielding her 'keen knife' and the brutal image of infanticide in Act One Scene Seven. Behind her steely and uncompromising façade is a woman who cannot commit the deed she has given her husband. This contradiction is the core of her tragedy. By humanising her, Shakespeare rejects a simplistic 'fair or foul' morality, instead revealing the internal conflict that makes her, and the play, psychologically resonant across centuries.

Themes

Ambition and power

Shakespeare presents two kinds of ambition in this scene. Macbeth's ambition is imaginative and self-consuming: he hallucinates daggers, hears voices, sees the oceans turning red. Lady Macbeth's ambition is pragmatic. She does not see blood; she sees 'daggers' that need to be 'laid ready'. She does not contemplate a prophecy; she rehearses a schedule. Her mind races – not through consequences but a checklist: guards drugged, weapons placed, alibi established. Shakespeare presents this not as a weakness but as a terrifying strength, until the moment she encounters her father's sleeping face. The ambition that could arrange murder now cannot perform it. The procedural mind, it turns out, still has a conscience it cannot overcome.

Guilt and conscience

Shakespeare complicates Lady Macbeth's earlier resolve by revealing a flicker of guilt. Her confession that she would have killed Duncan herself 'had he not resembled / My father as he slept' is a startling moment of humanity. This involuntary, familial association cuts through her projected 'direst cruelty,' exposing a conscience she cannot fully suppress. It is the first crack in her façade, foreshadowing her psychological collapse.

Appearance vs reality

In this scene, Shakespeare shows that Lady Macbeth is the sole architect of the deceptive appearance that will frame Duncan's guards. She has constructed the 'false face' that she earlier commanded Macbeth to wear. However, the reality of her own involvement is more ambiguous than she admits; her reference to her father proves that she is not as utterly 'unsexed' as she prayed to be, revealing a disparity between her brutal intentions and her lingering human instincts.

Analysis

Staging: sounds

Lady Macbeth's monologue is punctuated by sounds, which create a nervous tension. At this time of night, the castle should be very quiet, so any sound is a surprise.

The first noise is the shriek of an owl. In Shakespeare's plays, an owl is almost always a malevolent omen. Its appearance here connects beautifully with

Macbeth's soliloquy in the preceding scene, as in *The Rape of Lucrece* (1594) Shakespeare describes Tarquin's attack as happening on a night which is silent except for the 'death-boding cries' of owls.

Staging: recognitions

Failure to identify someone is a dramatic idea throughout the play, beginning with Duncan's question in Act One Scene Two: 'what bloody man is that?' Shakespeare presents us with a world of uncertainty, in which it is difficult to recognise friend or foe. Here, Lady Macbeth hears her own husband's voice, but seems not to recognise it.

Key quotation | 'I laid their daggers ready'

In Act One Scene Five, Lady Macbeth told her husband to 'leave all the rest to me'. In this scene, it is clear that she has taken complete control. Her meticulous orchestration provides compelling evidence in the critical debate over Macbeth's agency, positioning her not merely as an influence but as the primary engineer of Duncan's assassination. Lady Macbeth does not commit the crime, but she has arranged every detail of it.

PAUSE POINT

CONSOLIDATION

Ask students to 'read-reduce-rehearse-remember' our analysis of the key quotation (see 'How to use this book' page XIII).

Upon the stage

Directors and performers have approached the challenges of this scene in strikingly different ways:

- Goold (2010) had Kate Fleetwood portray a woman vibrating with growing panic, her agitation making the wait almost unbearable.
- Judi Dench (Nunn, 1979) whispered straight to camera, as if enlisting us in the deed. Her low, steady voice and her stillness convey an iron will attempting to conceal a profound inner terror.
- Samantha Spiro (Best, 2014) emphasised Lady Macbeth's exhilaration, pacing with a feverish intensity that blurred the line between excitement and panic.

Each interpretation navigates the same crucial balance: the mastermind of the plot is suffering under the weight of the evil she has summoned.

Show your students clips from each production: which do they find most impactful, and why?

CHAPTER 14
TO KNOW MY DEED, 'TWERE BEST NOT KNOW MYSELF
ACT TWO SCENE TWO (LINES 15 TO END)

At a glance

- **Plot and character development:** Macbeth enters, having killed Duncan. He is horrified and distracted by what he has done. Lady Macbeth takes charge and tidies up, before bringing Macbeth to bed.
- **Vocabulary:** Juxtaposition
- **Big question:** Why does Shakespeare emphasise Macbeth and Lady Macbeth's different responses to the murder?
- **Themes:**
  - Guilt and conscience
  - Disorder and the unnatural
- **Analysis:**
  - Text: shared lines
  - Text: imperative verbs
  - Motif: blood
- **Key quotation:** 'To know my deed, 'twere best not know myself'

PAUSE POINT

RETRIEVAL

In this extract, Macbeth feels separated from God. Use this speedy whiteboard quiz to check students' knowledge of the Divine Right of Kings.

1. The Divine Right of Kings is the belief that...?
   (a) The monarch should be chosen by the people.
   (b) There is a connection between church and state.
   (c) The monarch receives their power from God.
   (d) The monarch's oldest child should inherit the throne.
2. Which quotation shows that Macbeth is appalled by the thought of breaking the Divine Right of Kings?
   (a) 'This supernatural soliciting / Cannot be ill, cannot be good'
   (b) 'horrid image doth unfix my hair'
   (c) 'I have no spur / To prick the sides of my intent, but only / Vaulting ambition'
   (d) 'We will proceed no further in this business'
3. Which quotation shows that Macbeth is concerned about facing punishment in the afterlife?
   (a) 'The deep damnation of his taking off'
   (b) 'Why chance may crown me without my stir'
   (c) 'False face must hide what the false heart doth know'
   (d) 'Hear it not, Duncan, for it is a knell / That summons thee to heaven or to hell'

Answers: 1C, 2B, 3A

Plot and character development

Macbeth returns from Duncan's chamber a transformed man, immediately consumed by horror and guilt. He is haunted by the belief that he has 'murdered' his own ability to sleep and pray, and poetically agonises that not even all the water in the ocean can cleanse the blood – and the sin – from his hands.

Lady Macbeth's reaction provides a stark contrast. Her response is ruthlessly efficient. Discovering that Macbeth has brought the murder weapons from the scene of the crime, she takes charge, returning the weapons to frame the guards. Macbeth imagines that his hands are permanently stained with blood, but Lady Macbeth insists that 'a little water clears us of this deed.'

The scene concludes with a sharp knocking at the castle gate. Lady Macbeth, still in control, identifies the sound and ushers her distraught husband away to change clothes, insisting that their 'false faces' must hide the truth of their actions.

Vocabulary | Juxtaposition

Juxtaposition is a key method used by Shakespeare throughout the play. In this scene, Shakespeare clearly juxtaposes the protagonists' differing responses to the regicide. Discuss the word forms with your class, so that they are aware of how to use the term as both a noun and verb.

Definition:	**Word forms:**
Two contrasting ideas, characters, or images placed side by side.	Juxtaposition Juxtaposes Juxtaposed
Examples:	**Non-examples:**
A Christmas Carol (1843): Scrooge's misanthropic nature is juxtaposed to Fred's hospitable nature. *An Inspector Calls* (1946): Goole's socialism is juxtaposed with Birling's capitalism.	*A Christmas Carol* (1843): Fred's bonhomie is similar to Bob Cratchit's joy in the season. *An Inspector Calls* (1946): Sheila becomes Goole's mouthpiece, and is not contrasted with him.

Reading the scene

Sharing lines of iambic pentameter between the Macbeths allows Shakespeare to show the panic and the closeness between these characters.

Model the reading of the shared lines (see page 90). You and the student reading with you should almost cut across one another. Then give students time to rehearse in their triplets, giving them several opportunities to practice so they swap the parts between them. Finally, read the whole extract as a class.

PAUSE POINT

S-T-R-E-T-C-H

Both Macbeth and Lady Macbeth refer to 'nature' in this scene. Lady Macbeth says that she has drugged the guards, so that 'death and nature do contend about them'. Macbeth then refers to sleep as 'Nature's second course'. Later (in Act Two Scene Three) Macbeth describes Duncan's wounds as a 'breach in nature'.

Triplet discussion: How and why does Shakespeare use nature imagery in the play?

- Student A: Respond to the question by listing examples of nature imagery in the play.
- Student B: Respond to the question by considering the symbolic meaning of nature.
- Student C: Summarise the discussion.

Model answer:

By this point in the play, Shakespeare has employed nature imagery on several occasions to emphasise how the supernatural and then the Macbeths challenge the natural order. When the Witches first appear, Banquo comments on their 'withered' and 'wild' appearance, as well as on their unexpected 'beards'. Shakespeare uses these lines to portray the Witches as an unsettling force existing outside social norms, while their ambiguous gender connects with the play's exploration of unconventional women and power. The Witches' fair and foul prophecies seem to elicit an unnatural response in Macbeth, whose heart begins to beat 'against the use of nature'. This physical response reveals Macbeth's awareness that his thoughts of regicide will challenge political, social and moral order. Shakespeare revisits this theme in the moments leading up to Duncan's murder, as Macbeth comments that 'nature seems dead'. Macbeth's malevolent lust for power leads him to overturn the natural order and unleash a period of chaos.

Big question

Why does Shakespeare emphasise Macbeth and Lady Macbeth's different responses to the murder?

Shakespeare's stark juxtaposition of the Macbeths' reactions lays bare their immediate divergence. Macbeth is consumed by expansive, poetic regret, while Lady Macbeth's ruthless ambition manifests in pragmatic action. This contrast echoes their earlier, gender-focused argument: having goaded Macbeth by questioning his manhood, Lady Macbeth now assumes control of her panicked husband to secure their safety; all this despite being unable to commit the murder herself.

Through Macbeth's torment, Shakespeare issues a stark warning about the psychological and eternal consequences of regicide. His eventual possession of the 'golden round' will be a hollow victory. Conversely, Lady Macbeth's unnatural callousness illustrates the corrupting power of ambition. However, her steely efficiency can also be interpreted as a fragile façade for profound anxiety; this reading could establish a foundation for her own mental decline.

Analysis

Text: shared lines

This scene showcases Shakespeare's absolute mastery of verse, particularly through his use of shared lines. The iambic pentameter acts as a single, frantic breath of poetry split between the couple, creating an unbroken thread that heightens their intense connection and panic. Nowhere is this more electrifying than in their most famous exchange, where Shakespeare compresses four tense utterances into a single line of verse:

LADY MACBETH *Did not you speak?*

MACBETH *When?*

LADY MACBETH *Now.*

MACBETH *As I descended?*

N.B. The digital edition of the play provided in our online resources has been formatted to indicate all shared lines of verse.

Text: imperative verbs

As Lady Macbeth assumes the dominant role, she fires a rapid series of commands at her husband:

- 'Get some water'.
- 'Wash this filthy witness from your hand'.
- 'Carry [the daggers], and smear / The sleepy grooms with blood'.
- 'Give me the daggers'.
- 'Get on your nightgown'.

This sequence of imperatives underscores her absolute command of the situation and her husband.

Motif: blood

Macbeth's blood-stained hands become the 'filthy witness' to his irreversible crime. His immediate, horrified response is to imagine a cosmic cleansing, calling on 'great Neptune's ocean' to wash the guilt away. Yet, in a devastating reversal, he concludes that his guilt is so profound it would instead corrupt the entire natural world, turning the seas red with blood.

> *Will all great Neptune's ocean wash this blood*
> *Clean from my hand? No, this my hand will rather*
> *The multitudinous seas incarnadine,*
> *Making the green one red.*

Macbeth envisions a type of baptism, where his sins are washed away; he then forestalls this with the monosyllabic 'no', realising that he has crossed a threshold and therefore damned himself.

Shakespeare then sharpens the tragedy through brutal juxtaposition. Lady Macbeth's retort that 'a little water clears us of this deed' not only undercuts his existential despair with pragmatic coldness but also highlights a critical fissure in their partnership. Macbeth's solitary 'my hand' contrasts with her collective 'us,' sowing the early seeds of the profound isolation that will define their subsequent downfall.

PAUSE POINT

WRITING

The richness of the 'great Neptune's ocean' line means this is an ideal moment to practice analytical writing.

Prompt: How does Shakespeare present Macbeth's guilt following the regicide?

Whatever paragraph structure you use, here are some top tips:

- Writing on alternate lines means that students can easily edit their work, changing or adding in details. You can also mark it more easily.
- For reluctant writers, Jennifer Webb recommends marking how much you want them to write by putting a dot in the margin indicating the number of lines they should write. This gives them a clear target and reduces the fear of failure.
- Remind students to focus on Shakespeare's choices by including his name towards the start of sentences.
- For students working at greater depth, including brief quotations from other sections of the play can make their answers sparkle. For example, if they are writing about Shakespeare's presentation of Lady Macbeth's ambition, they could refer to the desire to attain 'the golden round'.
- Stretch students further by revisiting tentative and assertive language (see 'How to use this book' page XIII).

- Stretch these students further again by asking them to include a key concept: here, students could explain how Shakespeare dramatises Macbeth's trauma following the act of regicide in order to show the spiralling consequences of unchecked ambition.

Key quotation | 'To know my deed, 'twere best not know myself'

This line captures the profound psychological rupture Macbeth experiences immediately after the murder. He acknowledges that the horrific 'deed' he has committed is so antithetical to his former nature that to comprehend it fully would be to obliterate his own identity. The 'valiant cousin' praised by Duncan has been replaced by a murderer. This line juxtaposes these two sides of Macbeth's story.

His choice of the word 'deed' is significant. This euphemism, repeated throughout the scene, serves a dual purpose: it is a linguistic shield to distance himself from the brutality of 'murder,' and a stark acknowledgement of premeditated action, a deed to be 'done'. Unlike the reactive violence of the battlefield, this was a conscious, active choice; Macbeth recognises that the man he was cannot coexist with the murderer he has become.

PAUSE POINT

CONSOLIDATION

Triplet discussion: How does Shakespeare present Macbeth as a changing character?

- Student A: Consider how Macbeth was presented at the start of the play.
- Student B: Consider how Macbeth is presented at this point.
- Student C: Summarise the discussion.

Model answer:

At the start of the play, Shakespeare emphasised Macbeth's military prowess ('valiant Macbeth') and his allegiance to Duncan ('the service and the loyalty I owe'). However, following the prophecies Macbeth became increasingly introverted and ambitious. His aspiration is fuelled and redirected when he is denied the title of Prince of Cumberland, and this marks a further shift to secrecy and immorality as he dwells on his 'black and deep desires'. Shakespeare also indicates a change from masculine courage in the play's exposition, to submission to Lady Macbeth's commands in Act One Scene Five – commands which lead Macbeth to commit regicide and descend into psychological turmoil.

Upon the stage

Max Webster's Donmar production (2023) staged the play on a white platform. This, combined with Tennant and Jumbo's monochrome costumes, made the scene's blood particularly present and shocking. It stained their hands and their clothes; the scene was intimate and impressively tense. Other productions, like Nunn (1979), Best (2014) and Goold (2018) all feature varying quantities of blood, but it is almost always present and necessary.

Throughout whatever versions you share with your students, emphasise the importance of our seeing Lady Macbeth get her hands dirty, so that her sleepwalking scene makes sense in Act Five.

CHAPTER 15
THE PRIMROSE WAY TO THE EVERLASTING BONFIRE
ACT TWO SCENE THREE (LINES 1 TO 40)

At a glance

› **Plot and character development:** A drunken Porter enters to answer the knocking that ended the previous scene.

› **Social and historical context:** The Gunpowder Plot, Henry Garnet and equivocation

› **Vocabulary:** Equivocation

› **Big question:** Why does Shakespeare include this scene?

› **Themes:**

- Appearance vs reality
- Guilt and conscience

› **Analysis:**

- Staging: comic relief
- Text: prose

› **Key quotation:** 'The primrose way to the everlasting bonfire'

PAUSE POINT

RETRIEVAL

In Act Two Scene Two, Shakespeare dramatises Macbeth's horror at the act of regicide he has committed. Ask students to annotate the 'great Neptune's ocean' quotation from memory.

Explain that the opening of Act Two Scene Three will strike a contrasting note.

Plot and character development

The Porter only appears in this scene. He does not advance the plot and his primary function is to answer the knocking at the gate – to admit Macduff and Lennox. But Shakespeare gives him more than a door-keeper's role. His drunken ramble about sinners (the hanged farmer and the equivocator) holds a dark mirror to Macbeth himself, who has just committed treason and will soon equivocate about his guilt. The Porter imagines Macbeth's castle as a 'hell gate' and himself its 'devil porter', forcing the audience to laugh, here, at the threshold of damnation. He appears for comic relief, but this deepens – rather than diminishes – the horror.

Social and historical context

The Gunpowder Plot, Henry Garnet and equivocation

The Porter's speech is saturated with contemporary Jacobean anxieties. His references to equivocation are a direct allusion to the Gunpowder Plot. The Jesuit Henry Garnet famously defended the use of equivocation during his trial as a participant in the plot. For Shakespeare's audience, the 'equivocator' knocking at hell's gate would have been a clear and chilling reference to this recent treason. Furthermore, the speech's structure mirrors a 'hellgate play,' a common form of medieval drama in which a porter would admit various sinners to hell. The twist in *Macbeth* is that while the Porter complains about 'devil-porter[ing]' at the hellmouth that Macbeth's castle has become, he admits Macduff, who will avenge Macbeth's crimes. This cheeky scene provides a moment of tense laughter before the horror of Duncan's murder is discovered.

Vocabulary | Equivocation

Equivocation is the deliberate use of ambiguous language to mislead or deceive while technically avoiding a direct lie.

Definition:	Characteristics:
The use of ambiguous language to conceal the truth or to avoid committing oneself. It is a form of deception that relies on double meanings, allowing the speaker to mislead without technically lying.	• Ambiguity and double meanings. • Deliberate deception. • Often used to avoid oath-taking or direct accusations. • Exploiting the gap between literal truth and intended meaning.

Examples:	Non-examples (from *Macbeth*):
Macbeth (1606): The Witches' prophecies (e.g., 'none of woman born / Shall harm Macbeth'). This is literally true but deliberately misleading, as Macduff was 'from his mother's womb / Untimely ripped.' *A Treatise of Equivocation* (1851): Father Henry Garnet, a Jesuit involved in the Gunpowder Plot, wrote A Treatise of Equivocation to justify lying under oath to protect Catholics. His trial was a major public event.	Macduff's direct and honest grief when he discovers Duncan's body: 'O horror, horror, horror!' Duncan's genuine praise of Macbeth; he means what he says without deception.

Reading the scene

It can be difficult to capture this scene's complex mix of threat and comedy in the classroom. Show a clip from the Rupert Goold version of the play (2010) instead as it communicates the debased and disturbing nature of the Porter's character.

PAUSE POINT

S-T-R-E-T-C-H

Triplet discussion: The Porter imagines himself working at 'hell gate'. How else does Shakespeare use the metaphor of opening the door to unleash evil?

- Student A: List two examples of evil events within the play.
- Student B: List two additional examples of evil events within the play.
- Student C: Summarise the discussion.

Model answer:

The regicide is horrific, but what is yet to come is worse. The next killing is Banquo – Macbeth's friend and military companion. The child – Fleance – escapes, but soon more children are at risk as Macbeth decides to 'savagely slaughter' Macduff's family. The violence doesn't stop there: Malcolm says that 'Each new morn / New widows howl, new orphans cry'. Shakespeare also shows that Macbeth opens the gates of hell in his own sleepless mind: his psyche will soon be 'full of scorpions'. In the (2018) RSC production by Polly Findlay, the Porter remains on stage after this scene, chalking up deaths in an ominous tally until the wall surrounding the stage is covered with white lines.

Shakespeare's dramatisation of the hellish violence of Macbeth's rule is a warning against ambition: leaders who rule to satisfy their own lust for power become ruthless tyrants.

Big question

Why does Shakespeare include the Porter?

Shakespeare includes the Porter for three crucial dramatic purposes. First, it provides essential comic relief (see Analysis, page 97–8).

Second, his speech is packed with topical satire, most notably about 'equivocation,' discussed above.

Finally, and most profoundly, the Porter scene holds a dark mirror to the main action, transforming the Macbeths' castle into a literal and metaphorical hell. The Porter's speech universalises the specific horror of regicide by showing hell's gates opening for all manner of common sinners – from the greedy farmer to the petty thief. However, the most significant arrival is the equivocator, a figure who resonates on multiple levels: as a satirical jab at the Gunpowder Plotters, a reflection of the Witches' deceptive prophecies and an indictment of Macbeth himself, who has just sworn false loyalty to Duncan before murdering him. The Porter suggests that the castle is not just the site of a single crime, but a manifestation of a world turned upside down by sin and deceptive words, where the Macbeths have opened a portal to hell.

Themes

Appearance vs reality

The Porter's entire monologue is built on equivocation. He jokes about the sinner who 'could swear in both the scales against either scale,' a perfect description of the Witches' deceptive prophecies and Macbeth's own self-deception. The scene suggests the reality that the Macbeths' castle is not the gentle paradise that it appeared to Duncan, and is, in reality, a hell.

Guilt and conscience

The Porter's hell is not just a physical place but a state of being for those weighed down by their sins. The 'farmer that hanged himself on th' expectation of plenty' mirrors Macbeth, whose ambition for the crown (plenty) leads to the actions that bring about his downfall. The speech universalises Macbeth's crime, placing his specific guilt within a world of sin.

Analysis

Staging: comic relief

Comic relief provides the audience with a crucial emotional respite from the intense tension of the tragedy, making the subsequent return to horror even more powerful. For a Shakespearean audience, accustomed to long performances without intervals, these moments offered a necessary release.

Furthermore, this contrast often heightens the seriousness of the main plot. In *Macbeth*, the Porter's dark humour does not undermine the tragedy but instead holds a distorted mirror to it, deepening the thematic impact of sin and disorder.

Text: prose

Shakespeare primarily uses prose for characters of lower social status, comic relief, or moments of psychological disturbance. The Porter speaks in prose to signal his working-class role and the scene's comedic function, creating a stark tonal shift from the heightened verse of the preceding murder. Like Lady Macbeth, he has been drinking, but he is significantly more inebriated than she is. The switch from taut, brilliant verse to the Porter's drunken prose is a very deliberate change of tone.

Key quotation | 'The primrose way to the everlasting bonfire'

The phrase encapsulates the Porter's darkly comic role as hell's gatekeeper. Its mocking tone provides the scene's central humour, listing the 'primrose way' of easy sin. Yet, this comedy is deeply sinister, as the 'everlasting bonfire' is the literal consequence awaiting sinners like Macbeth. Delicate primroses are no match for the eternal fires of hell: this juxtaposition is therefore key: it balances the scene's jest with a profound moral warning, connecting the Porter's jest to the play's overarching themes of damnation and the fatal cost of ambition.

PAUSE POINT

CONSOLIDATION

Ask students to reduce the extract to a list of the five most important words or phrases. Discuss their choices, exploring what these words suggest or represent in the extract and the play as a whole.

Upon the stage

The Porter is Shakespeare's great test for directors. His jokes about farmers and equivocators land poorly for modern audiences; his timing is opaque, his references obscure. Yet cutting him entirely loses the play's only extended comic release. Productions must decide: is the Porter a breather between atrocities, or something more disturbing? In an extraordinary interpretation, Jamie Beamish performed this scene wearing multiple packages of dynamite and a lit fuse for the Royal Shakespeare Company (RSC) in 2011. The production, directed by Michael Boyd, gave the Porter a much more direct connection to the Gunpowder Plot and its equivocating terrorists. Beamish's Irish accent also played on more recent English anxieties about Catholic bombs and terrorists, making this a Porter more frightening than most. Footage of this performance is featured in James Shapiro's (2012) BBC documentary *The King and the Playwright*. The scene is usually less edgy, and a moment for comic relief. Boyd and Beamish pushed the Porter to a politically provocative precipice. Their extreme interpretation is valuable precisely because it forces us to ask just how dangerous the Porter might be.

CHAPTER 16
THERE'S DAGGERS IN MEN'S SMILES
ACT TWO SCENE THREE (LINE 40 TO END)

At a glance

- **Plot and character development:** Duncan's murder is revealed. All of his courtiers gather and react.
- **Social and historical context:** The real Duncan
- **Vocabulary:** Character foil
- **Big question:** Why does Shakespeare show Lady Macbeth fainting in this scene?
- **Themes:**
    - Appearance vs reality
    - Disorder and the unnatural
    - Guilt and conscience
    - Loyalty vs treason
- **Analysis:**
    - Dramatic irony
- **Key quotation:** 'There's daggers in men's smiles'

PAUSE POINT

RETRIEVAL

Who's who?

There are a lot of characters in this scene, and Shakespeare shows how they all respond to Duncan's death in different ways, depending on their background and situation.

Check the students' knowledge of the background and status of these characters:

- Malcolm
- Donalbain
- Lennox
- Macduff
- Banquo.

Plot and character development

The scene erupts into chaos when Macduff discovers Duncan's body. His cries of horror summon Lady Macbeth, Macbeth, Lennox and Ross. Macbeth launches into a performative, over-wrought speech lamenting the king's death. His theatrics, however, are punctuated by a rash and telling action: he reveals he has already killed the chamberlains, claiming it was an act of furious loyalty. This impulsive move eliminates the only other witnesses and frames the dead men, but its hastiness raises suspicion.

Lady Macbeth's role shifts dramatically. Initially, she feigns shock at the news. However, as Macbeth's story grows increasingly volatile, she intervenes with a calculated stunt, diverting attention from his performance. This underscores her continued role as the plot's strategic director, even as events spiral publicly.

The true political consequences unfold around Duncan's sons. Seeing their father murdered and the thanes in disarray, Malcolm and Donalbain confer in a hushed, pivotal aside. They correctly perceive the danger they are in and they decide to escape to England and Ireland respectively.

Macduff's character is also defined here; his genuine, grieved reaction and his pointed questions to Macbeth establish him as a figure of integrity and the first major threat to Macbeth's new, illegitimate authority.

Social and historical context

The real Duncan

The historical Duncan I (Donnchad mac Crinain) was quite unlike the venerable old king of Shakespeare's play. He became king of Scots in 1034, through a complex system of alternation between royal lines. His reign was notably unsuccessful; contemporary sources describe him as a weak and ineffective military leader, killed in battle by Macbeth rather than murdered in his sleep. Malcolm III, his son, did eventually win the throne, but only after killing Macbeth in 1057. (See Watson, 2010, for a complete account of the real history.) Duncan is primarily remembered today because of Shakespeare's tragic adaptation, which transformed a minor, flawed historical figure into a potent symbol of benevolent kingship.

PAUSE POINT

S-T-R-E-T-C-H

Triplet discussion: Why does Shakespeare deviate from the historical narrative, making Macbeth kill Duncan in his sleep rather than on the battlefield?

- Student A: Consider the significance of killing Duncan in his sleep.
- Student B: Imagine how the play would have been different if Macbeth killed Duncan on the battlefield.
- Student C: Summarise the discussion.

Model answer:

Shakespeare transforms the historical account of Macbeth killing Duncan in battle into a night-time assassination in order to vilify Macbeth's character and flatter his king. James I claimed Banquo as an ancestor, and so a play that depicted Banquo's killer as a treacherous assassin butchering a defenceless, sleeping king – rather than a worthy opponent on the battlefield – implicitly confirmed the Stuart claim to the throne. Shakespeare's transposition of the killing from public to private, with the royal victim asleep, emphasises the deviousness of Macbeth's betrayal. This shifts the audience's perception of Macbeth, who is no longer a hero slaying his foes in service of king and country, but an assassin who slinks into a darkened room. This lays the foundations for Macbeth's psychological torment later in the play.

Vocabulary | Character foil

Once you have taught this phrase, revisit it as you encounter more character foils in the play (such as Lady Macbeth and Lady Macduff).

Definition:	**Characteristics:**
A character who contrasts with the protagonist to highlight particular qualities, traits or themes through the juxtaposition of their differing natures, choices and outcomes.	• Creates a clear contrast. • Emphasises key traits of the main character. • Can highlight virtues by contrasting with vices (or vice versa). • Often serves to clarify a theme.
Examples:	**Non-examples (from *Macbeth*):**
Macduff as a foil to Macbeth: Macduff's loyalty, masculinity and motivation by righteous vengeance highlight Macbeth's treachery, his hollow 'masculinity' defined by violence, and his motivation by selfish ambition. *An Inspector Calls* (1946): Sheila is a character foil for Mr Birling, as she learns from Goole's visit while her father stubbornly holds on to his capitalist views.	The Witches in Macbeth: They are catalysts, not foils. Their purpose is not to contrast with Macbeth's character but to provoke his ambition. Lady Macbeth: Lady Macbeth is Macbeth's partner and ally, and while they have differences they are united in their desires.

Reading the scene

This large, chaotic scene is perfect for involving many students. As the teacher, you should take the role of Macbeth to maintain pace and convey his escalating panic. Key to this scene is its structure of public declarations punctuated by private asides. Assign students the parts of Macduff, Lennox, Banquo, Lady Macbeth and Donalbain. The remaining students can form the collective, murmuring voice of the other thanes and servants.

Instruct the readers to pay close attention to the stage directions for entrances and exits. When Macduff exits to wake the king, the tension builds through Lennox and Macbeth's conversation. Upon Macduff's return, his cries of 'O horror, horror, horror!' should trigger a wave of reaction from the 'crowd'.

Highlight the private conversations that break out within the chaos: Macbeth's frantic aside to Lennox about the guards, and most importantly, the brief but critical exchange between Malcolm and Donalbain. Lady Macbeth's role, while brief, is pivotal. Position her reader slightly apart. When she enters, she must appear to survey the entire room with a detached, 'birds-eye view,' and she must give a compelling performance of innocence that contrasts with the genuine panic of everyone else.

Once you have read the scene, check students' understanding of these key events:

1. Who discovers Duncan's body, and what is his reaction?
2. Who kills the guards, and why?
3. Why does Lady Macbeth faint?

4. What do Malcolm and Donalbain decide to do, and why?

As you read the scene a second time, ask students to complete this table contrasting Macbeth and Macduff.

Macbeth	Macduff
Façade of distress. Slow to act at first. Long, complex speeches using a lot of imagery.	Overwhelmed by genuine horror. Quick to act – rings the bell and wakes up the castle. Short, direct lines. Asks questions.

PAUSE POINT

ORACY

Triplet discussion: 'Shakespeare suggests that Macduff would be a more effective leader than Macbeth.' How far do you agree?

- Student A: Argue that Macduff is the more effective leader.
- Student B: Argue that Macbeth is the more effective leader.
- Student C: Summarise the discussion.

Model answer:

Shakespeare first introduces Macduff in Act One Scene Two, where he is described as 'Bellona's bridegroom' who foiled a second attack by the Norwegians and captured the Thane of Cawdor. Therefore, like Macbeth, he is presented as a valiant military leader who risked his life to defend his country.

Now Shakespeare re-introduces Macduff as he arrives to accompany his King on the next leg of his journey, only to find Duncan's bloody corpse. Shakespeare emphasises that Macduff is openly appalled at the murder, and the challenge to the Divine Right of Kings. He cries 'horror, horror, horror' and laments the 'most sacrilegious murder'. Unlike the villainous Macbeth, Macduff is presented as moral. He is also quick to act, whereas we watched Macbeth's indecision during the second half of Act One. We also notice Macduff's quick intelligence in this scene. As he asks Macbeth why he killed Duncan's guards, does the Thane of Fife already suspect something? He is certainly quick to leave the castle in the next scene and does not attend Macbeth's coronation.

Big question

Why does Shakespeare show Lady Macbeth fainting in this scene?

Lady Macbeth's faint is a calculated act of theatrical diversion, not genuine weakness. It occurs at a critical juncture: immediately after Macbeth delivers an overly elaborate and suspiciously dramatic speech justifying his impulsive murder of the guards, claiming it was an act of passionate loyalty. This rash act risks exposing them, as it destroys the very men they had framed.

The scene's immense importance lies in the public, chaotic transfer of power. With Duncan's heirs, Malcolm and Donalbain present, the question of succession is paramount. Lady Macbeth's faint successfully shifts the focus away from her husband's volatile performance and the princes' growing suspicion. By creating a new crisis, she halts further interrogation, allowing the thanes to regroup and ultimately enabling Macbeth to be named king once the heirs flee. Her feigned collapse is thus the final, crucial move in securing the crown, a masterful piece of staging that underscores her control even as Macbeth's begins to unravel.

Themes

Appearance vs reality

Macbeth and Lady Macbeth construct elaborate public performances to conceal their guilt. His lengthy, melodramatic speech and her feigned fainting spell are strategic deceptions designed to manipulate the thanes' perceptions, presenting a façade of outrage and shock that starkly contrasts with the horrific reality of their treachery.

Disorder and the unnatural

The discovery of Duncan's murder immediately unleashes political and natural disorder. The chaotic reactions of the thanes, the sounding of the alarm bell and the flight of the king's appointed successor, Malcolm, symbolise the complete breakdown of the natural order. Shakespeare reveals how the castle, a seat of power, is transformed into a site of confusion and fear, reflecting the macrocosmic chaos now unleashed upon Scotland. Even before Duncan's murder is announced, Macbeth and Lennox discuss the disorder in the natural world, summarised in Macbeth's pithy line 'twas a rough night'.

Guilt and conscience

While Macbeth's outwardly projects rage, his overexplained justification for killing Duncan's guards suggests a guilty conscience. In contrast, Macduff's stark, horrified reaction ('O horror, horror, horror!') embodies a true moral response. This juxtaposition highlights Macbeth's psychological unravelling while establishing Macduff as a figure of authentic feeling, setting the stage for his role as Macbeth's foil and an agent of righteous vengeance.

Loyalty vs treason

The scene forces every character to choose a side. Macduff's immediate grief and his pointed question to Macbeth ('Wherefore did you so?') signal burgeoning suspicion and an allegiance to the crown rather than whoever holds it. The flight of Malcolm and Donalbain, a pragmatic act of self-preservation, will be interpreted as an admission of guilt. This will allow Macbeth to consolidate his illegitimate power by branding the loyal heirs as traitors.

Analysis

Dramatic irony

The dramatic irony in this scene is at its most extreme and agonising. The audience knows Macbeth is the murderer, and this makes his every action a grotesque performance. His melodramatic grief and his impulsive execution of the guards – under the guise of loyal vengeance – are actually desperate acts to cover his crime. The true irony lies in the thanes' misinterpretation: they witness a man seemingly overcome with righteous fury, while we see a tyrant fabricating evidence. Ironically, Macbeth is convincing enough to be made king!

Key quotation | 'There's daggers in men's smiles'

Donalbain's line brilliantly condenses the scene's core themes into a single, potent image. The word 'daggers' immediately echoes both the hallucinated weapon that spurred Macbeth to action and the very real ones used to kill Duncan, charting the entire course of bloody events. More profoundly, the phrase encapsulates the theme of appearance vs reality. A smile – the universal signal of goodwill – is reimagined as a mask for treachery. Macbeth's performative grief hides his guilt, while Lady Macbeth's faint conceals her complicity. The line signals that their crime has unleashed a universal mistrust, poisoning all of Scotland. The political realm has become a landscape of concealed violence, exactly as the Witches' 'fair is foul' foretold.

PAUSE POINT

CONSOLIDATION

This scene features many characters who are responding to Duncan's murder in different ways. Support students in consolidating their understanding by asking them to complete this table.

Character	What is their reaction to Duncan's death?	Why do they react in this way?
Macduff		
Macbeth		
Lady Macbeth		
Banquo		
Malcolm and Donalbain		

Upon the stage

This scene's chaos is often amplified or condensed by directorial choices. Webster's (2023) Donmar Warehouse production used its small space to create a palpable sense of collective panic, with Tennant and Jumbo masterfully portraying the Macbeths' performative grief amidst the turmoil.

A key non-textual addition in this and many productions is a silent coronation at the scene's end. This directorial flourish is smart: it can visually underscore the terrifying speed with which Macbeth fills the power vacuum. The chaos of Duncan's death is immediately supplanted by the chilling order of Macbeth's ascent, making his usurpation feel both inevitable and alarmingly swift.

CHAPTER 17
DARK NIGHT STRANGLES THE TRAVELLING LAMP
ACT TWO SCENE FOUR

At a glance

- **Plot and character development:** Ross, Macduff and an Old Man discuss Macbeth's election and the state of Scotland.
- **Social and historical context:** An eclipse in 1605
- **Vocabulary:** Pathetic fallacy
- **Big question:** How does Shakespeare present the natural world's response to Macbeth becoming king?
- **Themes:**
  - Disorder and the unnatural
- **Analysis:**
  - Staging: a different perspective
- **Key quotation:** 'Dark night strangles the travelling lamp'

PAUSE POINT

RETRIEVAL

In this scene, Shakespeare employs a range of unnatural imagery, which links to the unnatural killing of King Duncan.

Check students' understanding of the ideas connected with natural and unnatural images (see Appendix B).

Plot and character development

This short but vital scene, set outside Macbeth's castle, depicts Scotland's reaction to the king's murder under its new ruler. An Old Man and Ross discuss the unnatural portents following Duncan's death: a falcon killed by an owl and Duncan's horses turning wild and cannibalistic. This symbolic disorder reflects the political chaos.

Macduff arrives and reveals that Macbeth has been named king and has gone to Scone to be crowned. Crucially, Macduff reports his own decision not to attend the coronation, instead returning to his home in Fife. This act of quiet defiance marks him as the first major threat to Macbeth's illegitimate rule and establishes him as the key figure of resistance, while the unnatural imagery confirms that Scotland itself has been sickened by the regicide.

Social and historical context

An eclipse in 1605

The context of the Gunpowder Plot profoundly intensified the Jacobean audience's perception of regicide as a crime against the Divine Right of Kings: this sin was so profound it was believed nature itself would rebel. A total solar eclipse over London in October 1605, weeks before the Plot's discovery, served as a real-world omen, an example of 'dark night strangling the travelling lamp.' By echoing this recent, terrifying event in *Macbeth*, Shakespeare immediately legitimises the play's unnatural imagery, grounding Scotland's descent into chaos in the very real anxieties of his audience.

Vocabulary | Pathetic fallacy

Students often develop reductive understandings of pathetic fallacy. Use the table below to stretch students' knowledge and address misconceptions.

Definition:	**Misconceptions:**
A form of personification where the natural world is described as though it responds to human events, typically mirroring the emotional state of characters or the narrative's tone.	• Pathetic fallacy does not have to involve negative emotions: the natural world can reflect positive emotions too. • Pathetic fallacy does not have to involve the weather: it is about giving emotions to the natural world.

Examples (from *Macbeth*):	**Non-examples (from *Macbeth*):**
'The night has been unruly.' (Act Two Scene Three) The storm reflects the disorder of Duncan's murder.	'The moon is down.' (Act Two Scene One) This is a simple statement of fact; it is night-time.
'Dark night strangles the travelling lamp.' (Act Two Scene Four) The eclipse symbolises evil triumphing over good.	A description of a sunny day that is merely setting the scene, with no emotional weight.

Reading the scene

This scene is a conversation between three characters: the Old Man, Ross and Macduff, so it is perfect for reading in triplet groups.

Instructions for the group:

1. Assign the three roles within your group.
2. Read the scene aloud once through.
3. Work together to find and highlight the specific information listed in the table below. Each character reveals crucial details.

Information Hunt:

Character	**Find the line:**
Old Man	1. Describing the unnatural behaviour of the falcon and owl.
	2. Describing what Duncan's horses have done.
Ross	3. Explaining how the world has become diseased following Duncan's murder.
Macduff	4. Explaining where Malcolm and Donalbain have gone and why people suspect them.
	5. Revealing what Macbeth is doing and where he has gone.
	6. Revealing Macduff's own plan, and his attitude towards the new king.

Discussion question (after reading):

Based on the information you gathered, what is the overall mood of Scotland now that Macbeth is king?

PAUSE POINT

S-T-R-E-T-C-H

At the end of the scene, Ross announces that he will go to Macbeth's coronation at Scone. Macduff replies: 'Well, may you see things well done there. Adieu! / Lest our old robes sit easier than our new.'

Shakespeare often uses rhyming couplets to highlight important ideas that he wants the audience to notice.

Triplet discussion: Shakespeare uses rhyming couplets to draw attention to Macduff's words. Why is that?

- Student A: Explain what Macduff's words mean.
- Student B: Consider why Shakespeare used rhyming couplets.
- Student C: Summarise the discussion.

Model answer:

Shakespeare revealed that Macduff had incipient suspicions of Macbeth in Act Two Scene Three when he asked why Macbeth had killed Duncan's guards. Now he says that he hopes the coronation – and the beginning of Macbeth's reign – goes well. However, Shakespeare uses the clothing image to indicate that Macduff fears for the future.

Shakespeare's use of the clothing motif reminds the audience of similar images earlier in the play. Shakespeare presents Macbeth's awareness that by donning the crown and robes of the king, he is illegitimately seizing power. [See Appendix B for more.]

Big question

How does Shakespeare present the natural world's response to Macbeth becoming king?

Shakespeare uses the rebellion of the natural world to condemn Macbeth's reign as a violent perversion of the natural order. The Old Man's reports are crucial: an owl, a creature of darkness and a clear echo of the owl heard after Duncan's murder, kills a falcon, a noble bird of day. This signifies the triumph of a predatory usurper over rightful majesty. Furthermore, Duncan's well-bred horses turning wild and cannibalistic serves as a metaphor for his loyal followers (the Scottish thanes) descending into chaotic infighting now that their master is gone. The Old Man explicitly describes these events as unprecedented, telling Ross that they are as unnatural as 'the deed that's done.' This collective disorder portrays Scotland itself as a body politic sickened by Macbeth's crime.

Themes

Disorder and the unnatural

This short scene is entirely dedicated to illustrating the catastrophic consequences of Macbeth's regicide on the world itself. The conversation between the Old Man and Ross serves no plot-advancing purpose other than to catalogue the unnatural chaos that has engulfed Scotland since Duncan's murder. The specific, symbolic events are not random portents but direct reflections of the political upheaval: the rightful king has been overthrown by a treacherous subject and the state has descended into self-destructive chaos.

Analysis

Staging: a different perspective

The measured blank verse of this scene provides a calmer perspective following the castle's internal chaos. Shakespeare often uses ordinary figures like this Old Man to ground tragedy in human experience. This scene's dialogue, detailing unnatural events in the wider world, confirms that the horror is not confined to the castle. Scotland itself has been sickened by the regicide, offering a sobering overview of the national catastrophe Macbeth has unleashed.

Key quotation | 'Dark night strangles the travelling lamp'

This line is the scene's central metaphorical statement and a culmination of the play's motif of darkness and light. Ross's description of an eclipse, where night actively 'strangles' the sun (the 'travelling lamp'), transforms a natural phenomenon into a violent, unnatural act. It marks the total, cosmic victory of the evil that Macbeth and Lady Macbeth privately summoned, which is now manifesting over all of Scotland. The darkness of treason has not merely obscured but actively obliterated the light of divine kingship represented by Duncan. The verb 'strangles' is particularly effective, echoing Macbeth's own violent actions and suggesting a deliberate, suffocating oppression. The image confirms that the disorder is not just political but universal: the rightful, life-giving order has been extinguished and a brutal, dark tyranny has taken its place.

PAUSE POINT

S-T-R-E-T-C-H

Shakespeare's depiction of an unnatural darkness falling upon Scotland after Duncan's murder directly parallels the account of the Crucifixion in the Gospel of Luke (23: 44-45), where darkness likewise covers the land.

Triplet discussion: Why would Shakespeare allude to the death of Jesus when dramatising the events following the regicide?

- Student A: Respond to the question by making one suggested interpretation.
- Student B: Respond to the question by making a second suggested interpretation.
- Student C: Summarise the discussion.

Model answer:

Shakespeare's allusion builds upon a foundation of holiness he has carefully constructed for Duncan. Throughout the early acts, characters describe the king in virtuous and sacred terms. Macbeth, in his soliloquy, concedes that Duncan's 'virtues / Will plead like angels, trumpet-tongued, against / The deep damnation of his taking off.' Macbeth is not merely killing a political rival, but a man of exceptional goodness. The subsequent allusion to the darkness after the Crucifixion elevates this 'deep damnation' from a personal fear to a universal symptom. In echoing this specific phenomenon from the Bible, Shakespeare frames Duncan's murder not just as a treasonous act, but as a sacrilegious one.

PAUSE POINT

CONSOLIDATION

As Act Two draws to a close, this is a good opportunity to revisit the protagonists' journey so far.

Ask students to create a timeline for the Macbeths' ascent to power. They should include key vocabulary, quotations and events in the play.

Upon the stage

This scene is often cut in performance, but Kenneth Branagh and Rob Ashford (Manchester, 2013) staged it very cleverly. Its three speakers conversed while Duncan's funeral cortege passed through the entire playing space. As Macduff revealed that Macbeth was to become king, the procession revealed the Macbeths, now crowned and moving towards their thrones. The change, in which Duncan's funeral parade became Macbeth's coronation, was a smart theatrical choice, showing how quickly power changes hands in the play – and how most people stay on the sidelines and merely observe.

CHAPTER 18
THOU HAST IT NOW
ACT THREE SCENE ONE (LINES 1 TO 46)

At a glance

- **Plot and character development:** Banquo voices his suspicions about Macbeth.
- **Social and historical context:** Paranoia in 1606 England
- **Vocabulary:** Paranoia
- **Big question:** Does Shakespeare present Banquo as suspecting Macbeth?
- **Themes:**
  - Appearance vs reality
  - The Divine Right of Kings
- **Analysis:**
  - Text: formal language
  - Staging: sennet
- **Key quotation:** 'Thou hast it now'

PAUSE POINT

RETRIEVAL

This activity builds students' ability to make connections across the text.

Give students a copy of the grid and ask them to link boxes by drawing and annotating arrows.

Crown	Milk	Daggers
Birds	Darkness	Serpent
Hands	Flower	Blood

Plot and character development

This scene marks a crucial transition in the presentation of Macbeth's character: he changes from a reactive, manipulated thane to a proactive, manipulative king. The initial courtly dialogue with Banquo reveals Macbeth's insecurity; his kingship feels empty and threatened. He is already gathering intelligence on his former friend. Banquo appears to have suspicions and hopes of his own: he fears Macbeth 'play'd most foully' to earn the crown, but perhaps the Witches' final prophecy will also come true.

Social and historical context

Paranoia in 1606 England

In 1606, England was a nation steeped in paranoia. In the wake of the very recent Gunpowder Plot, King James I's court saw Catholic conspiracies in every shadow. This pervasive fear of hidden traitors and regicide was amplified by a belief in a fragile cosmic order, where a subject's disloyalty could unravel the very fabric of the state. This atmosphere of suspicion and impending chaos is the essential context for Macbeth, a play that dramatises a king's murder and the tyrannical paranoia that inevitably follows.

Vocabulary | Paranoia

In Act Three, Shakespeare presents Macbeth as increasingly paranoid. In this scene his specific, repeated inquiries about Banquo's afternoon ride and, crucially, 'Goes Fleance with you?' show that he is making a plan. Teaching this word is an excellent opportunity to revisit other key texts to strengthen students' knowledge.

Definition:	**Characteristics:**
A state of irrational and persistent fear, suspicion and mistrust of others, often leading to the belief that one is being persecuted or threatened by a conspiracy.	• Irrational fear: Macbeth's fear of Banquo is based on a prophecy, not an active threat. • Perceived threat: his entire soliloquy fixates on Banquo's 'royalty of nature'. • Feeling of persecution: he believes he has damned his soul only for Banquo's descendants to benefit. • Preemptive action: the decision to murder Banquo and Fleance is a preemptive strike driven by suspicion, not evidence.

Examples:	**Non-examples:**
Macbeth (1606): Macbeth's 'fears in Banquo / Stick deep'.	*Macbeth* (1606): Banquo's wariness of the Witches' prophecies demonstrates healthy mistrust.
Animal Farm (1945): Napoleon is paranoid about threats to his power, and consequently eliminates Snowball.	*Animal Farm* (1945): Boxer trusts the pigs completely.

Reading the scene

This scene has two parts: Banquo's soliloquy and his conversation with the Macbeths. Each has a particular function:

- Banquo's soliloquy: this reveals the danger he poses to Macbeth, as he suspects foul play and considers his own ambitions for his family.
- Macbeth's arrival: the trumpets and attendants announce Macbeth's authority. This contrasts with Banquo's isolation and relative powerlessness. Macbeth's questions introduce a menacing tone.
- Introduce these functions by 'staging' the scene within your classroom.

Preparation:

- Set up a sennet sound effect. Cue a student to play it when Banquo says 'hush, no more'.
- Banquo stands alone at one end of the classroom.
- Macbeth wears a crown and is surrounded by attendants at the other end of the classroom.

Reading:

- Model reading Banquo's soliloquy: place the stress on 'my oracles' and 'set me up in hope' (to contrast with Macbeth's use of 'them' in his soliloquy later on).
- The student reads Banquo's soliloquy, followed by the sennet sound effect.
- Macbeth and his attendants 'enter' the scene and read up to 'exuent'.

Big question

Does Shakespeare present Banquo as suspecting Macbeth?

Shakespeare reveals that Banquo strongly suspects Macbeth, but he bides his time because he lacks proof. His short soliloquy acknowledges that the witches predicted Macbeth would be king, and now 'thou art,' but he pointedly adds, 'I fear / Thou played'st most foully for't.' This is a direct and private accusation of foul play. But Banquo immediately connects his own destiny to Macbeth's, recalling the prophecy that his sons, not Macbeth's, will be kings. His soliloquy confirms his mistrust: he hopes his part of the prophecy will also come true, but not through the same evil means Macbeth may have used.

PAUSE POINT

S-T-R-E-T-C-H

Shakespeare presents Banquo as a character foil to Macbeth: both receive prophecies in Act One Scene Three and both are welcomed and praised by Duncan in Act One Scene Four. However, Shakespeare gives them different paths: Macbeth commits the 'horrid deed', while Banquo bides his time. Surprisingly, in Shakespeare's source (Holinshed's *Chronicles*, 1587), Banquo helps Macbeth to murder Duncan.

Triplet discussion: Why does Shakespeare present Banquo so differently to the historical source?

- Student A: List the differences between Shakespeare and Holinshed's presentations of Banquo.
- Student B: Explain why Shakespeare presents Banquo differently.
- Student C: Summarise the discussion.

Model answer:

Unlike Holinshed, Shakespeare does not present Banquo as a co-conspirator and murderer, but as a loyal soldier who is also a victim of Macbeth's relentless ambition. Perhaps, Shakespeare adapted the source material due to a need to please King James I, who believed he was descended from Banquo. An alternative explanation could be that the change highlights Banquo's function as a character foil to Macbeth, highlighting the alternative path he could have taken. Like Macbeth, Banquo receives a prophecy, but he chooses honour above ambition.

PAUSE POINT

ORACY

Triplet discussion: Shakespeare builds tension between Macbeth and Banquo. How does he do this?

Students could consider how Shakespeare presents:

- Banquo's private suspicions, voiced in his soliloquy.
- Macbeth's ceremonial entrance, flaunting his newfound status.
- Macbeth's planning, through his pointed questions about Banquo's movements.
- Banquo's worries, shown through his evasive responses.

Themes

Appearance vs reality

The first exchange is entirely performative. Macbeth and Banquo speak with formal, courteous language, masking their true thoughts. Banquo hides his suspicions, while Macbeth conceals his murderous intent beneath the guise of a gracious host and king. He blatantly lies to Banquo when he says he 'thinks not' of the Witches.

The Divine Right of Kings

The Scottish system of tanistry – election of the worthiest candidate rather than automatic succession – has worked in Macbeth's favour, particularly since Malcolm and Donalbain have fled. But Banquo now legitimately wonders if the Witches' prophecies will come true for him and that his children will be kings. The question of succession is always at work in Shakespeare's plays and was a particular fixation for King James I. He abolished tanistry in the 1600s, insisting on the Divine Right behind his reign. No wonder that it is a theme that dominates *Macbeth*.

Analysis

Text: formal language

Shakespeare's use of formal, courtly language between Macbeth and Banquo signifies their growing suspicion, creating a façade of loyalty to mask their true intentions. This polished rhetoric ('chief guest,' 'indissoluble tie') is a performance. Each carefully chosen word heightens the dramatic irony, revealing the schism between their respectful public dialogue and private suspicions. This section echoes the courtly language used by Duncan and Lady Macbeth in Act One Scene Six, reminding the audience that this kind of heightened, flattering diction probably masks more sinister intentions.

Staging: sennet

The 'sennet' is a trumpet call exclusively for a king's stage entrance. Its use here shows Macbeth manipulating the symbols of royalty to perform and consolidate his new power.

Key quotation | 'Thou hast it now'

Opening with 'Thou hast it now' is a profound grammatical choice, revealing Banquo's inner conflict. As Macbeth's subject, he should use the formal 'you.' The intimate 'thou' signals that Banquo is speaking to his friend and comrade, not his king. It frames his accusation not as treason, but as a friend's horrified conclusion: Macbeth 'played'st most foully for't.' The adverb 'foully' subtly recalls the Witches' 'fair is foul', showing how their influence is spreading through Scotland.

PAUSE POINT

CONSOLIDATION

How does Shakespeare present Macbeth and Banquo's changing relationship?

Students could think-pair-share or free write their responses to this question.

Alternatively, provide students with this list of prompts and ask them to provide supporting evidence and examples:

- Banquo and Macbeth's closeness in Act One Scene Three.
- Banquo's cautionary words to his friend ('to win us to our harm...').
- Macbeth retreating into soliloquies when he hears the prophecies.
- The tense conversation in Act Two Scene One.
- Mutual suspicions in Act Three Scene One.

Upon the stage

Kenneth Branagh's (2013) Manchester production seamlessly linked the end of Act Two and this first scene of Act Three with the royal parade described in the previous chapter. As the Macbeths processed through the space, Banquo's soliloquy provided a wry commentary. The soliloquy operated almost like a voiceover, and hearing it while we watched the newly-crowned Macbeths created intense dramatic irony. The audience was forced to view the new king and queen through the lens of Banquo's suspicion, undermining their authority and power from the very start of their reign.

Directors choose to stage soliloquies in a variety of ways – the soliloquy can be staged as a speech given directly to the audience or camera, a commentary on the action or a character musing aloud to themselves. On screen they can even be presented as a voiceover. Which of these methods of staging a soliloquy do you think is most effective, and why?

CHAPTER 19
A FRUITLESS CROWN
ACT THREE SCENE ONE (LINES 47 TO 71)

At a glance

- **Plot and character development:** Macbeth, alone after dismissing his court, reveals the profound emptiness of his achievement and identifies Banquo as the next threat to his security.
- **Social and historical context:** Royal flattery
- **Vocabulary:** Resentful
- **Big question:** Why does Shakespeare present Macbeth, as king, still consumed by fear?
- **Themes:**
  - Guilt and conscience
  - Kingship
- **Analysis:**
  - Macbeth's soliloquy
  - Mark Antony
- **Key quotation:** 'A fruitless crown'

PAUSE POINT

RETRIEVAL

At this point in the play, Shakespeare presents Macbeth as tormented by the horror of committing cold-blooded murder to attain the crown.

Ask students to discuss and rank these statements from the most to the least accurate, based on the last time we encountered Macbeth in Act Two Scene Three.

A. Shakespeare presents Macbeth as completely consumed by guilt.

B. Shakespeare emphasises Macbeth's desperation as he tries to maintain his façade of innocence.

C. Shakespeare reveals Macbeth's continued reliance on Lady Macbeth's direction and support.

Plot and character development

Alone after dismissing his court, Macbeth reveals the profound emptiness of his ill-gotten kingship. He confesses that 'to be thus is nothing, / But to be safely thus,' revealing that his power is meaningless without absolute security. He fixates on Banquo, whose 'royalty of nature' and 'dauntless temper' feel like a direct threat. Macbeth's characterisation deepens into bitter resentment as he contemplates the Witches' prophecy: he realises he has damned his own soul and murdered the 'gracious Duncan' only to place a 'fruitless crown' upon his own head and a 'barren sceptre' in his grip. This realisation (that he has no heir and that Banquo's sons will be kings) propels him from anxious king to determined murderer, as he resolves to challenge fate itself and assassinate Banquo – and Fleance.

Social and historical context

Royal flattery

Shakespeare wrote this soliloquy not merely for character development, but as a piece of strategic royal flattery. By having Macbeth articulate that his own crown is 'fruitless' and 'barren,' while simultaneously venerating Banquo and his promised lineage, he indirectly asserts the Stuart claim. The speech dramatises the futility of any threat to Banquo's heirs, assuring the audience – and most importantly, King James I, Banquo's supposed descendant – that the Stuart line is protected by the Witches' prophecy.

PAUSE POINT

S-T-R-E-T-C-H

Challenge students to recall other uses of natural imagery in the play (see Appendix B).

Vocabulary | Resentful

Fearing the prophecy that Banquo's heirs will inherit the crown, Macbeth feels increasingly resentful towards him. His own childlessness makes this threat feel all the more acute. Discuss the connected words with your class to support students in using a range of vocabulary and avoiding repetition.

Definition:	**Use it in a sentence:**
Feeling anger towards someone perceived as having an undeserved advantage, which threatens one's own status or desires.	1. Macbeth is resentful of Banquo because... 2. Macbeth is resentful of the Witches because...
Related words:	**Opposite words:**
Bitter, aggrieved, dissatisfied, hostile, hateful	Joyful, harmonious, appreciative

Reading the scene

Introduce visual symbols of kingship, perhaps using a picture of King Charles' coronation. Discuss the crown, sceptre, orb, the Stone of Scone and the robes the king wears. You could link this to the motif of clothing used throughout the play.

Read the soliloquy to the class and ask them to highlight symbols of kingship:

- 'fruitless crown'
- 'barren sceptre'.

Both adjectives hint that Macbeth will not be father to a line of kings.

Re-read the soliloquy. This time, ask students to highlight the pronouns 'him' and 'them'.

Discuss the repetition of these pronouns, demonstrating Macbeth's resentment that he has destroyed his mind for someone else's family. Compare with Banquo's use of the intimate 'thou' in his soliloquy.

Ask students to rehearse these lines in their triplets: 'For Banquo's issue I have fil'd my mind; / For them the gracious Duncan have I murdered'. Ask students to vary the emotions they inject into these words: bitterness, despair, hatred and anger.

Discuss which interpretation students think is the most appropriate for this point in the play.

Big question

Why does Shakespeare present Macbeth, as king, still consumed by fear?

Macbeth is consumed by fear because his crown is illegitimate, stained with blood and psychologically 'fruitless.' He realises that committing the 'horrid deed' has only given him a temporary throne. If, as Macbeth clearly believes, the Witches' prophecy about Banquo's lineage will also come true, it means that he has destroyed his own soul and peace of mind merely to be a 'barren' placeholder for Banquo's descendants. His crown is hollow and he fears not just losing power, but that his sacrifice will have been for nothing.

Themes

Guilt and conscience

Paranoia is a manifestation of Macbeth's guilt. After murdering Duncan, his conscience leads him to irrational and paranoid fear, leaving his mind 'full of scorpions.' Macbeth goes from a general sense of insecurity ('To be safely thus') to an obsessive preoccupation with one man ('There is none but he / Whose being I do fear'). He sees Banquo's every virtue as a threat and interprets the prophecy as a trick designed to rob him of his ill-gotten gains. Macbeth is now morally bankrupt, planning to murder his friend to protect what he gained through the previous murder. The chain of violence is unfolding before him.

Kingship

The crown has brought Macbeth no peace. In his soliloquy, he dwells not on power enjoyed but on heirs he cannot have: 'Upon my head they placed a fruitless crown.' The verb is telling: the crown is *placed*, not *given*, as though kingship were a borrowed thing. Under tanistry, Macbeth's reign is lawful, yet it brings him nothing but anxiety. Where Duncan's kingship suggested divine ordinance and natural order, Macbeth's is maintained only by anticipating the next threat. Banquo need not even accuse him; his very existence as a father is enough. Shakespeare shows us, in this scene, a king who holds the sceptre but has lost all security.

Analysis

Macbeth's soliloquy

Shakespeare begins this soliloquy with Macbeth qualifying his kingship: 'to be thus is nothing, but to be safely thus'. This substitution echoes his earlier euphemisms and immediately draws the audience into his paranoid state of mind. He confesses his fear stems not from Banquo's actions, but from his innate 'royalty of nature.' Macbeth acknowledges that Banquo's 'dauntless temper' and 'wisdom' are the very qualities of a true king, making his own 'genius' – his guiding spirit – feel 'rebuked' or humiliated in comparison.

His language grows increasingly agitated, marked by frantic rhetorical questions ('Why, upon this...?') that propel him deeper into his fears. The soliloquy's emotional core is his bitter fixation on the prophecy, which he now views not as a promise but a personal threat. This culminates in the devastating revelation of the 'fruitless crown' and 'barren sceptre' – powerful symbols of a sterile reign that will die with him, rendering his monstrous crimes futile unless he acts.

The soliloquy concludes with a decisive shift to the metaphor of a medieval tournament. When Macbeth commands, 'come fate into the list, / And champion me to the utterance,' he is issuing a formal challenge. The 'list' is the jousting arena and 'fate' is the opponent he dares to face. To 'champion me to the utterance' is a call for a fight to the death – the 'utterance' meaning the outrance, or the very end. In this moment, Macbeth arrogantly casts himself as the righteous knight, demanding a final, violent confrontation with the very destiny that foretold Banquo's lineage would reign.

Mark Antony

Shakespeare's reference to Mark Antony is apt. He alludes to the historical moment when Octavian (the future Caesar Augustus) overcame his rival, Mark Antony, to found not just a lasting dynasty but an empire. Macbeth fears an identical fate: Banquo, or his children, may usurp him and establish a new line. This parallel was understandably fresh in Shakespeare's mind, as he wrote his *Antony and Cleopatra* in the same year as *Macbeth*.

Key quotation | 'A fruitless crown'

The 'fruitless crown' is the soliloquy's central revelation: Macbeth's reign will be sterile and end with him. This fear of irrelevance, echoing his earlier allusion to Mark Antony's eclipse, transforms his anxiety into a specific, murderous resolve. He now understands the hollow victory the Witches have granted.

PAUSE POINT

S-T-R-E-T-C-H

In Act One Scene Four, Shakespeare uses the language of cultivation, as Duncan says he has 'begun to plant[ed] thee' Macbeth and will make him grow. In contrast, Shakespeare emphasises Macbeth's 'fruitless[ness]'. Significantly, when Malcolm is crowned in Act Five, he revives his father's metaphor, describing the work ahead of him as what 'would be planted newly with the time'.

Triplet discussion: Why does Shakespeare associate Duncan and Malcolm with growth and Macbeth with barrenness?

- Student A: Respond to the question with reference to Duncan and Malcolm.
- Student B: Respond to the question with reference to Macbeth.
- Student C: Summarise the discussion.

Model answer:

Shakespeare's use of imagery of nature and growth suggests that Duncan and Malcolm are the rightful rulers of Scotland: they will nurture their country, bringing prosperity and harmony. In contrast, Shakespeare reveals that Macbeth's reign, defined by barrenness, represents a blight – a period of moral and political decay that yields no lasting legacy.

However, Shakespeare introduces a subtle ambiguity with Malcolm. Duncan's trust in Macbeth proved fatal, raising the question: is Malcolm's promise to 'plant' a sign of wise rule, or could his judgment also be flawed? Shakespeare leaves this tension unresolved to preserve the prophetic space for Banquo's lineage. The audience is left to wonder if Malcolm's reign will be secure, or merely a temporary pause before Fleance (or his heirs) ascend to the Scottish throne.

PAUSE POINT

CONSOLIDATION

Revisit the statements from the beginning of the chapter. Have your students' opinions changed?

Upon the stage

This extraordinary soliloquy is a risky moment for the character – and the actor playing him. As Macbeth contemplates Banquo's death, we could very easily turn away from him. Compare the performances of three great actors in this scene; Stewart (Gould, 2010), McKellen (Nunn, 1979) and Tennant (Webster, 2023).

Which is the most convincing? Which is the most disturbing? Do we still feel any sympathy or connection to Macbeth even as he plots his friend's murder?

CHAPTER 20
IT IS CONCLUDED
ACT THREE SCENE ONE (LINES 72 TO END)

At a glance

- **Plot and character development:** Macbeth orchestrates Banquo's murder with cold, political precision, deliberately excluding his wife.
- **Social and historical context:** Royal flattery (continued)
- **Vocabulary:** Tyrant
- **Big question:** Why does Macbeth not murder Banquo himself?
- **Themes:**
  - Violence and masculinity
  - Ambition and power
  - Fate vs free will
- **Analysis:**
  - Role reversal
- **Key quotation:** 'It is concluded: Banquo, thy soul's flight, / If it find heaven, must find it out tonight'

PAUSE POINT

RETRIEVAL

Explore these questions, focusing on Shakespeare's representation of masculinity:

- How does Shakespeare present stereotypes of masculinity Act One Scene Two?
- How does Shakespeare present Lady Macbeth's manipulation of Macbeth in Act One?

Plot and character development

Two Murderers enter. Macbeth skillfully manipulates them, questioning their manhood and blaming Banquo for their misfortunes. He instructs them to murder Banquo and Fleance, insisting that there be no survivors. The scene concludes with Macbeth asserting his newfound autonomy, pointedly withholding the plan from Lady Macbeth.

Social and historical context

Royal flattery (continued)

Banquo was a fictional creation in Holinshed's *Chronicles* (1587), but for James and the Stuart court, he was considered a mythical ancestor. Recognising this, Shakespeare portrays Banquo as a noble figure worth mourning, whose murder is a crime against the king's own line. To amplify the horror of this crime, Shakespeare has Macbeth dehumanise the hired Murderers, dismissing them as beings less than 'dogs'. By framing them as animals, he highlights the savagery of killing the royal Banquo: it is another flattering allegory for James.

Vocabulary | Tyrant

As Macbeth turns his mind to the murder of his friend and companion-in-arms, he graduates from illegitimate king to murderous tyrant. Contrast Macbeth's tyranny with other examples of leadership in the play, as suggested in the table below.

Definition:	**Characteristics:**
A ruler who seizes power illegally and exercises it in an absolute, cruel and oppressive manner, often through fear and violence. Related words: Oppressor, dictator, totalitarian leader	• Violence: gains throne by murdering the legitimate king (Duncan). • Rules by fear: uses spies, violence and intimidation to control his thanes. • Paranoia: isolates himself and trusts no one, fearing loss of power. • Violence as policy: orders murders to eliminate perceived threats (Banquo, Macduff's family).
Examples:	**Non-examples (from *Macbeth*):**
Macbeth (1606): Macbeth is a tyrant who orders the murders of women and children to consolidate his power. *Animal Farm* (1945): Orwell presents Napoleon as a tyrant who rules by fear.	King Duncan: A lawful, hereditary monarch who rules with gratitude and honour. Edward the Confessor: A king whose 'healing' power symbolises his divine right and virtuous nature.

Reading the scene

This is a lengthy and complex section of the play. If you choose to read this with your class, take the role of Macbeth yourself to maintain the pace and correct pronunciation. If you choose to skip the reading, focus on the lines highlighted in our online version of the text.

PAUSE POINT

S-T-R-E-T-C-H

Triplet discussion: Does Shakespeare present Macbeth as a more effective manipulator than Lady Macbeth?

- Student A: Argue that Macbeth is a more effective manipulator.
- Student B: Argue that Lady Macbeth is a more effective manipulator.
- Student C: Summarise the discussion.

Model answer:

We can directly compare Shakespeare's presentation of Macbeth's actions here to his portrayal of Lady Macbeth's manipulation in Act One Scene Seven. She questioned his manhood and love for her, using personal taunts and emotional blackmail. It is arguable, however, that Macbeth is the more effective manipulator as he operates with a colder, more political precision. For example, Shakespeare emphasises Macbeth's use of a shared enemy in his discussion with the murderers. Instead of personal insults, he frames Banquo as the 'common enemy', thus creating a bond of shared grievance. Shakespeare amplifies this sense of Macbeth's mastery of manipulation when he questions the Murderers' class and humanity: he doesn't just call them cowards, but asks if they are so passive and 'gospell'd' that they will accept their lowly status, attacking their very sense of self-worth.

Big question

Why does Macbeth not murder Banquo himself?

Macbeth's choice to delegate Banquo's murder marks a pivotal shift in his character, moving him further from the honourable warrior he once was. Unlike his visceral, public violence on the battlefield, the murder of Duncan required him to kill in cold blood – an act that left him psychologically shattered, his mind 'full of scorpions.' Having been traumatised by his own hands-on regicide, he now seeks to insulate himself from further guilt by hiring assassins. This evasion is compounded by his personal relationship with Banquo; as a fellow soldier and companion-in-arms, Banquo's death represents a more intimate betrayal. Shakespeare shows that to kill Banquo directly would be to cross a moral threshold that even the sleepless, traumatised Macbeth cannot face.

Themes

Violence and masculinity

Violence is no longer a means to an end; it has become the primary instrument of Macbeth's rule. Having committed murder to gain the crown, Macbeth now reflexively uses it to maintain power. His shift from committing the act himself (Duncan) to *commissioning* it shows a more calculating, political and sinister approach to tyranny, maintaining a layer of deniability. Ironically Macbeth questions the Murderers' masculinity – just as Lady Macbeth previously questioned his – as he enjoins them to take on the job of murdering Banquo.

Fate vs free will

Spurred by the prophecy that Banquo's sons will be kings, Macbeth actively tries to wrestle control of his destiny. The decision to murder Fleance is a direct assault on the future articulated by the Weird Sisters. Shakespeare reveals that Macbeth will no longer be a passive recipient of fate but an active, defiant agent trying to secure his authority with blood.

Ambition and power

There is no longer any hesitation. The Macbeth who could not say 'Amen,' who heard voices cry 'Sleep no more,' who clutched at air-drawn daggers: that man has vanished. In his place stands a king who summons murderers as a master calls upon servants, itemising Banquo's faults with cool efficiency. The language is managerial, almost bureaucratic; there is no trace of the supernatural horror that accompanied Duncan's death. Ambition, once a fever, has hardened into prerogative. The first murder may have cost him his peace, but this one costs him nothing – yet. Shakespeare shows us, in this transformation, that the true corruption is not the murder, but the ambitious zeal for power that requires Macbeth to kill again in order to maintain it.

Analysis

Role reversal

The scene's conclusion completes the reversal of roles between Macbeth and Lady Macbeth. Shakespeare emphasises how Macbeth has not only adopted his wife's manipulative tactics but has upgraded them into something even more dehumanising. Where Lady Macbeth questioned Macbeth's manhood, asking if he was 'afeard' to be the same in act as desire, she ultimately appealed to his ambition and spirit. Macbeth, however, goes further with the Murderers. He doesn't just question their manhood ('in the catalogue you go for men'), but their very humanity, rhetorically asking if they have so little agency that they will 'pray for this good man' like passive, 'gospell'd' creatures. He redefines true courage as the brutal willingness to 'have...a score' like animals, reducing them from men to attack dogs he can unleash upon his enemy.

Key quotation | 'It is concluded Banquo, thy soul's flight, / If it find heaven, must find it out tonight'

This couplet comes with considerable finality, firmly resolving the scene's tense interactions. Shakespeare uses it to indicate Macbeth's transformation from a tormented conspirator to a cold, autonomous tyrant. 'It is concluded,' gives a stark closure to his manipulation of the Murderers, highlighting his newfound authority. Shakespeare ends the scene with a death sentence for Macbeth's former friend and also usurps a divine right: judging a soul's final destination is a task reserved only for God. This declaration shatters his 'barren sceptre' soliloquy, replacing anxious fear with resolute, blasphemous action. In planning this without Lady Macbeth, he widens the fracture in their partnership, isolating himself from his friend and his wife at once.

PAUSE POINT

CONSOLIDATION

Ask students to explore the similarities and differences between these quotations.

Act Two Scene One:

'I go, and it is done. The bell invites me.
Hear it not, Duncan, for it is a knell
That summons thee to heaven or to hell.'

Act Three Scene One:

'It is concluded. Banquo, thy soul's flight,
If it find heaven, must find it out tonight.'

Students could consider how Shakespeare presents:

- A sense of finality in both quotations, heightened by the use of rhyming couplets.

- The difference in killing a friend and committing regicide.
- Lady Macbeth's (lack of) involvement.
- References to the afterlife.
- Macbeth's role in the murder.

Upon the stage

Max Webster (2023) directed David Tennant to enlist and motivate the two Murderers against Banquo with chilling and entertaining efficiency. The intimacy of the scene, enabled by the production's headphone-based sound design, was particularly compelling, right down to the final couplet sealing Banquo's fate. Tennant here achieved the remarkable feat of staying charming even as he arranged his friend's murder. Show your students other interpretations (Nunn, Goold or Godwin) to see how actors navigate this difficult moment; ask whether this is a moment where an audience might turn away from Macbeth.

Consider each production: which is the most effective, and why?

CHAPTER 21
WE HAVE SCORCHED THE SNAKE, NOT KILLED IT
ACT THREE SCENE TWO

At a glance

- **Plot and character development:** Lady Macbeth and Macbeth descend from triumphant conspiracy to paranoia and anxiety.
- **Social and historical context:** Succession
- **Vocabulary:** Emotional anguish
- **Big question:** Who does Shakespeare present as being more troubled in this scene, Macbeth or Lady Macbeth?
- **Themes:**
  - Appearance vs reality
  - Guilt and conscience
  - Violence and masculinity
- **Analysis:**
  - Role reversal (continued)
  - Motif: sleep
  - Motif: darkness and light
- **Key quotation:** 'We have scorched the snake, not killed it'

PAUSE POINT

RETRIEVAL

How does Shakespeare present the couple's relationship?

Ask students to think-pair-share the ideas, including supporting quotations.

Students could consider how Shakespeare presents:

- The passionate nature of the relationship in Act One.
- Lady Macbeth's concerns about her husband's courage and masculinity.
- Lady Macbeth's dominance and manipulation of her husband's masculinity.
- Their differing responses to the murder.

Explain that in Act Three Scene One, Shakespeare highlights how Macbeth isolates himself from his wife.

Plot and character development

Lady Macbeth, troubled by her own growing anxiety, seeks out her husband, who is obsessed with the threat posed by Banquo and Fleance. She urges him to be cheerful for his guests at the banquet that night. Macbeth, revealing his tormented state, tells her to mask their true feelings: 'make our faces vizards [masks] to our hearts'. Crucially, he withholds the specific details of his plan to murder Banquo: this signals his new autonomy and a growing distance in their relationship.

Social and historical context

Succession

Macbeth's earlier reference to his 'fruitless crown' and 'barren sceptre' speaks directly to the Jacobean concern with lineage and succession. A monarch's legitimacy was tied to their ability to found – or continue – a dynasty. Without an heir, and threatened by Banquo's line, Macbeth acknowledges the ultimate futility of his crime. He has shattered the natural order not for a lasting legacy, but for a 'fruitless' title that he cannot even leave to children of his own.

Vocabulary | Emotional anguish

Students often struggle to describe the Macbeths' psychological torment using appropriate and nuanced terminology. Act Three Scene Two provides an opportunity to address this issue.

Definition:	**Use it in a sentence:**
Significant mental suffering and pain.	Macbeth's soliloquy in Act One Scene Seven reveals his mental anguish about... Shakespeare reveals Macbeth's emotional anguish after the murder by...
Related words:	**Opposite words:**
Turmoil, torment, distress, despair	Joy, happiness, exuberance, delight

Reading the scene

This scene contrasts with two earlier ones: Act One Scene Five (Lady Macbeth's soliloquy and Macbeth's entrance), and Act Three Scene One (their entrance as king and queen).

Remind your students of these scenes. In the first, Lady Macbeth is focused on achieving their joint ambition for the 'golden round' – even if this means manipulating her husband. When Macbeth enters, they express their devotion to each other: 'great Glamis, worthy Cawdor', and 'my dearest love'. In Act Three Scene One, they enter together as king and queen, accompanied by the sound of trumpets and attendants.

The relationship has changed significantly by the start of Act Three Scene Two. Read the scene, asking students to notice signs of the fractured marriage. They might consider:

- Lady Macbeth's use of the phrase 'the king' when she asks permission to speak to her husband.
- The lack of affection between the couple when Macbeth enters.
- Lady Macbeth's question: 'why do you keep alone?'.
- The shift from 'dearest partner in greatness' to 'dear wife'.
- Secrets: Lady Macbeth withholds her anxiety and Macbeth withholds his plan to murder Banquo.

PAUSE POINT

ORACY

Triplet discussion: 'Shakespeare now presents Lady Macbeth as being less powerful than her husband.' How far do you agree?

- Student A: Respond to the question.
- Student B: Provide evidence or examples to support Student A.
- Student C: Summarise the discussion.

Model answer:

In this scene, Shakespeare clearly presents Lady Macbeth's loss of determination: she now lives in 'doubtful joy', uncertain of her future, she gains no pleasure from being queen. Her loss of confidence is accompanied by her failure to control Macbeth, even when she employs the manipulative methods that worked so effectively in Act One. Macbeth now ignores her imperatives ('sleek', 'be'), and he actively withholds information about the planned killing of Banquo. Shakespeare also uses names to indicate a clear shift in the power dynamic. Lady Macbeth is no longer her husband's 'dearest partner of greatness', but is now reduced to his 'dearest chuck'.

Big question

Who does Shakespeare present as being more troubled in this scene, Macbeth or Lady Macbeth?

While Shakespeare presents Macbeth as visibly more agitated, giving voice to his 'scorpions,' Lady Macbeth's earlier strength also seems to be receding. Her opening line, ''Tis safer to be that which we destroy / Than by destruction dwell in doubtful joy,' reveals an incipient despair. They have achieved their goal but are finding no happiness in it. Macbeth is tormented by active fear, while Lady Macbeth is succumbing to a quiet, passive anguish, foreshadowing her eventual breakdown.

PAUSE POINT

S-T-R-E-T-C-H

Read-reduce-rehearse-remember (see 'How to use this book' page XIII).

The contrast Shakespeare creates between Macbeth and Lady Macbeth's emotional states introduces dissonance – a discordant or unresolved clash between elements. In this scene, the dissonance is multifaceted: between the Macbeths' public faces and private torment ('make our faces vizards to our hearts'); between their achieved goal and their profound lack of happiness and security ('doubtful joy'); and between Macbeth's kingly title and his 'fruitless,' barren state. This tension is the engine of the scene's psychological drama.

Themes

Appearance vs reality

Shakespeare reveals the performance of kingship as a desperate façade. Macbeth's command to 'make our faces vizards to our hearts' shows that their reign is a carefully staged lie. The cheerful, secure monarchs they present to the court are a complete fiction, masking their paranoid and guilt-ridden state.

Guilt and conscience

Macbeth's revelation that his mind is 'full of scorpions' is the emotional core of the scene. This visceral metaphor for paranoia conveys a mind poisoned from within, tormented by stinging, inescapable thoughts of fear and guilt. The spur that pricked the sides of his intent has now been transformed into a nest of scorpions, stinging him constantly. What Lady Macbeth described as 'doubtful joy' has been replaced by Macbeth's 'terrible dreams,' showing that, as a couple, their consciences torment them, punishing them more effectively than any external force.

Violence and masculinity

Shakespeare shows how Macbeth seizes agency in his grim resolution to commit further violence. By telling Lady Macbeth to 'be innocent of the knowledge,' he excludes her, framing his actions not as a shared conspiracy but as his own brutal, solitary duty. This redefines his masculinity around autonomous, ruthless action and is the first major signal of their crumbling relationship.

Analysis

Role reversal (continued)

This scene continues the important reversal of roles: Macbeth and Lady Macbeth effectively trade personalities. Initially, she was the driving force, manipulating his ambition and directing the plot. Now it is Macbeth who tells his wife that they must 'make our faces vizards to our hearts / Disguising what they are.' Shakespeare has Macbeth plan the next murders alone, relegating Lady Macbeth to the sidelines. The shift is most evident when he pointedly excludes her from his plans for Banquo, telling her to 'be innocent of the knowledge, dearest chuck.' This condescending term demotes her from 'dearest partner in greatness' to a powerless, conventional wife, highlighting his newfound autonomy and the fracturing of their partnership. Lady Macbeth is left to confront the 'doubtful joy' of their success, realising too late that the power they sought has corrupted everything, including their bond.

Motif: sleep

The Macbeths' world is now devoid of restorative sleep, which they recognise as a permanent casualty of their crimes. Macbeth explicitly links their actions to a perpetual state of torment, telling his wife they will 'sleep / In the affliction of these terrible dreams / That shake us nightly.' The 'innocent sleep' Macbeth mourned after Duncan's murder has now been wholly replaced by nightmares and chronic insomnia. This is not mere restlessness, but a profound psychological punishment; sleep, a symbol of a clear conscience and divine favour, has abandoned them.

Motif: darkness and light

The motif of darkness evolves from a cover for crime to a symbol of the Macbeths' moral state. Macbeth's plea for nightfall – 'Come, seeling night… with thy bloody and invisible hand / Cancel and tear to pieces that great bond' – is a chilling invocation. His beautiful, yet sinister, description of light thickening as the 'crow makes wing to the rooky wood' poetically captures a world succumbing to gloom. This is no longer a temporary cloak but their permanent element.

Key quotation | 'We have scorched the snake, not killed it'

This line is the scene's crucial metaphor, crystallising Macbeth's destructive psychology. The 'snake' represents the enduring threat of Banquo's lineage, which the prophecy promised would inherit the Scottish crown. By killing Duncan, Macbeth made his way to the throne, but this only temporarily blocks Banquo's descendants from the crown. It's a wound to the snake – the lingering, wriggling potential in the prophecy – but this has disabled it only temporarily. Macbeth feels he must kill the snake in order to be secure. This understanding fuels his paranoia and propels him toward the next murder: it reveals that the initial kill was not an endpoint but a catalyst. Securing a bloody crown requires perpetual violence, as one deed inevitably demands another. Blood, as Macbeth will soon tell us, will have blood.

Note: some editions of the play will read 'we have scotched the snake'. This is an emendation from an 18th century editor; while it is an attractive idea to use this Scottish-sounding word, the Folio text insists that the snake is *scorched*.

PAUSE POINT

CONSOLIDATION

Revisit the play's key concept: Shakespeare explores how unchecked ambition acts as a corrupting force, eroding a person's morality and sanity.

Ask students to explore how the start of Act Three provides evidence to support this idea.

Students could consider how Shakespeare presents:

- Macbeth's mental anguish.
- The fracturing of Macbeth and Lady Macbeth's relationship.
- Macbeth's descent into tyranny.
- Macbeth's plan to murder Banquo, representing the spread of violence and chaos.

Upon the stage

This scene dramatises the fracture in the Macbeths' partnership, as Macbeth alone seizes control of their campaign. He can be a figure of ruthless energy (Webster, 2023), exhausted pragmatism (Godwin, 2024) or desperate vulnerability (Norris, 2018). Godwin highlighted Lady Macbeth's dawning isolation by moving her 'Naught's had, all's spent' speech until after Macbeth's exit; this allowed Indira Varma to begin with dominance, her dismay slowly growing more apparent as she realised she was being excluded.

Show your students a variety of interpretations and see whose performances move them most. Pay particular attention to how each actor says the word 'assailable'?

CHAPTER 22
FLY, GOOD FLEANCE
ACT THREE SCENE THREE

At a glance

- **Plot and character development:** Three murderers attack Banquo and Fleance.
- **Social and historical context:** Staging murder
- **Vocabulary:** Unscrupulous
- **Big question:** Who is the third Murderer?
- **Themes:**
  - Violence and masculinity
  - Conflict
- **Analysis:**
  - Motif: darkness and light
- **Key quotation:** 'Fly, good Fleance'

PAUSE POINT

KNOWLEDGE CHECK

Ask students to think-pair-share what they remember about the offstage deaths of key characters so far. Remind students that regicide could not be depicted onstage for legal reasons and that it was impractical to stage busy, violent battles early in the play.

In contrast to these earlier deaths, Shakespeare places Banquo's murder on stage – he is killed by hired assassins, not Macbeth. By staging Banquo's murder, Shakespeare draws our attention to Macbeth's growing desperation as he uses violence to cling on to power.

Plot and character development

Three Murderers attack as darkness approaches. Banquo dies protecting his son, but Fleance escapes. This ensures that the Witches' prophecy can still come true, Banquo's children can someday be kings.

Social and historical context

Staging murder

Staging Banquo's murder was unusual, as Jacobean drama typically relegated violence to offstage. For King James, a supposed descendant of Banquo, this choice would have been profoundly shocking, making the attack on his lineage visceral and immediate, and framing Macbeth's tyranny as an affront to the crown itself.

Vocabulary | Unscrupulous

The earlier killings reveal either Macbeth's patriotism (Macdonwald) or his ambition (Duncan), but the unscrupulous murder of Banquo reveals that the tragic hero has crossed another moral threshold, descending further into tyrannical corruption.

Definition:	**Morphology:**
Completely lacking morality and integrity.	Prefix: un = not Root: scrupulus (Latin) = small stone Imagine how irritating it is to have a small stone in your shoe. This is a metaphor for your conscience. Add the negative prefix un- and Macbeth has no conscience.
Examples:	**Non-examples:**
An Inspector Calls (1946): Priestley presents Mr Birling as an unscrupulous capitalist who callously fires Eva Smith. *A Christmas Carol* (1843): Initially, Scrooge's financial dealings are unscrupulous, as he does not care about driving people to misery.	*Dr Jekyll and Mr Hyde* (1886): Stevenson portrays Utterson as a scrupulous character, who embodies morality and goodness. *Macbeth* (1606): Banquo scrupulously wishes to keep his 'allegiance clear' (Act Two Scene One).

Reading the scene

The pacing of this scene is important, as it moves from suspicion (up to 'then stand with us'), to tense waiting ('let it come down'), to action (the murder).

Talk to the students about these three sections and how they can use their voices to communicate the shifts in emotion.

- Suspicion – speaking at normal volume and pace.
- Tense waiting – the murderers whisper, Banquo speaks at normal volume.
- Action – each reader should start speaking even as the previous reader finishes their line. This will increase the pace and sense of confusion.

Choose four readers and rehearse this in front of the class. Pause and give students direction where necessary. Then split the class into groups of four to rehearse the scene. Bring the class back together, choose another four readers and read the scene again.

Added bonus: if you have a torch, bring this to illustrate the shifts in lighting.

Big question

Who is the third Murderer?

The appearance of a third Murderer is a notable anomaly in the text – and his identity has prompted considerable speculation. While its dramatic function is clear (to heighten the tension and ensure Fleance's escape) the Murderer's identity remains an open question: is he:

- Hired by Macbeth: sent to ensure the job is done, highlighting Macbeth's distrust of everyone, even his own hired killers?
- Macbeth himself: showing his hands-on descent into violence and his consuming need for control over his fate?
- A supernatural figure: a witch (or a demon) ensuring the prophecy's survival, ensnaring Macbeth as a pawn in a larger, evil design?

Analysis

Motif: darkness and light

This scene begins in twilight, as is indicated by the first murderer, who mentions that 'the west yet glimmers with some streaks of day'. When Banquo enters, he cries for a 'light', as the sun is fading fast. The darkness of the scene echoes the staging of Act One Scene One, Act Two Scene One, Act Two Scene Two, and the beginning of Act Two Scene Three, thus symbolising how the 'instruments of darkness' poison Macbeth's mind and his consequent malevolence infects all of Scotland.

PAUSE POINT

ORACY

This is a quick, 60 second activity to help students recap key images in the play.

- Students work in pairs: one chooses light, the other darkness.
- The students take turns in saying a connotation linked to their chosen symbol. The first student to 'drop the ball' loses the game.

Key quotation | 'Fly, good Fleance'

Shakespeare uses this desperate command from a dying father to amplify the human anguish caused by Macbeth's tyranny. The murder of Banquo and the attack on his son, Fleance, marks a new level of unscrupulous cruelty; children have become fair game in Macbeth's frantic consolidation of power. However, in this moment, Macbeth's plan to kill 'the snake' fails, as Fleance's escape ensures the threat lives on. This crucial glimmer of hope ensures the seed of Macbeth's own destruction has been sown.

PAUSE POINT

CONSOLIDATION

Shakespeare uses this scene to demonstrate a turning point in Macbeth's character: he has become an unscrupulous tyrant, prepared to order the murder of his friend and a child.

Ask students to write a summary of how Shakespeare presents Macbeth's changing character, including these key words:

- malevolent
- manipulative
- resolute
- façade
- character foil
- paranoia
- resentful
- tyrant
- emotional anguish.

Upon the stage

It is always worth watching to see how a production casts the third Murderer, as discussed above. Joel Coen (2021) had Ross (Alex Hassell) join the two Murderers, before rescuing Fleance and putting him in hiding. This Ross is more active than most and appears to have substantial plans for the boy he saves. Coen's film also makes a bold visual choice in having Banquo fight for his life with his blazing torch. Given how many lines Banquo has that mention candles, torches and light, this is a brilliant and textually responsive approach.

In another unusual choice, Rufus Norris had the Porter play the third Murderer, showing startling menace both in this scene and in the murder of Macduff's family. Having been introduced as the comic relief after Duncan's murder, it was chilling to see him enlisted as a core member of Macbeth's kill squad as the play progressed.

These choices have strong implications for their characters; Coen's Ross became an essential player in Scotland's future, rescuing Fleance so he can reappear in the film's closing image, while Norris' Porter was revealed not just as a drunken servant but as a lethal operative.

With your students, consider casting the role of the third Murderer.

If the third Murderer were played by another character from the play (since doubling was common practice in Shakespeare's theatre), who would you cast, and why?

- **Ross** – loyal thane, double agent, or man with his own agenda?
- **Seyton** – Macbeth's silent aide, quietly enabling every atrocity?
- **The Porter** – comic relief turned cold-blooded killer?
- **A Witch** – supernatural interference in human violence?
- **Lady Macbeth** – refusing to be sidelined and now getting her hands very dirty?
- **Fleance** – a son killing his own father?
- **Donalbain** – returned in secret, carving a path to the throne?
- **Your own bold choice** – who else might be lurking in the wings?

CHAPTER 23
BLOOD WILL HAVE BLOOD
ACT THREE SCENE FOUR

At a glance

- **Plot and character development:** Macbeth's coronation feast is shattered when he alone sees the ghost of the murdered Banquo. His hysterical reaction terrifies the Scottish lords and confirms his guilt, while Lady Macbeth struggles to maintain control.
- **Social and historical context:** Ghosts on stage
- **Vocabulary:** Frenzy
- **Big question:** Does Shakespeare present the Ghost as real or as a hallucination?
- **Themes:**
  - Appearance vs reality
  - Guilt and conscience
  - Disorder and the unnatural
  - Violence and masculinity
- **Analysis:**
  - Motif: blood
  - Motif: names
- **Key quotation:** 'Blood will have blood'

Plot and character development

This pivotal scene marks Macbeth's irreversible public unravelling. The feast, meant to cement his kingly status, becomes the stage for his downfall. As Macbeth welcomes his lords, one of the murderers arrives to report Banquo's death and Fleance's escape. The news unsettles Macbeth, but he tries to resume his role as host. However, upon seeing the ghost of

Banquo – visible only to him – he erupts into a terrified, guilty frenzy. Lady Macbeth's attempts to explain his behaviour as a harmless infirmity grow increasingly desperate. She eventually dismisses the guests in disarray. Alone, Macbeth reveals his descent into a bloody mindset, vowing to consult the Witches again and already plotting his next move against Macduff.

Social and historical context

Ghosts on stage

In Shakespeare's theatre, ghosts were potent, conventional figures, not psychological hallucinations. They often emerged from a stage trapdoor, visually marking them as inhabitants of the underworld. Their primary role was to demand revenge, a tradition set by the ghost in Thomas Kyd's *The Spanish Tragedy* (1587) and elevated by the morally complex Ghost in Shakespeare's *Hamlet*. Unlike these vocal spirits who drive the plot, Banquo's ghost does not speak. Shakespeare subverts convention and lets the ghost's silence be its own chilling rebuke.

Vocabulary | Frenzy

Macbeth's psychological state deteriorates further in this scene. By building on the vocabulary for emotional anguish, you can support students in writing nuanced explanations of Macbeth's changing emotions.

Definition: Overwrought emotions lead to wild and uncontrolled behaviour.	**Related words:** Delirious, turmoil, uncontrollable, mania, wildness
How to use this word: In Act Three Scene Four, Shakespeare portrays Macbeth's frenzied state of mind. Macbeth descends into a frenzy. When he sees Banquo's ghost, Macbeth works himself into a frenzy.	**True or false?** 1. Macbeth is frenzied when he 'carve[s]' his way to Macdonwald in battle. 2. Lady Macbeth is in a frenzy when she cries 'unsex me here'. 3. Lady Macbeth is in a frenzy when she tries to wash the blood from her hands in Act Five Scene One.

Answers to 'True or false?': 1. False, 2. False, 3. True

PAUSE POINT

S-T-R-E-T-C-H

Read-reduce-rehearse-remember (see 'How to use this book' page XIII).

The significance of Act Three Scene Four

Act Three Scene Four functions as a corruption of royal spectacle. Shakespeare reveals how the banquet is staged by Macbeth as a public celebration of his kingship – a calculated display of power and legitimacy, designed to secure the loyalty of his thanes. But it systematically unravels into a spectacle of its very opposite: psychological disintegration and political illegitimacy. This becomes starkly apparent when contrasted with Duncan's court in Act One Scene Four.

Shakespeare showed how Duncan's authority was rooted in a natural economy of reciprocity and grace; he 'planted' his thanes, lavished them with praise and tangible rewards and fostered a cohesive body politic. Macbeth's court, by contrast, is presented as sterile and paranoid. Shakespeare highlights how Macbeth's attempts at hosting devolve into a fractured dialogue with an empty stool, exposing the profound schism between his public persona and his haunted interiority. The ghost of Banquo – the one guest he cannot control – becomes the true centre of the feast, a visible manifestation of Macbeth's guilt and his failure to consolidate power.

Reading the scene

This is one of the most theatrically thrilling and psychologically complex scenes in the play. Its power rests on the staging of the ghost. The scene's rhythm is a rollercoaster of tension and release, building to the catastrophic breakdown of the feast and Macbeth's political authority.

Given the visual power of this spectacle, it is best to watch it first. The Rupert Goold (2010) version clearly communicates Macbeth's mental turmoil and Lady Macbeth's loss of power.

When reading this scene, it is important that students understand who Macbeth is speaking to and – crucially – who does not hear or see his interlocutors (Macbeth and the murderer have a private conversation; Macbeth and Lady Macbeth have private conversations; no other character on stage can see Banquo's ghost). For this reason, take the role of Macbeth yourself and use your body language and tone of voice, or indeed your position in the classroom, to indicate who hears and does not hear your lines.

PAUSE POINT

ORACY

Triplet discussion: 'Shakespeare presents Act Three Scene Four as a key turning point in the play.' Why is this?

- Student A: Respond to the question.
- Student B: Provide evidence or examples to support Student A's response.
- Student C: Summarise the discussion.

Model answer:

Shakespeare uses this scene to mark the transition from Macbeth's private fears to his public descent into madness: he shouts 'never shake thy gory locks at me' at an unseen ghost, in the presence of his thanes. These confused onlookers ask questions of their new king, inquiring 'What is't that moves your Highness' and receiving unsatisfactory responses from both Macbeth and Lady Macbeth. The thanes exit in confusion, and in Act Three Scene Six will begin to discuss Macbeth's growing tyranny: he has lost power over his followers.

This scene is also a turning point, as it confirms Lady Macbeth's loss of power over her husband. Her manipulative attacks on his masculinity ('are you a man?') have no effect, and the scene concludes with the irrevocable fracture of the marriage. When Macbeth insists that he is 'in blood / Stepped in so far that [...] Returning were as tedious as go o'er.', his wife has little to say by way of comfort or direction. We never see the couple on stage together again.

Big question

Does Shakespeare present Banquo's ghost as real or as a hallucination?

Shakespeare deliberately leaves this ambiguous. In a play full of witches and visions, a real supernatural apparition is possible. However, that only Macbeth can see it strongly suggests it is a psychological projection of his overwhelming guilt – a 'painting' of his fear, as Lady Macbeth calls it. The Ghost appears directly after Macbeth mentions Banquo, and its mutilated state reflects the brutality of the murder Macbeth ordered. Whether a demonic trick or a figment of a tormented mind, its effect is the same: it exposes Macbeth's crime to the entire court.

Themes

Appearance vs reality

The feast is a façade of royal legitimacy, masking the brutal reality of Macbeth's rule. Macbeth performs the role of gracious host, but this appearance shatters when Banquo's ghost reveals the bloody truth he alone can see, exposing the murderer beneath the crown. Lady Macbeth makes a desperate attempt to hide the reality of Macbeth's breakdown, but eventually she has to give up and dismiss everyone.

Guilt and conscience

Shakespeare presents Banquo's ghost as the terrifying embodiment of Macbeth's guilt. His horrified reaction is not feigned; these are the convulsions of a tortured conscience, visually manifesting the psychological burden of his crimes and making his internal torment horribly public.

Disorder and the unnatural

Banquo's ghost is profoundly unnatural, a violation of the natural order where the dead should remain so. Macbeth grimly comments that 'when the brains were out, the man would die'. The ghost's appearance causes immediate disorder, shattering the state banquet and proving Macbeth's own unnatural acts have doomed his reign to chaos.

Violence and masculinity

The language of masculinity is central to this scene, directly echoing the earlier manipulation that spurred Macbeth to murder. Lady Macbeth once again uses the idea as a weapon, asking 'Are you a man?' Her contempt frames Macbeth's terror as unmanly weakness, a shameful infirmity that undermines them both.

In response, Macbeth redefines the concept. He swears he dares to face any mortal threat ('What man dare, I dare') be it a tiger or a bear. But Shakespeare shows that confronting this supernatural embodiment of his guilt is entirely different. Echoing his earlier maxim, 'who dares do more is none', Macbeth believes that to 'dare' to look upon Banquo's ghost is not to be more than a man, but to be less: to be utterly unmanned by a conscience he thought he had silenced.

Analysis

Motif: blood

Here blood evolves from a removable stain into an active, spectral force. It literally manifests on Banquo's ghost, proving the violence of Macbeth's reign is now a visible, inescapable part of his world. This marks a shift from hidden guilt to public accusation: blood is the foundational element of Macbeth's rule, which can no longer be cleansed but only perpetuated.

Motif: names

The names Macbeth and Lady Macbeth use for one another are important. When we first see them together, Lady Macbeth cries 'great Glamis, worthy Cawdor', and Macbeth calls his wife 'my dearest partner in greatness' and 'my dearest love'. Directly after the murder, Lady Macbeth calls Macbeth 'my husband', emphasising how they are united in ambition and guilt. However, by Act Three Scene Two, Lady Macbeth asks for the 'king' and Macbeth calls her 'dearest chuck'. Now, at the conclusion of Act Three Scene Four, Lady Macbeth calls her husband 'sir'; she appears to have accepted the reversal of roles which has led to Macbeth's dominance in their marriage.

PAUSE POINT

ORACY

Ask students to think-pair-share their ideas on the motifs of blood, masculinity and names in the play.

Then discuss how each motif changes as the play progresses.

See Appendix B for more information.

Key quotation | 'Blood will have blood'

This line echoes a grim, proverbial law. Macbeth introduces it as something 'they say,' a direct allusion to Genesis 9:6: 'Whoso sheddeth man's blood, by man shall his blood be shed.' The irony is stark: a murderer quotes the Bible to comment on his situation. Macbeth's initial crime has inevitably bound him to a future of further bloodshed.

PAUSE POINT

CONSOLIDATION

Ask students to make a 'three-two-one' summary of the scene. List:

- Three quotations that provide evidence of Macbeth's frenzied behaviour.
- Two details Macbeth notices about Banquo's ghost.
- One way in which Lady Macbeth tries to calm her husband.

Upon the stage

Based on his experience in the 1979 Trevor Nunn production, Ian McKellen has argued that the audience really should not see Banquo's ghost in this scene (see Curry, 2010). The (2023) Donmar production by Max Webster, whose entire set became a large dining table, likewise had no visible ghost. Norris (2018), Godwin (2024) and Best (2014) all have blood-soaked Banquos appear at the feast, visible only to their respective Macbeths. Consider the alternative stagings of this scene: is it more dramatically effective to have the ghost appear onstage – even if it is invisible to most of the characters – or is it better to have Macbeth alone 'see' the apparition?

CHAPTER 24
MORTALS' CHIEFEST ENEMY
ACT THREE SCENE FIVE

At a glance

- **Plot and character development:** Hecate visits the Witches and scolds them.
- **Social and historical context:** Witch-plays in the aftermath of Macbeth
- **Big question:** Does this scene matter?
- **Themes:**
  - Disorder and the unnatural
  - Fate vs free will
  - Appearance vs reality
- **Key quotation:** 'mortals' chiefest enemy'

Plot and character development

Back on the heath, Hecate, the goddess of witchcraft, scolds the Witches for interfering with Macbeth without her. She takes command, plotting to use illusions of security to lead the overconfident Macbeth to his ruin.

Social and historical context

Witch-plays

Following the success of *Macbeth*, Jacobean theatre saw a wave of witch-plays, all capitalising on this popular thematic material. The trend was heavily influenced by King James I's own obsession with witchcraft, making the subject a fashionable and lucrative choice for playwrights.

Reading the scene

If you read this scene, take the role of Hecate yourself so that students hear the correct pronunciation of the lines. Before reading, ask students to listen for the rhymes. Then discuss how the rhyming couplets continue the incantatory tone heard in the other scenes featuring the Witches.

Big question

Does this scene matter?

Many productions and teachers skip this scene, but it is worth double-checking your specification before making a decision about whether or not to teach it. It doesn't advance the main plot in any crucial way and you can easily grasp Macbeth's growing overconfidence from his own actions in the surrounding scenes.

The song Hecate requests, 'Come away,' actually appears in Middleton's play, *The Witch* (c. 1613). The scene's tone and melodic focus align more with Middleton's style than Shakespeare's, and it was possibly inserted when the play was printed in the First Folio. For an extended discussion of this issue, see Appendix 2 of the Arden edition, or the Textual Analysis essay in the New Cambridge Shakespeare edition of the play.

Key quotation | 'Mortals' chiefest enemy'

This line shows that Hecate's strategy isn't just prophecy but psychological manipulation. She will weaponise Macbeth's overconfidence, making him feel invincible. This false sense of security leads him directly to his downfall.

Upon the stage

This scene is invariably cut in performance. Godwin (2024) used portions of the text, including our key quotation, but redistributed the lines among the Witches during the dramatic and bloody staging of Banquo's murder. The Witches supervised the killing, but did not participate, and the Hecate lines instead became a commentary on Banquo's 'security'.

Why might a director keep this scene, despite its dubious authorship?

CHAPTER 25
ALL WHICH WE PINE FOR NOW
ACT THREE SCENE SIX

At a glance

- **Plot and character development:** Lennox discusses the state of Scotland with a Lord who reveals Macduff's whereabouts.
- **Social and historical context:** Tyrants and King Edward
- **Vocabulary:** Tyrant (revisited)
- **Big question:** Whose side does Shakespeare suggest Lennox supports?
- **Themes:**
  - Disorder and the unnatural
  - The Divine Right of Kings
  - Kingship
  - Tyranny
- **Analysis:**
  - Staging: an outside perspective
  - Motifs: multiple
- **Key quotation:** 'All which we pine for now'

PAUSE POINT

RETRIEVAL

In this scene, Shakespeare dramatises a discussion between Lennox and the Lord about events which occurred earlier in the play. They also refer to new characters we have not yet encountered. Check students' knowledge of these characters before reading.

Character	What has happened to them?	What are they doing at the moment?
Duncan		
Banquo		
Fleance		
Malcolm		
Donalbain		
Duncan's guards		
Macduff		
Edward the Confessor		
Siward (Earl of Northumberland)		

Plot and character development

Lennox and an unnamed Lord discuss the recent murders. The Lord reports that Macduff has fled to England to join Malcolm and raise an army with King Edward's support. Significantly, we hear the word tyrant aloud for the first time in this scene: *both* characters use it to describe Macbeth.

Social and historical context

Tyrants

For Shakespeare's audience, the word tyrant was not just an insult but a precise legal and moral classification. Shakespeare has already introduced the word, as did we in Chapter 20, but now it defines Macbeth as a usurper, who has taken the crown by illegitimate means. He is ruling without divine sanction; the rebellion against him will be a righteous and necessary act.

King Edward

Edward the Confessor (c.1003–1066), here called 'the pious Edward,' was a historically holy figure. He possesses the divine grace to heal scrofula, 'the king's evil.' He contrasts directly with Macbeth, the unholy murderer, embodying the legitimate, God-ordained monarchy that Macbeth has violently destroyed.

Vocabulary | Tyrant (revisited)

Give students a blank copy of the Frayer model from Chapter 20: Act Three Scene One and check their recall.

Reading the scene

This scene is short and does not feature any major characters. It is a useful turning point because it shows the tide of opinion turning in Scotland, but need not be a prolonged episode in your journey through the play.

PAUSE POINT

S-T-R-E-T-C-H

Write a report from the perspective of a Scottish citizen, explaining how the country has changed since Macbeth became king.

Use the following headings and your knowledge of the play to structure your report:

- Leadership and the court: How is Macbeth's rule different from Duncan's?
- Crime and safety: What major crimes have occurred? Who is responsible? How safe do people feel?
- The supernatural: What unnatural events have been reported? How have these affected the atmosphere?
- The economy and daily life: How does the Lord's speech hint at the impact on ordinary life? (Think of 'our tables meat' and 'sleep to our nights').
- Hope and the future: According to this scene, where is hope now? Who is challenging Macbeth?

Challenge:

- Use key quotations from Act Three Scene Six (e.g. 'tyrant,' 'bloody knives,' 'free honours').
- Use key vocabulary (e.g. malevolent, vengeful, resolute, façade, paranoia, resentful, unscrupulous, frenzy).

Big question

Which side does Shakespeare suggest Lennox supports?

Shakespeare has shown Lennox rise through the ranks over the course of the play so far; he is by now one of Macbeth's right-hand men. Shakespeare presents another side of him in this scene; his allegiance is revealed through his masterful use of sarcastic irony. Although his words technically praise Macbeth's actions, he also seems to question the assumption that Malcolm,

Donalbain and Fleance killed their fathers. His inquiry about Macduff and his closing prayer to save Scotland from Macbeth's 'accursed hand' confirm he is more aligned with the rebellion, cautiously navigating the dangers of such a treasonous conversation.

Analysis

Staging: an outside perspective

As at the end of Act Two, Shakespeare presents a new, anonymous character who speaks for the wider community in Scotland. The unnamed Lord's explicit condemnation of Macbeth as a 'tyrant' and his longing for liberation reveal widespread dissent, confirming Macbeth's political isolation.

Motifs: multiple

This scene consolidates several key motifs, highlighting Macbeth's tyranny. The lord yearns for sleep and 'free honours,' untainted by the 'bloody knives' of Macbeth's reign, directly linking bloodshed and insomnia to his illegitimate rule.

Key quotation | 'All which we pine for now'

This line, spoken by the Lord, expresses Scotland's collective yearning for everything Macbeth has destroyed: peaceful sleep, safe feasts and true honour. It defines his rule as a tyranny and implicitly justifies the rebellion being plotted, all in a single, poignant lament.

PAUSE POINT

CONSOLIDATION

Display the following quotations on screen and ensure that students have secure knowledge of the word 'tyrant'. Then ask students what these quotations have in common (they all present Macbeth as an irredeemable tyrant, who has lost the loyalty of his followers).

- 'the tyrant's feast'
- 'this tyrant'
- 'our suffering country'
- 'a hand accursed'.

Triplet discussion: How does Shakespeare present the thanes' changed attitudes to Macbeth?

- Student A: Respond to the question.
- Student B: Provide evidence and examples to support Student A's response.
- Student C: Summarise the discussion.

Model answer:

Macbeth was once described as 'valiant' and 'noble', but now Lennox and the Lord refer to him as a 'tyrant' responsible for the 'suffering' of all Scotland. Shakespeare uses the motif of the hand as a symbol of Macbeth's callous leadership, but it also serves as a reminder of how he attained the crown: through the violent actions of his bloodstained hands. The adjective 'accursed' also has multiple meanings here. Lennox uses it to emphasise just how brutal and ungodly Macbeth's reign has become; but the word also carries a deeper resonance, reminding the audience that Macbeth's actions have bound him to the Witches' prophecy in horrifying ways.

Upon the stage

The (2010) Rupert Goold film staged a heavily edited version of this frequently-cut scene, casting Lennox as a violent interrogator, torturing the lord for information. His equivocal language became a script of forced loyalty, starkly revealing Macbeth's deepening paranoia and tyrannical control.

Contrast this with the full text of the scene. Which side do your students think he is on?

CHAPTER 26
DAMNED ALL THOSE THAT TRUST THEM
ACT FOUR SCENE ONE

At a glance

- **Plot and character development:** As the Witches brew a fiendish potion, Macbeth arrives and they show him a series of visions.
- **Social and historical context:** Witchcraft
- **Vocabulary:** Equivocation (continued)
- **Big question:** Does Shakespeare present the Witches as controlling Macbeth, or does he choose his own fate?
- **Themes:**
  - Appearance vs reality
  - Fate vs free will
  - Disorder and the unnatural
- **Analysis:**
  - Motif: children
  - Motif: the crown
  - Staging: the supernatural
- **Key quotation:** 'Damned all those that trust them'
- **Handle with care:** This scene contains elements deliberately designed to be offensive, as well as imagery to do with traumatic childbirth and violence against children.

PAUSE POINT

RETRIEVAL

Reactivate students' knowledge of the Witches by revisiting these key quotations: 'fair is foul and foul is fair' and 'all hail, Macbeth'. Develop this into an oracy activity by asking students to work in pairs. Each participant chooses a quotation, which they annotate independently. Students share their thoughts before feeding back to the class.

Students could consider how Shakespeare:

- Uses the Witches to establish the theme of appearance and reality at the outset of the play. Students should connect these to other relevant moments in the text (see Appendix A).
- Has the Witches present apparently 'fair' truths to Macbeth and Banquo, which in reality lead the tragic hero into 'foul' actions.
- Uses alliteration, repetition and trochaic tetrameter to create an incantatory tone in Act One Scene One.
- Alludes to Judas Iscariot's betrayal of Jesus ('hail').
- Uses the word equivocation.

Plot and character development

Macbeth finds the Witches brewing a fearsome potion. They refuse to explain its purpose, but he demands further information. Summoning 'their masters,' they show Macbeth a series of apparitions. An 'Armed Head' warns him to beware Macduff. A 'Bloody Child' assures him that 'none of woman born shall harm Macbeth,' and a 'Child Crowned, with a tree in his hand' promises he will be safe until Birnam Wood marches to Dunsinane. These visions fill Macbeth with a reckless confidence, which is instantly shattered by a final vision: a parade of kings led by Banquo's ghost, confirming the prophecy that Banquo's line will inherit the crown. Enraged and embittered, Macbeth resolves to attack Macduff's castle and slaughter his family, in a decisive turn from paranoid king to merciless tyrant.

Social and historical context

Witchcraft

This scene would have been intensely exciting for its Jacobean audience, especially King James I. Most would have recognised the grotesque ingredients of the 'charmed pot' as the authentic paraphernalia of black magic – these are described in substantial detail in episodes 43 and 44 of the *Macbeth* series of *The Hamlet Podcast* (Hanratty, 2023) – validating widespread beliefs about witchcraft. The climactic vision of the eight Stuart kings, led by Banquo, served as direct political flattery, visually legitimising James's claimed lineage on stage. Crucially, the scene stages the ultimate temptation: the chance to learn one's fate with the help of witchcraft.

Vocabulary | Equivocation (continued)

Equivocation was introduced in the play's opening paradox ('fair is foul') and now reaches its full, destructive potential. The Witches' prophecies are the pinnacle of this deceptive 'double talk.' They use euphemistic language that suggests certain victory for Macbeth even as they tell him what will destroy him: being harmed by a man not 'of woman born' sounds impossible and a forest 'marching' seems absurd. Macbeth believes the apparently positive meaning of the Witches' words but fails to comprehend the dangerous reality behind them.

Ask students to work together to complete a blank copy of the equivocation Frayer model from Chapter 15: Act Two Scene Three (see online resources). Use this as an opportunity to address any gaps in students' knowledge and any misconceptions before progressing.

Reading the scene | Part one

This is a long scene, so we recommend reading it in two sections: lines 1 to 43 and 44 to end.

Lines 1 to 43

Remind students that Shakespeare has written the Witches' lines as incantations or chants. He uses trochaic tetrameter again, now recognisable as a rhythm for things supernatural. Rehearse the repeated lines to illustrate this ('Double, double, toil and trouble; / Fire burn, and cauldron, bubble'). The class will read these lines in unison during the scene.

Choose your readers. The remainder of the class will join in when the text says 'all'.

Read the extract once through.

As you prepare to read it for a second time, instruct your students to consider what the ingredients have in common. (They are mostly body parts from living beings – either animals or humans.)

PAUSE POINT

S-T-R-E-T-C-H

Focus on the key quotation that you have just rehearsed: ('Double, double, toil and trouble; / Fire, burn and cauldron, bubble').

Read-reduce-rehearse-remember (see 'How to use this book' page XIII).

In these lines, Shakespeare suggests that the Witches are increasing the strength of their magic by adding more ingredients to their potion. In turn, this indicates that their power over the tragic hero Macbeth is also growing. In some versions of the text, when Hecate enters the scene, she brings three additional witches onto the stage; this doubles the number of witches, again amplifying our sense of the power of the magic being brought against Macbeth. This almost creates a sense of pathos for Macbeth, now seemingly ensnared by magical forces beyond his control.

The word 'double' also evokes the concept of equivocation. The witches equivocate throughout the play, telling Macbeth half-truths, but manipulating the true meaning of their words. In a sense, they are speaking 'double'.

PAUSE POINT

ORACY

In the next section of the scene, Shakespeare revisits the play's key motifs.

Before reading the next section of the scene, ask students to work in their triplets to discuss three motifs which reoccur in Act Four Scene One. See Appendix B for a list of relevant quotations.

- Student A: Where has Shakespeare used the motif of children in the play? What does he use children to symbolise?
- Student B: Where has Shakespeare used the motif of blood in the play? What does he use blood to symbolise?
- Student C: Where has Shakespeare used the motif of the crown in the play? What does he use the crown to symbolise?

Model answer:

Shakespeare introduces the symbolic significance of children in Act One Scene Three. The Witches catalyse a division between the childless Macbeth and the father Banquo, who will be the progenitor of a line of kings. Shakespeare later revisits the topic of Macbeth's childlessness: for example, in Act Three Scene One, he obsesses over his 'fruitless crown' and is tormented by the thought that 'Banquo's issue' will inherit the throne. This leads directly to the attempted murder of Fleance. In this context, children symbolise the ability to found a powerful dynasty. Elsewhere, Shakespeare uses children to symbolise innocence and vulnerability. Lady Macbeth's claim that she would have "dash'd the brains out" of her baby underscores her ruthless determination. After the Witches goad Macbeth by showing him apparitions in the form of children in Act Four Scene One, he responds by orchestrating the killing of more children: Macduff's family are slaughtered at Macbeth's command, and he himself kills Siward's son in the play's final act.

Shakespeare also employs blood as a motif throughout the play, using it in two distinct ways: on the one hand, the legitimate shedding of blood symbolises an individual's loyalty to the true king but, on the other hand, illegitimate bloodshed represents betrayal. In Act One Scene Two, Macbeth's sword 'smok[es] with bloody execution' as he patriotically hacks his way through the invading army: this act is handsomely rewarded in Act One Scene Four. Yet when Macbeth spills blood again in Act Two, it is an act of deception and treachery that leads to guilt and torment. His 'hangman's hands' are no longer celebrated, but have instead become a 'filthy witness' to his illicit actions. References to blood multiply in Acts Two and Three, culminating in the dramatic appearance of Banquo's ghost at the banquet: as he shakes his 'gory locks' at the murderer Macbeth, the tragic hero is overwhelmed with horror and guilt.

Finally, Shakespeare uses the crown to symbolise the Macbeths' ambition for absolute power. In Act One Scene Five, Lady Macbeth's description of the crown as the 'golden round' evokes its irresistible allure. Yet by Act Three Scene One, the crown is no longer 'golden' but 'fruitless'. This shift reinforces Macbeth's despair at his childlessness (as discussed above) and implies the futility of his sacrifice: he has condemned his soul for a temporary taste of power. In Act Four Scene One, the Witches taunt Macbeth with a vision of what he cannot attain: a 'child crowned' and a line of kings that ends with Banquo himself wearing a crown.

Reading the scene | Part two

Lines 44 to end

Prepare a picture of each apparition to show on the screen or to hold up at the appropriate moments. Read the scene, asking listening students to highlight the new prophecies Macbeth is given.

After reading, clarify the meaning of each prophecy:

- Armed head: Macbeth should be wary of Macduff.
- Bloody child: Macbeth can only be killed by someone who has not been 'born of woman'.
- Crowned child: Macbeth cannot be killed until Birnam Wood comes to Dunsinane.
- Banquo's heirs: the Witches indicate that the prophecy about Banquo's children is true.

There is a significant shift in tone and atmosphere when the Witches vanish and Lennox enters. Perhaps signal this through changing the lighting: dim the lights for the section involving the Witches and flick them on when Lennox enters.

PAUSE POINT

ORACY

The Witches are the great equivocators of the play and they have already made a number of ambiguous prophecies.

Ask students to work in pairs to consider the meaning of these key lines: what do the Witches leave unsaid?

Line	What do the Witches leave unsaid?
'Hail to thee, Thane of Glamis!'	
'Hail to thee, Thane of Cawdor!'	
'that shalt be king hereafter!'	
'None of woman born shall harm Macbeth.'	
'Macbeth shall never vanquished be until Great Birnam Wood to high Dunsinane Hill shall come against him.'	

Big question

Does Shakespeare present the Witches as controlling Macbeth, or does he choose his own fate?

It could be argued that the Witches control Macbeth's fate. From their first scene, the Witches declare a prearranged 'meeting' with Macbeth, strategically intercepting him at his moment of triumph. Their calculated prophecies and deceptive equivocation not only foresee his future, but actively place him on his path to destruction.

However, a more convincing argument is that the Witches do not control Macbeth's fate; their ambiguous prophecies set a trap and Macbeth willingly walks into it. He interprets their riddles through the lens of his paranoia, hearing only the reassurance he desperately desires. The vision that warns him to 'beware the Thane of Fife' is not a command to kill Macduff's family, yet by the end of the scene Macbeth has resolved to do so. His decision to 'make assurance double sure' through this gratuitous violence is a conscious, if tyrannical, choice. Ultimately, the Witches give Macbeth a series of partially-true hints of what his future holds, but Macbeth himself chooses how to interpret them – and how to act thereafter.

Themes

Appearance vs reality

The core of the scene is the deceptive nature of the Apparitions. They appear to offer comfort and guarantee Macbeth's safety, but their statements are double-edged: each masks a truth that will lead to his destruction.

Fate vs free will

Macbeth's return to the Witches is a decisive, voluntary choice. He comes to these 'black and midnight hags' unsummoned and unbidden, conjuring them 'by that which you profess' and demanding more information. He can no longer blame fate for what happens to him; he has sought this knowledge by his own free will. Yet the prophecies do not bind him: they are open-ended, allowing for many interpretations. They offer the illusion of security while leading him toward his doom. This is the scene's cruelest equivocation: Macbeth's free will is not an illusion; it is the very instrument of his destruction. He is not fate's victim but its complicit participant.

Disorder and the unnatural

In this scene, Shakespeare creates a symphony of the unnatural, inverting images of growth to highlight Macbeth's corruption. The Witches' Brew is a perverse anti-fertility ritual, a concoction of death and blasphemy they call 'a charm of powerful trouble.' The 'Bloody Child' speaks of a man not 'of woman born,' a concept Macbeth dismisses as impossible, overlooking the literal truth. The third prophecy presents an image that seems utterly unnatural: an uprooted forest marching. Macbeth interprets it as another impossibility as well as a guarantee of safety; for the audience, it signifies nature itself rising up against the usurper.

Analysis

Motif: children

The three visions are all child-like, perverting the natural image of infancy into monstrous portents. The 'bloody child' is a horrific image of birth trauma, symbolising a baby ripped unnaturally from the womb and directly foreshadowing Macduff. The 'child crowned' carries a tree, a symbol of growth, directly opposing Macbeth's barren reign. The scene culminates in the procession of eight kings – a visualisation of Banquo's thriving, unbroken lineage. Banquo's ghost, smiling and pointing, emphasises his paternal legacy, confirming this is a future from which Macbeth is entirely excluded. It confirms his worst fear from his 'fruitless crown' soliloquy: he has no legacy and his throne is merely a temporary seat for Banquo's line.

Motif: the crown

The 'child crowned' is a devastating image for Macbeth. It shows a child – a symbol of the future – already in possession of the crown. This visually asserts that true, lasting kingship belongs not to him, but to a lineage he cannot touch. The crown on Macbeth's own head becomes meaningless in the face of the crowned child and the line of future kings. His kingship appears more as an interruption in the natural line of succession, not its culmination.

Staging: the supernatural

Staging this elaborate conjuring ritual underscores the demonic influence over Macbeth's world. His voluntary engagement with this dark magic signifies his complete moral surrender and alignment with – and attempt to control – these evil forces.

Key quotation | 'Damned all those that trust them'

On the surface, this is a bitter curse aimed at the 'juggling fiends' who have teased Macbeth with their wordplay. Yet, in a moment of supreme dramatic irony, this line is the scene's ultimate truth and Macbeth is its primary, self-cursing subject. He damns himself with his own words.

This line is crucial because it transcends the immediate plot to articulate the scene's core theme: the spiritual and psychological mechanics of damnation. The Witches do not damn Macbeth; they simply present possibilities. Macbeth, in his desperate hunger for security, willingly believes what he hears. He trusts their promises of safety ('none of woman born') while ignoring their warnings ('beware Macduff'), cherry-picking from the Apparitions to suit his own desires. His tragedy is not that he was fated to fall, but that he chose to trust the 'instruments of darkness', activating his own destruction.

PAUSE POINT

CONSOLIDATION

This is a complex scene containing a lot of key plot information. Use this activity as an opportunity to allow students to pause and consolidate their knowledge of the key plot details. Ask students to:

- List five ingredients the Witches put in their potion.
- List four prophecies the Witches give Macbeth.
- List three words to describe Macbeth's response to the witches.
- List two words to describe the Witches.
- List one action Macbeth is going to take as a result of hearing the prophecies.

Upon the stage

The theatrical tradition of calling *Macbeth* 'The Scottish Play' treats its title as a kind of spell, an unnameable force akin to the Witches' own 'deed without a name.' This superstition stems from the play's potent staging of the occult, from its charmèd pot to its ghostly parade of future kings. The myth was expanded in the 1920s when Max Beerbohm fabricated outrageous tales of a curse (and even the death of the original 1606 Lady Macbeth) just to invigorate ticket sales. The lore grew to infamy with Orson Welles's (1936) 'Voodoo Macbeth,' where the sudden death of a hostile critic was widely attributed to 'real' black magic performed by some of the production's drummers. Ironically, the play's alleged curse often signals not supernatural danger but financial trouble; when the play's title is heard in a theatre, it can be a sign that the company needs a sure-fire hit. The curses and portents that surround the play may be fiction, but the superstitions they inspire in theatre folk are very real.

Consider how you would stage the supernatural elements of the play: how would you communicate the Witches' evil to a modern audience?

CHAPTER 27
HE HAS KILLED ME, MOTHER
ACT FOUR SCENE TWO

At a glance

- **Plot and character development:** Lady Macduff and her children are left vulnerable by Macduff's journey to England.
- **Social and historical context:** Family loyalty in Jacobean Scotland
- **Vocabulary:** Pathos
- **Big question:** Does Shakespeare present Macduff as responsible for the murder of his own family?
- **Themes:**
    - Tyranny
    - Appearance vs reality
    - Disorder and the unnatural
- **Analysis:**
    - Motif: children
- **Key quotation:** 'He has killed me, mother: / Run away, I pray you'
- **Handle with care:** This scene is the most brutal in the play; a child is murdered onstage.

PAUSE POINT

RETRIEVAL

Ask students to think-pair-share their understanding of stereotypes of femininity in Shakespeare's time. Students could consider:

- The expectation for women to remain in the domestic sphere.
- Stereotypes which associate women with physical weakness, innocence and nurture.
- How these ideas were beginning to change, as Elizabeth I had ruled independently.

Plot and character development

At Macduff's castle, Lady Macduff angrily tells Ross that her husband's flight to England has left his family vulnerable. She then confides in her son, who wittily defends his father. A Messenger urgently warns them to flee, but then the Murderers enter, accuse Macduff of treason and kill the young boy. Lady Macduff escapes the stage, but the Murderers pursue her and kill her offstage.

Social and historical context

Family loyalty in Jacobean Scotland

For a Jacobean audience, the family was the foundational unit of a stable kingdom. The slaughter of Lady Macduff and her children was therefore more than a personal tragedy; it was a symbol of the state itself being torn apart by tyranny. The murder of a child violated the most profound natural and moral laws, showing Macbeth as a monster who attacked the very future of the nation. Furthermore, Lady Macduff's complaint that her husband lacks 'the natural touch' highlights a contemporary conflict: a man's duty to protect his own household versus his duty to the wider country, a tension made acute by the threat of a monstrous ruler.

Vocabulary | Pathos

Shakespeare builds pathos through the tender, witty exchange between Lady Macduff and her son; it makes them relatable and sympathetic. The murder of this boy, who dies defending his father's honour, is designed to generate audience outrage against Macbeth and solidify his status as a tyrant.

Definition:	Characteristics:
A quality that evokes pity, sympathy or sorrow in the audience. It is a technique used to make the audience emotionally invested in a character's suffering.	• A focus on innocence and vulnerability. • Highlights injustice or undeserved suffering. • Often involves children, family bonds or defeat of the helpless.
Examples:	**Non-examples:**
Macbeth (1606): In this scene, the boy's witty courage and his desperate cry, 'He has kill'd me, mother,' are designed to wring the audience's heart and generate maximum outrage. *A Christmas Carol* (1843): Dickens's depiction of Tiny Tim, hopeful and generous despite all of his troubles, is a source of great sorrow.	*Macbeth* (1606): Macbeth's soliloquy about his 'fruitless crown' evokes intellectual understanding of his anxiety, but not pity for his situation. *A Christmas Carol* (1843): Dickens's presentation of Scrooge's initial refusal to give to charity provokes anger or disapproval in the reader.

Reading the scene

This scene is complex because there are several shifts in tone. Beginning with Lady Macduff's exasperation at her husband's unexplained absence, it progresses to a tender and witty exchange with her son, and then defiance and finally terror when the murderers arrive.

Ask students to work in triplets to rehearse key lines from the scene before reading. Use a timer to keep these rehearsals fast-paced and focused.

- Student A: Lady Macduff (60 seconds)
  - Anger: 'to leave his wife, his babes'.
  - Tenderness and love: 'Now God help thee, poor monkey. But how wilt thou do for a father?'
  - Defiance: 'I hope in no place so unsanctified / Where such as thou mayst find him.'
- Student B: Son (30 seconds)
  - Childish innocence: 'what is a traitor?'
  - Defiance: 'thou liest, thou shag-haired villain!'
- Student C: Murderer (20 seconds)
  - Threat and violence: 'What, you egg!'

Choose the strongest performers and read the scene.

PAUSE POINT

S-T-R-E-T-C-H

Triplet discussion: 'Shakespeare presents Lady Macbeth and Lady Macduff as complete opposites of one another.' How far do you agree?

- Student A: Respond to the question.
- Student B: Provide evidence to support Student A's response.
- Student C: Summarise the discussion.

Model answer:

At first glance, Shakespeare presents Lady Macbeth and Lady Macduff as character foils. Lady Macbeth is politically ambitious, rejecting her own maternal potential to help her husband achieve 'the golden round'. In contrast, Lady Macduff is a mother defending her 'babes'. She embodies the domestic order that Macbeth's regime destroys; her murder, alongside her children, is a profound violation of moral codes. Her complaint that Macduff lacks 'the natural touch' underscores the era's expectation that a man's primary duty was to protect his family.

However, Shakespeare reveals that both women suffer because of their husbands' choices. Macbeth isolates himself from his wife; the growing emotional distance between them is a catalyst for her descent into madness. After Macbeth's rejection of his wife's assistance in the banquet scene, we never see them together again. Lady Macduff is similarly isolated from her husband, who puts the needs of the nation above those of his family. Ultimately, both women find themselves vulnerable and alone.

Big question

Does Shakespeare present Macduff as being responsible for the murder of his own family?

Shakespeare presents Macduff's journey to England as a necessary political act to help Scotland, but also as a conscious choice that leaves his family defenceless against a ruthless tyrant. Lady Macduff's accusation that he lacks 'the natural touch' underscores this; by the era's standards, a man's primary duty was to protect his household, a duty Macduff sacrifices for the national cause.

Shakespeare shows that Macduff's error of judgement means that although he makes a calculated risk for the greater good, his family pays the ultimate price. The scene's horror lies in this impossible conflict: the path to liberating a nation required the destruction of its most fundamental unit, the family. Therefore, Macduff becomes a hero burdened with the horrific, unintended cost of his own heroism.

Themes

Tyranny

The scene moves the consequences of Macbeth's rule from the political sphere to the personal and domestic. It is no longer about thanes fearing for their positions, but about the slaughter of the innocent and vulnerable. It shows that tyranny ultimately destroys the most fundamental unit of society: the family.

Appearance vs reality

This theme is central to the dialogue between mother and son. Macduff's son understands that traitors are not always as they appear, asking 'was my father a traitor, mother?' He intuitively grasps that the world's labels ('liar and swearer') can be deceptive, a moment of childish wisdom that highlights the moral inversion of Macbeth's Scotland, where the actual traitor is the king himself.

Disorder and the unnatural

Lady Macduff's complaint that her husband lacks the 'natural touch' establishes the scene's core conflict. She frames a man's duty to protect his family as the natural order. Macduff's abandonment of this duty is an unnatural act, which is then catastrophically followed by the murderers' invasion of his home and the killing of his family. Shakespeare forces the audience to question whether his choice was noble or a fatal betrayal.

Analysis

Motif: children

Shakespeare uses the child's on-stage killing to demonstrate Macbeth's new ruthlessness; having been outwitted by Fleance's escape, he now pre-emptively destroys future threats at their source. The boy's courageous defence of his father contrasts with his brutal death. In the previous scene we heard a bloody child tell Macbeth to beware the Thane of Fife, and now, in a grim contrast, we hear the Thane of Fife's son defending his father even as he is murdered.

Key quotation | 'He has killed me mother: / Run away, I pray you'

This dying cry from Macduff's son is the emotional and thematic heart of the scene. Its power lies in its devastating simplicity. The first half, 'He has killed me, mother,' is a stark, simple announcement of the ultimate unnatural act, the murder of a child. It makes the horror undeniably real. The boy's final words are the scene's climax. In dying to protect his mother he becomes a tragic mirror of his father, who has sacrificed his family to save Scotland. Shakespeare uses this small, domestic tragedy to reflect the larger, national one, compounding the pathos of Macduff's loss.

PAUSE POINT

CONSOLIDATION

Ask students to rank these statements from the most to the least convincing. Challenge them to include quotations or references to the text to support their reasoning.

1. Shakespeare uses this scene to highlight women's weaknesses.
2. Shakespeare includes this scene to dramatise Macbeth's descent into tyranny and brutality.
3. This scene is important because it lays the foundations for Macduff's desire for revenge.
4. Shakespeare uses this scene to suggest how Macbeth has changed from a courageous warrior to a man traumatised by bloodshed.

Upon the stage

Most productions generate pathos by having a child actor play Macduff's son. Garry Hynes' (2025) production for Druid Theatre Company made a profoundly different casting choice. Liam Heslin, playing Macduff, also portrayed Macduff's son, while Marty Rea, playing Macbeth, appeared as the murderer. This doubled the impact of the killing in this scene; the audience saw Macbeth personally destroy Macduff's family, making their final conflict a viscerally immediate reckoning. The audience had already watched one man kill the other; the final combat became an overdue execution for Macbeth's crimes.

CHAPTER 28
AN UNTITLED TYRANT BLOODY-SCEPTRED
ACT FOUR SCENE THREE (LINES 1 TO 138)

At a glance

- **Plot and character development:** In England, Macduff urges Malcolm to lead a force against Macbeth. Malcolm, suspicious, tests Macduff's loyalty.
- **Social and historical context:** The Divine Right of Kings
- **Vocabulary:** Virtue and vice
- **Big question:** Why does Shakespeare present Malcolm lying so elaborately to Macduff?
- **Themes:**
  - Appearance vs reality
  - Tyranny
  - Loyalty vs treason

Analysis:

- Motif: disease and medicine
- Motif: sin and virtue

- **Key quotation:** 'An untitled tyrant, bloody-sceptred'
- **Handle with care:** Malcolm speaks at length about depravity and immorality.

PAUSE POINT

RETRIEVAL

Ask students to think-pair-share the qualities of a good leader.

Students could consider:

- bravery on and off the battlefield
- wisdom
- ability to inspire others
- kindness and compassion
- determination and confidence
- good judgement.

Read the following summary with the class:

Shakespeare portrayed Duncan as having many of these good qualities, but also as overly trusting and lacked good judgement – which led to him being betrayed not just by Macbeth, but also by Macdonwald and the previous Thane of Cawdor. In contrast, Macbeth initially embodies bravery, the ability to inspire others and determination, but he is easily manipulated and betrays those closest to him.

Plot and character development

In England, Malcolm and Macduff discuss Scotland's suffering under Macbeth's tyranny. Malcolm is suspicious of Macduff, fearing he may be an agent of Macbeth. To test Macduff's integrity, he deliberately lies about his own character, claiming insatiable lust, greed and a lack of kingly virtues. He suggests he would be a worse tyrant than Macbeth, but Macduff's loyal, honest disgust at this possibility is enough to convince Malcolm that they are on the same side.

Social and historical context

The Divine Right of Kings

For a Jacobean audience, this scene was a masterclass in political theory, reflecting King James I's own writings. A true king was seen as God's lieutenant on earth, and his virtue was essential for the nation's health. Malcolm's list of vices, and his lack of 'king-becoming graces', contravene the Jacobean ideal of a pious, just and temperate ruler. James had laid these out in another book, *Basilikon Doron* ('The Gifts of Kings') written for his son in 1599. The scene debates what makes a legitimate monarch: is it merely birthright, or is it moral character?

Shakespeare is yet again flattering King James with an allusion to another of his published works; in this scene a rightful Scottish King sits at the English court and contemplates what becomes a monarch most.

Vocabulary | Virtue and vice

The scene functions as a political and moral debate, systematically juxtaposing the 'king-becoming graces' of virtue against a detailed catalogue of vice to define the very soul of a legitimate ruler.

	Virtue	Vice
Definition	Moral goodness, or righteousness. In this political context, it encompasses the specific qualities ('graces') expected of a legitimate ruler.	Immoral or malevolent behaviour.
Examples	Justice, verity, temperance, stableness, bounty, perseverance, mercy, lowliness, devotion, patience, courage, fortitude.	Envy, sloth, lack of self-control, gluttony, jealousy, greed, lust.

Reading the scene

Before reading, explain that unlike Duncan, Malcolm is suspicious of those around him. When Macduff arrives, Malcolm decides to test his loyalty. He does this by pretending to be a worse tyrant than Macbeth.

Ask students to work in triplets to discuss Macduff's possible responses to Malcolm's insistence that he is immoral. You could leave this as an open discussion, or ask students to rank the following possibilities from the most to the least likely.

A. Macduff is distraught as he believes there is no hope for Scotland, even if Macbeth is killed and Malcolm takes the throne.	B. Macduff is concerned, but he decides to try to change Malcolm into a more moral and honourable leader.
C. Macduff is not concerned and agrees to support Malcolm, despite his immorality.	D. Macduff is happy that Malcolm is immoral; he will support him in every way, because he is the rightful king.

Explain that the correct response is A: Macduff is distraught. Malcolm takes this as proof of Macduff's honour and morality. Malcolm then reveals that he is actually not a tyrant and will do his best to be a good king.

This is a challenging section to read with the class, full of ideas and potential rather than action, so take the role of Malcolm yourself to maintain the pace. Use your voice to emphasise key moments.

PAUSE POINT

S-T-R-E-T-C-H

At the climax of his speech about his supposed iniquities, Malcolm declares 'I am as I have spoken'.

Triplet discussion: Why does Shakespeare present Malcolm as making this false claim?

- Student A: Respond to the question.
- Student B: Add another idea.
- Student C: Summarise the discussion.

Model answer:

This simple statement is the chilling climax of Malcolm's test. It is technically a lie, solidifying his false appearance as a sinful reprobate who might be worse even than Macbeth. Yet, in the deeper context of the scene, it becomes a profound assertion of control. Shakespeare presents Malcolm as transforming from a passive refugee into an active, strategic prince who is testing Macduff's loyalty. Shakespeare shows that Malcolm proves he can wield the tools of deception not for selfish gain, like Macbeth, but as a *medicine* to diagnose loyalty to secure a virtuous future. Malcolm's cunning strategy highlights the difference between him and the overly-trusting Duncan; it also establishes him as the legitimate counter-force to Macbeth.

Big question

Why does Shakespeare present Malcolm lying so elaborately to Macduff?

Malcolm's elaborate lie is not cruelty but a necessary test of political survival. When we last saw Malcolm, his father had just been assassinated. In the 'diseased' state of Scotland, where 'fair is foul' and trust is a risk, Malcolm cannot afford to take Macduff's loyalty at face value. By painting himself as a monster of vice, worse even than Macbeth, he forces Macduff to make a critical choice: does he seek merely any king to replace the tyrant, or does he truly desire a virtuous one? Macduff's horrified, despairing reactions ('O Scotland, Scotland!' 'Bleed, bleed, poor country!') prove his authentic patriotism, confirming that he will be a trustworthy ally, loyal to the nation's soul, not just to its throne.

Themes

Appearance vs reality

Malcolm crafts a false appearance of utter depravity, presenting himself as a creature of insatiable lust and avarice. This façade serves as a test of the reality underlying Macduff's intentions. In a world where the trustworthy Thane of Cawdor was a traitor and the new king is a murderer, Malcolm understands that he cannot trust mere claims of loyalty. He uses a monumental lie to uncover a more profound truth, ensuring that Macduff's allegiance is to the virtuous idea of kingship itself.

Tyranny

The dialogue moves beyond a simple power struggle into a theoretical debate. Malcolm's fictional confession provides a detailed catalogue of a tyrant's vices, which he explicitly contrasts with the 'king-becoming graces' of justice, stability and mercy. Shakespeare creates a stark political spectrum: on one end is Macbeth, the usurping tyrant whose rule is characterised by violent paranoia; on the other is the hypothetical monster Malcolm claims to be, who would be even worse. Macduff's despair at this prospect confirms that true kingship is not a title but a moral condition – a blend of legitimate birth and virtuous character that Macbeth definitely lacks and that Malcolm proves he embodies.

Loyalty vs treason

Shakespeare shows that by abandoning his family, Macduff has committed what seems like a profound betrayal of his domestic duty. Now, Malcolm's test confronts him with an even greater potential betrayal: pledging allegiance to a king who would destroy Scotland. Macduff's refusal to support the monstrous persona Malcolm presents ('Fit to govern? / No, not to live') expands his loyalty from the personal (to a prince) to the national (to Scotland itself). Shakespeare frames his flight from home not as an act of cowardice or disloyalty, but rather as a sacrifice for a higher cause, forging an alliance purified of all suspicion and grounded in a shared, patriotic loyalty.

Analysis

Motif: disease and medicine

In this scene Shakespeare frames Macbeth's tyranny as a sickness infecting Scotland, a 'disease' rotting the body politic. Malcolm, the rightful heir, is positioned as the potential cure, the 'physician.' His elaborate lies to Macduff act as a diagnostic test to prove his own moral health, ensuring he is not a deadlier strain of the same malady. This verbal purification is a necessary prelude to the physical cure of restoring rightful, healthy rule.

Language: sin and virtue

The scene's dense catalogue of vices and virtues is the moral core of the play's political resolution. Shakespeare transforms a political negotiation into an ethical debate, forcing both Macduff and the audience to define what constitutes a legitimate king. Malcolm's elaborate fiction, confessing boundless lust, violent avarice and a lack of 'king-becoming graces', clearly lists the sins of a tyrant. This rhetoric does more than test loyalty. It purges their alliance of mere ambition, re-founding the future kingship of Scotland not on bloodline alone, but on a bedrock of demonstrable virtue.

Key quotation | 'An untitled tyrant bloody-sceptred'

Shakespeare presents Macduff's despair for Scotland, now ruled by a violent usurper who has unleashed terror and suffering upon its people. In this damning condemnation, Macduff highlights Macbeth's illegitimacy, reminding the audience that the new king seized power by murdering his predecessor. Shakespeare uses the image of a 'blood-stained sceptre' to communicate how a symbol of God-given authority has been corrupted by violence. Finally, Shakespeare employs a potent pun: 'untitled' means without a legal claim, forming a direct antithesis to the 'entitlement' that Malcolm holds by birth.

PAUSE POINT

CONSOLIDATION

Within this scene, Shakespeare presents Macduff and Malcolm lamenting Scotland's suffering under Macbeth's tyrannical rule.

Triplet discussion: 'Shakespeare presents Macbeth and Macduff as character foils.' How far do you agree?

- Student A: Respond to the question.
- Student B: Provide evidence to support Student A's response.
- Student C: Summarise the discussion.

Model answer:

Whilst both Macbeth and Macduff are described as valiant heroes in Act One Scene Two, after this point Shakespeare presents them as character foils. Whilst Macbeth betrays Duncan, Macduff maintains his loyalty, articulating the absolute 'horror' of the act of regicide. Then when Macbeth ascends onto the throne of Scotland he becomes a tyrannical, ruthless ruler, whereas Macduff retains his compassion, which is demonstrated through his grief at the suffering of his 'poor country'. His sense of responsibility to the people of Scotland is so great that he has put public responsibility above private concerns – a decision which ultimately leads him to cut Macbeth down at the denouement.

Upon the stage

In Ninagawa Yukio's remarkable Japanese production (1980), this scene was dominated by fierce, oversized statues of Buddhist temple guardians, who embody divine protection and righteous strength. The imposing presence of these idealised heroes stood in stark, visual contrast with Malcolm's lengthy confession of his own fictional vices of cowardice, lust and avarice. The statues represented towering ideals which Malcolm must live up to, and from which Macbeth has fallen. This setting highlighted the vast gulf between the kingdom Scotland should be and the diseased state it had become under Macbeth's tyranny. Productions sometimes cast England in a softer, flattering light (as Nunn did in 1979), but Ninagawa used the scene to interrogate the ideals of power and masculinity that Malcolm is testing in Macduff.

Consider how you would stage the shift from Scotland to England if you were the director: how would you use the setting and lighting to signal a change in location and atmosphere?

CHAPTER 29
THIS GOOD KING
ACT FOUR SCENE THREE (LINES 139 TO 160)

At a glance

- **Plot and character development:** Macduff and Malcolm discuss Edward the Confessor, the king of England and a paragon of virtuous leadership.
- **Social and historical context:** The king's touch
- **Vocabulary:** Semantic field
- **Themes:**
  - Kingship
  - The Divine Right of Kings
- **Analysis:**
  - Motif: hands and touch
- **Key quotation:** 'This good king'

Plot and character development

Following Malcolm and Macduff's discussion, a Doctor enters, bringing news that a group of 'wretched souls' await the king of England (Edward the Confessor).

Social and historical context

The king's touch

King Edward the Confessor, the historical English monarch known for his piety, was believed to cure 'the king's evil' (scrofula) with his touch (Bloch, 1973). By including this 'good king,' Shakespeare accomplishes two things. First, he creates a perfect character foil to the 'bloody-sceptered' Macbeth. Second, and just as importantly for the 1606 audience, he flatters the reigning monarch, King James I, who had also claimed the power of the 'king's touch' and saw himself as a similarly pious and legitimate ruler. The scene thus legitimises James's own rule by associating it with a saintly predecessor, while demonising the Scottish tyrant.

Vocabulary | Semantic field

Definition:	**Characteristics:**
A toolkit of related words.	• Words have similar connotations. • The words can be from different word classes (e.g. nouns, verbs, adjectives etc.). • The words convey a particular image or meaning.
Examples:	**True or false?**
A Christmas Carol (1843): Dickens uses a semantic field of cold to convey Scrooge's misanthropy in Stave One. *An Inspector Calls* (1946): Priestley uses a semantic field of affluence in the opening stage directions, describing the Birlings' house.	1. A semantic field must be made up entirely of adjectives. 2. Writers use a semantic field to drag the reader in.

Answers to 'True or false?':

1. False – semantic fields can be made up of different types of words.
2. False – a common misconception. Semantic fields have precise effects, as explored in the activity below.

PAUSE POINT

S-T-R-E-T-C-H

Ask students to highlight the semantic fields in the following extracts:

- Semantic field of holiness and heaven: Act Four Scene Three, from the Doctor's line 'Ay sir...' to Malcolm's line '...full of grace' (lines 161 to 181).
- Semantic field of evil and hell: Act Two Scene One, from 'I see thee still...' to '...heaven or hell' (lines 57 to 77).

Once students have identified the semantic fields, explore the differences in the ways Shakespeare presents Edward the Confessor and Macbeth. He does this to heighten our awareness of Macbeth's malevolent tyranny, and warn the audience about the consequences of unchecked ambition.

Analysis

Motif: hands and touch

Shakespeare builds on imagery of hands and touch, culminating in the description of Edward's healing power. Malcolm's line 'He hath not touched you yet' is part of this pattern. It prepares the audience to think of royal power in terms of physical contact. Edward's 'healing benediction' and healing 'touch' contrasts all the more powerfully with how we know Macbeth has 'touched' Macduff in the previous scene.

Key quotation | 'This good king'

With this reverential phrase, Shakespeare introduces Edward as the antithesis of Macbeth's tyranny. Edward, 'full of grace,' possesses a 'healing benediction' that restores health and spiritual order, symbolising legitimate, God-appointed kingship. This stands in stark contrast to the 'hell-kite' Macbeth, whose 'blood-stained' hands can only inflict wounds and murder, and who has 'touched' Macduff by slaughtering his family. In a play obsessed with unnatural corruption, Edward embodies the restoration of natural order. His goodness directly opposes the demonic inversion Macbeth embodies, offering Scotland a tangible vision of the righteous monarchy for which Malcolm and Macduff must fight.

Upon the stage

Although this section is often cut, the Trevor Nunn version (1979) presented it very effectively. Echoing the sound design of the opening scene, a church bell tolled in the background as Malcolm (Roger Rees) described King Edward and his piety. The crucial difference was that the juxtaposed cacophony of the Witches, so present in Scotland, was absent in this tranquil England. Given that this play emerged in a time that was so obsessed with witchcraft, piety and the difference between England and Scotland, Nunn's interpretation remains a clever choice.

Consider how you would stage this scene, were you the director: what setting, props, lighting or sound effects would you employ to portray England as a place of peace?

CHAPTER 30

BE THIS THE WHETSTONE OF YOUR SWORD

ACT FOUR SCENE THREE (LINES 161 TO END)

At a glance

- **Plot and character development:** Ross arrives from Scotland with news that initially seems hopeful, but quickly turns to devastating tragedy.
- **Social and historical context:** Masculinity in Jacobean England
- **Vocabulary:** Nemesis
- **Big question:** How does Shakespeare present Macduff as being changed by the murder of his family?
- **Themes:**
  - Violence and masculinity
  - Loyalty vs treason
- **Analysis:**
  - Dramatic irony
  - Motif: birds
- **Key quotation:** 'Be this the whetstone of your sword'
- **Handle with care:** This portion of the scene deals with intense grief and the murder of women and children.

PAUSE POINT

RETRIEVAL

Ask students to think-pair-share their understanding of male stereotypes in the Renaissance era.

Students could consider:

- The stereotype of male courage and violence (as depicted by Shakespeare in Act One Scene Two).
- The expectation that men would act as the patriarch of the family.
- The stereotype that men were less emotional than women.

Plot and character development

Ross arrives with news from Scotland. He cautiously tells Malcolm that the country is in a state of deep misery under Macbeth's rule, but that the people are ready to rise up. However, this slight hope is shattered when Macduff asks after his family. After a moment of equivocating hesitation, Ross reveals the horrific truth: Macbeth has slaughtered Macduff's wife, children and servants. Macduff is utterly broken by the news. Malcolm urges him to 'dispute it like a man' – to channel his sorrow into revenge. But Macduff insists that he must also 'feel it as a man.' The scene concludes with Malcolm rallying the troops: Macbeth is 'ripe for shaking' and they will attempt to cut him down.

Social and historical context

Masculinity in Jacobean England

In Jacobean England, masculinity was a public performance of honour, courage and authority. A man was expected to be the resolute head of his household and to demonstrate martial valour, defending his name and property. This ideal was intensely social, with reputation being a cornerstone of male identity. It is within this conflicted context that Macduff's grief – his insistence on feeling his sorrow 'as a man' – becomes a powerful, albeit controversial, assertion that true manhood can encompass profound emotional depth.

Vocabulary | Nemesis

By the end of this scene, Macduff desires vengeance against Macbeth and becomes his nemesis – ready to bring justice against the tyrant who has 'savagely slaughtered' his family.

Definition:	**Characteristics:**
A rival or enemy. Also an agent of retribution; an inevitable, unstoppable force of justice or vengeance that brings about the downfall of a tragic hero, often due to the hero's own flaws and actions.	• Brings justice and vengeance. • A powerful character. • Opposes and mirrors the protagonist. • Conflict leads to the protagonist's downfall.
Examples:	**Non-examples (from *Macbeth*):**
The Iliad: Achilles brings about Hector's downfall. *Frankenstein* (1818): The Creature is Frankenstein's nemesis, bringing about his downfall.	Duncan Malcolm Banquo The Witches

Reading the scene

There are many tonal shifts in Act Four Scene Three as Macduff moves from anxiety, to disbelief, despair and finally a desire for vengeance. Before reading the extract, enhance students' understanding of these by rehearsing key lines with the appropriate emotion.

Quotation	What is the character's emotion?
Macduff: 'My children too?' 'My wife killed too?'	Disbelief
Malcolm: 'Dispute it like a man' 'Be this the whetstone of your sword'	Encouragement, determination
Macduff: 'I must also feel it as a man'	Despair
Macduff: 'this fiend of Scotland'	Hatred

N.B. Students may misunderstand the word 'niggard' in line 181. Before reading with students, pronounce the word carefully and explain that this word means 'miser'.

PAUSE POINT

S-T-R-E-T-C-H

Triplet discussion: Why does Shakespeare show Ross equivocating before delivering the news of the murders?

- Student A: Provide evidence of Ross's equivocation.
- Student B: Give two reasons why Ross might equivocate at this point.
- Student C: Summarise the discussion.

Model answer:

Ross is the messenger throughout the play, but here his role reaches its most agonising peak. His initial report of Scottish resistance seems like good news, but his stumbling equivocation ('They were well at peace when I did leave 'em') is a grim use of dramatic irony. Having witnessed the murders, the audience understands Ross's reluctance to speak. This hesitation reflects a stark social reality: in an age without swift communication, a messenger bore the full personal burden of delivering catastrophic news, often facing the raw, unpredictable fury of the recipient. Ross's delay is not just a dramatic device; it is a profoundly human response, making the eventual revelation all the more devastating.

PAUSE POINT

ORACY

In one of the many poignant lines in this scene, Macduff says 'he has no children'. But who might the 'he' Macduff refers to be? Is it the childless Macbeth who has callously slaughtered Macduff's family; the unmarried Malcolm who is refusing to give Macduff time to process his grief or the bereaved Macduff himself?

Prepare students for a triplet discussion. Each member of the triplet will make their case for who they think the pronoun 'he' refers to.

Stretch students by reminding them to use tentative language (see Chapter 5).

We explore this debate further in the rest of the chapter.

Big question

How does Shakespeare present Macduff as being changed by the murder of his family?

Shakespeare uses Macduff's loss to redefine him as an agent of personal vengeance, a role shaped by the stark contrasts with every other major character. While Banquo's and Duncan's sons all escape to secure their futures, Macduff's children are all slaughtered. This absolute loss is sharpened by the nature of his enemy. Macbeth, haunted by his 'fruitless crown,' and Lady Macbeth, having 'unsexed' herself, represent a barren, sterile evil. Macduff, the father, confronts the childless tyrant. His cry, 'He has no children,' is a moment of horrific clarity: Macduff is a man defined by paternal love, facing a tyrant incapable of comprehending such a loss. This makes his vengeance a deeply personal mission; he is not just saving Scotland but avenging his own family.

Themes

Violence and masculinity

Malcolm's initial command to 'dispute it like a man' by channeling grief into violent action represents the traditional, martial view of masculinity. Macduff's response – 'I must also feel it as a man' – is surprising. He does not reject violence as a tool, but insists that for it to be righteous, it must be fuelled by authentic, deeply felt sorrow. His vengeance will not be a dispassionate political duty (like Macbeth's killing of Macdonwald in Act One) but a personal crusade, establishing a new paradigm for heroic action in the play's final act.

Loyalty vs treason

Here, the very definitions of loyalty and treason are agonising and purified. Macduff's personal tragedy removes any remaining ambiguity. His loyalty is no longer a complex negotiation between family and state; it is now an absolute, singular drive for revenge that aligns perfectly with the cause of Scotland. To be loyal to Scotland is to be disloyal to Macbeth, and vice versa. The scene erases any middle ground, transforming Macduff's quest from a political rebellion into a moral imperative. His 'treason' against the sitting king is now the highest form of loyalty to the nation and the natural order; it justifies the coming war and frames the final act as a clear-cut battle between justice and tyranny.

Analysis

Dramatic irony

The dramatic irony here is excruciating, rooted entirely in our knowledge of the slaughter of Macduff's family. As Ross delivers the news in slow, painful increments, the audience is forced to watch Macduff remain in a state of ignorant hope. We are made to endure the agonizing gap between the horrific reality and the devastating truth Ross struggles to speak, magnifying the emotional impact of the blow when it finally lands.

Motif: birds

The play's bird imagery, which has consistently symbolised the natural order and its disruption, culminates in this scene with its most vulnerable iteration. Earlier in the play, Shakespeare contrasted sparrows and eagles as well as the mousing-owl and the falcon, and he also gave us crows and ravens. These images charted a descent from royalty to dark and treacherous conflict. Now, we get an attack on domestic vulnerability. Macduff's heartbroken cry – 'All my pretty chickens?' – reduces his wife and children to helpless chicks, utterly defenceless against the predator Macbeth has become.

Key quotation | 'Be this the whetstone of your sword'

Shakespeare uses Malcolm's line to mark the pivotal moment where Macduff's grief is weaponised. A whetstone does not change the fundamental nature of the sword; it sharpens it, making it infinitely more lethal and effective. Malcolm urges Macduff to use his personal loss not to dull his resolve with despair, but to hone his purpose into a sharper, more focused instrument of revenge. This metaphor perfectly captures Macduff's transformation. His love for his family, now a source of pain, is not discarded. Instead, it is channeled, becoming the very thing that will give his subsequent violence its edge and moral certainty.

PAUSE POINT

CONSOLIDATION

Shakespeare has now set the stage for Macbeth's downfall. He is presented as a merciless tyrant whose indiscriminate reign of terror does not spare innocent victims. In contrast, Shakespeare reveals that Malcolm has the support of the king of England and Siward, Earl of Northumberland, and that Macduff has a personal reason to pursue revenge.

Act Five swiftly brings the play to its denouement, so before you begin ensure students' knowledge is secure: ask them to map out the locations, states of mind and actions of the key characters.

- Macbeth
- Lady Macbeth
- Macduff
- Malcolm
- Edward the Confessor and Siward.

Upon the stage

Patrick O'Kane's Macduff in the (2018) Norris production was particularly compelling. Within the grubby landscape and contemporary setting, O'Kane gave a very moving account of Macduff's grief. Compare and contrast with Ben Turner in the Godwin production (2024) – also excellent – and Edward Bennett's rather cooler interpretation in Findlay (2018). Which of these most seems to 'feel it as a man'? The juxtaposition of violence and masculinity is a theme we discuss throughout the play; this scene is one of its most theatrically important instances.

Encourage your students to discuss this: is it more masculine to show emotion, to hide it, or to channel it into Macduff's approaching revenge?

CHAPTER 31
ALL THE PERFUMES OF ARABIA WILL NOT SWEETEN THIS LITTLE HAND
ACT FIVE SCENE ONE

At a glance

› **Plot and character development:** A Doctor and a Gentlewoman observe a sleepwalking Lady Macbeth, who unconsciously reveals the murders of Duncan, Banquo and Lady Macduff as she tries to clean imaginary blood from her hands.

› **Social and historical context:** Madness in Shakespeare

› **Vocabulary:** Psychosomatic

› **Big question:** Why does Shakespeare portray Lady Macbeth sleepwalking?

› **Themes:**

- Guilt and conscience
- Appearance vs reality
- Disorder and the unnatural

› **Analysis:**

- Motif: blood
- Motif: darkness and light
- Text: prose
- Staging: witnesses

› **Key quotation:** 'All the perfumes of Arabia will not sweeten this little hand'

› **Handle with care:** This scene depicts a severe mental health crisis. Be mindful of students who may have experience with sleepwalking, OCD or who have been affected by trauma.

PAUSE POINT

RETRIEVAL

In Chapter 21 we explored the meaning of the phrase emotional anguish. Check students' understanding of this term so that they can use it to describe Lady Macbeth's state of mind in this scene.

Hinge question: Which of these statements contains the correct use of the phrase emotional anguish?

1. Shakespeare emphasises Macbeth's emotional anguish in Act One Scene Three, when he is 'rapt' following the witches' prophecies.
2. In Act One Scene Five, Shakespeare presents Lady Macbeth as full of emotional anguish as she calls on the spirits to 'unsex' her.
3. Following the regicide, Shakespeare emphasises Macbeth's torment; the source of his emotional anguish is his frustration at his 'fruitless crown'.
4. Shakespeare shows that when Macbeth meets with Banquo's murderers, he is afflicted by emotional anguish.

The correct response is 3.

Plot and character development

The formidable, calculating queen of the play's first half has completely disintegrated. Shakespeare reveals her breakdown not through a soliloquy, but through a devastating public performance she cannot control. The Gentlewoman's report and the Doctor's observation provide a clinical framework for a scene of profound psychological horror.

Social and historical context

Madness in Shakespeare

Scenes of frenzy or madness appear in nearly a quarter of Shakespeare's plays, from Lear's raging grief in *King Lear* to Ophelia's lovesick despair in *Hamlet*. However, *Macbeth* is unique in its portrayal of a character walking in her sleep. For a Jacobean audience, such a 'great perturbation in nature', especially in a character who has already invoked evil spirits, would not have been seen as a simple medical condition. Instead, it would have been a clear sign of a soul tormented by the very forces it had summoned, or haunted by the variety of crimes to which it has been privy.

Vocabulary | Psychosomatic

In Act Three, we introduced the term emotional anguish to describe Macbeth's torment. In this scene, we see its ultimate physical manifestation in Lady Macbeth. Her suffering is not just in her mind; it has a tangible, physical component, which can be described as psychosomatic.

Definition:	**Morphology:**
A physical illness or condition caused or aggravated by a mental factor such as internal conflict or stress.	Prefix: psyche- = mind or soul Root word: soma- = body
Examples:	**Non-examples:**
Macbeth (1606): Lady Macbeth's sleepwalking and compulsive hand-washing are psychosomatic manifestations of her guilt. *Of Mice and Men* (1937): Lennie's anxiety can cause him to have physical outbursts he cannot control.	*Macbeth* (1606): The Sergeant's wounds in Act One Scene Two are from physical trauma, not a mental state. *A Christmas Carol* (1843): Scrooge's coldness is a metaphor, not a physical illness.

Shakespeare portrays Lady Macbeth's overwhelming emotional anguish through psychosomatic symptoms. Her sleepwalking and her desperate attempts to clean the invisible 'damned spot' from her hands are physical symptoms caused by the psychological burden of her guilt.

Reading the scene

This extract can be challenging due to the level of emotion Lady Macbeth demonstrates. For this reason, you may wish to take the role of Lady Macbeth yourself. Read the extract twice through.

On the second reading, ask students to highlight relevant motifs (blood, hands, light and darkness). Then discuss how Shakespeare has used these motifs to highlight Lady Macbeth's despair: she has been involved in an unnatural murder, which has plunged her into moral and psychological darkness.

PAUSE POINT

S-T-R-E-T-C-H

Revisit Act Two Scene Two and compare the imperatives that Lady Macbeth speaks in this scene with those in Act Five Scene One.

Model answer:

Shakespeare uses Lady Macbeth's frantic command, 'Out, damned spot! out, I say!' as a direct echo of her earlier, cool-headed instruction to Macbeth to 'Go get some water, / And wash this filthy witness from your hand.' Similarly, 'To bed, to bed' mirrors her earlier, decisive order 'Retire we to our chamber.' These echoes occur because her unconscious mind is now tormented by the same practical details of the crime she earlier managed with ruthless efficiency. For the Doctor and Gentlewoman, these specific, repeated imperatives reveal her direct involvement in the murder.

Big question

Why does Shakespeare portray Lady Macbeth sleepwalking?

Lady Macbeth's sleepwalking demonstrates that her guilt is no longer a conscious feeling but a subconscious and inescapable affliction, an uncontrollable torment in her soul that plays on an endless loop. This indicates the utter collapse of the ruthless persona she so fiercely constructed, reducing the woman who once commanded dark spirits to a fragile, childlike figure desperately seeking light – and absolution. Furthermore, the sleepwalking makes her private torment dangerously public; the shocked observations of the Doctor and Gentlewoman transform her internal anguish into a documented fact that threatens to expose the rotten core of Macbeth's reign. Finally, her nightly walk unites the play's central motifs: her obsession with the 'damned spot' is a final, harrowing evolution of the blood motif, while her constant need for a candle hauntingly inverts her earlier invocations of 'thick night' to conceal the deed.

PAUSE POINT

ORACY

Triplet discussion: 'In Act Five Scene One, Shakespeare presents Lady Macbeth as a changed character: instead of being powerful and determined, she has become weak and remorseful.' How far do you agree?

Student A: Argue that Lady Macbeth has become weak.

Student B: Provide evidence or examples to support Student A.

Student C: Summarise the discussion.

Model answer:

Shakespeare initially presents Lady Macbeth as dominant and confident: her ruthless determination propelled Macbeth towards regicide, her orchestration of details (drugging the guards, providing the daggers, ringing the bell) revealing a mind in full control. Yet now Shakespeare reveals a mind tormented by guilt. Apparently abandoned by her husband, Lady Macbeth compulsively revisits her crimes: the blood that no washing can cleanse, the sight of 'the old man' she helped murder, the ghost of Banquo, and the elimination of Lady Macduff. Where once she could defiantly state that 'my hands are of your colour', now she laments the smell of blood on her 'little hand'. The diminutive signals her changed character: the hands that would have dashed out a baby's brains are now vulnerable, stained and powerless.

Themes

Guilt and conscience

This scene is the final, devastating verdict on the power of conscience. Shakespeare externalises Lady Macbeth's internal guilt through her compulsive, unconscious actions. The Doctor observes that 'Unnatural deeds / Do breed unnatural troubles,' concluding that her psychological torment is the direct consequence of her crimes. Her sleepwalking is the physical manifestation of a mind 'infected' by its own deeds. The guilt with which she daubed the faces of Duncan's grooms now permanently stains her own hands.

Appearance vs reality

Lady Macbeth's public persona has become a fragile lie. Here, in private, her guilt-ravaged reality is exposed. The loyal Gentlewoman refuses to repeat what she has heard because she knows the deadly gap between Lady Macbeth's public persona and her private truth.

Disorder and the unnatural

The Doctor initially notes that sleepwalking is not, in itself, a sign of deep disorder, while observing that it is 'a great perturbation in nature, / to receive at once the benefit of sleep, and do the effects of watching.' Lady Macbeth's unwitting disclosures suggest that her sleepwalking is not a peculiarity of the body, but instead a symptom of a soul in torment. The final diagnosis (that she more needs 'the divine than the physician') confirms that her problem is not physical but spiritual.

Analysis

Motif: blood

The blood motif reaches its climax in Lady Macbeth's subconscious. Her obsession with the 'damned spot' is an answer to her earlier command to Macbeth after Duncan's murder: 'I'll gild the faces of the grooms withal, /

For it must seem their guilt.' In that moment, her hands became stained, but she was in control, actively using the blood as a tool to frame others. Now, the blood has returned as a permanent, hallucinatory stain on her own hands: the motifs of blood and guilt coagulate in a stain she can no longer command, control or wash away.

Motif: darkness and light

In a powerful inversion, Shakespeare shows that Lady Macbeth, who once summoned 'thick night' to hide her deeds, now compulsively carries a taper (candle). Her desperate need for light symbolises her soul's craving for grace and truth after living in moral darkness. The Gentlewoman notes she has 'light by her continually,' a telling detail that highlights her newfound paranoia.

Text: prose

Unlike the Porter in Chapter 15, whose prose signalled lower status and drunkenness, Lady Macbeth's shift to prose here signals a shattering of her high status and mental cohesion. Where iambic pentameter represents the conscious, public world of the court, prose becomes the medium for unfiltered truth. Lady Macbeth's frantic speech reveals the murders of Duncan, Banquo and Lady Macduff.

Staging: witnesses

In both Act Two Scene Four and Act Three Scene Six we hear from outsiders who comment on the state of affairs in Scotland. The Gentlewoman and the Doctor perform a similar function here, almost like a Greek chorus, commenting on the tragedy and interpreting it for the audience.

Key quotation | 'All the perfumes of Arabia will not sweeten this little hand'

Shakespeare uses this line to mark the tragic and complete transformation of Lady Macbeth's character. The pragmatic woman who once coolly assured her husband that 'a little water clears us of this deed' is now consumed by a guilt of unimaginable scale, believing that not even 'all the perfumes of Arabia' could remove the scent of blood from her hand. This shift from a simple, physical solution to an insoluble affliction charts her descent from cold practicality into profound emotional anguish. Unlike Macbeth, who feared his guilt would corrupt the oceans, her focus on masking the scent reveals her despairing belief that the stain is permanent and she is beyond true cleansing.

The poetic expanse of 'all the perfumes of Arabia' echoes Macbeth's own exaggerations ('the multitudinous seas incarnadine') – but Shakespeare uses this to indicate how their roles have reversed. He initially presented Lady Macbeth as the cool-headed orchestrator who kept her head in a crisis, but now shows how her guilt has caused her to unravel. As we will see in coming scenes, he portrays Macbeth as the opposite; his earlier conscientiousness is replaced with a nihilistic resignation to the horrors on which he 'sups'.

Shakespeare cements Lady Macbeth's hopelessness in the definitive phrase 'will not.' This is not a wish but a statement of absolute certainty. She is convinced that redemption is impossible, acknowledging in her subconscious torment that she is damned. Finally, the word 'little,' which she once used to describe the negligible amount of water needed, now describes her own hand. This subtle repetition underscores her devastating diminishment from a figure of formidable will to a vulnerable, broken soul. In this single, haunting line, Shakespeare masterfully evokes pathos for a character finally destroyed by the conscience she once bravely – and foolishly – believed she could silence.

PAUSE POINT

S-T-R-E-T-C-H

In Act Two, Shakespeare shows Lady Macbeth cautioning her husband not to think on their deeds, lest it 'make us mad'. In Act Five Scene One, Shakespeare reveals the truth of this warning.

Triplet discussion: 'In Act Five, Scene One, Shakespeare reveals that Lady Macbeth's character has completely changed.' How far do you agree?

- Student A: Explain how Lady Macbeth's identity has changed.
- Student B: Provide evidence to support Student A's ideas.
- Student C: Summarise the discussion.

Model answer:

By Act Five, it has become clear that Lady Macbeth's character has irrevocably changed. In Act One Scene Five, Shakespeare showed Lady Macbeth's willingness to destroy her female identity – the command 'unsex me here' was an articulation of her frustration at the limitations of gender stereotypes which threatened to thwart her ambitions. However, Shakespeare reveals the disastrous consequences of Lady Macbeth's unconventional behaviour, as she is now tormented by guilt and unable to liberate herself from sin ('will these hands ne'er be clean?'). She is alone, abandoned by her husband, lacking the power she wielded so effortlessly over him earlier in the play.

PAUSE POINT

CONSOLIDATION

At the end of this scene, the Doctor summarises the current situation:

> *Foul whisp'rings are abroad. Unnatural deeds*
> *Do breed unnatural troubles: infected minds*
> *To their deaf pillows will discharge their secrets.*

Think-pair-share: Using these lines as a starting point, what are the consequences of regicide?

Students could consider Shakespeare's presentation of how regicide has caused:

- Lady Macbeth's 'infected mind'.
- Lady Macbeth's isolation from her husband.
- Distrust and secrecy ('foul whisperings').
- Chaos and disruption in society.
- More violence (such as the 'unnatural' slaughter of Macduff's family).

Upon the stage

Judi Dench's performance of this scene (Nunn, 1979) was a masterclass in hollowed-out despair. Her voice was a thin, papery whisper, and her movements slow and ghostlike, as if she was already dead. In contrast, Indira Varma (Godwin, 2024) delivered the speech with a more violent, volatile intensity, maintaining her stylish, elegant performance but without the steely control she has exhibited until now.

Show students both versions: which interpretation is more powerful, and why?

CHAPTER 32
NOW DOES HE FEEL / HIS SECRET MURDERS STICKING ON HIS HANDS
ACT FIVE SCENE TWO

At a glance

- **Plot and character development:** The Scottish thanes prepare to meet the approaching English army.
- **Social and historical context:** Rebellion against tyranny
- **Vocabulary:** Tyrant (revisited)
- **Big question:** Why does Shakespeare show us the Scottish lords' perspective before the battle?
- **Themes:**
    - Appearance vs reality
    - Disorder and the unnatural
    - The Divine Right of Kings
- **Analysis:**
    - Motif: disease and medicine
    - Motif: clothing
    - Text: iambic pentameter
- **Key quotation:** 'Now does he feel / His secret murders sticking on his hands'
- **Handle with care:** In this scene Shakespeare uses the adjective 'dwarfish' to indicate Macbeth's diminished character and reputation. We would never use this word in this way today, since it seems to equate a physical condition with immorality. Pause and reflect on how society has progressed in its understanding of how language should be used inclusively and to empower people.

PAUSE POINT

RETRIEVAL

This scene provides crucial information relating to how the Witches' seemingly impossible prophecies in Act Four Scene One will come true.

Revisit these prophecies with your class, highlighting Shakespeare's use of dramatic irony to build tension as we progress towards the denouement.

Plot and character development

This short scene serves as a military briefing before the final showdown. The once-loyal Scottish thanes (Meinteith, Angus, Lennox and Caithness) are now unified in their rebellion, indicating the collapse of Macbeth's political support. They discuss Macbeth's deteriorating state, his fortified position in Dunsinane and the universal hatred his rule has inspired, framing the final confrontation.

Their dialogue builds tension, describes the 'hardened' state of their opponent and justifies the imminent invasion as a righteous cause. Macbeth is no longer a king, but a 'tyrant,' whose grip on power seems both desperate and brittle.

Social and historical context

Rebellion against tyranny

Tyranny and rebellion were important political issues for a Jacobean audience. While the Divine Right of Kings was a sacred doctrine, political theorists argued that a ruler who became a tyrant or destroyed the commonwealth forfeited his right to rule. Recalling the Divine Right of Kings discussed in Chapter 5, the thanes now view Macbeth not just as a criminal, but as a heretic. Their language justifies their rebellion not as treason, but as a 'medicine' for the sick country, articulating their duty to 'pour we, in our country's purge / Each drop of us.' Their allegiance has transferred to Duncan's appointed heir, Malcolm, whose presence with an English army is not an invasion but a liberation.

Vocabulary | Tyrant (revisited)

The term 'tyrant' has been used cautiously before, but now Menteith openly uses it for Macbeth. Ask students to think-pair-share examples of tyrannical behaviour in the play.

Reading the scene

The value of this short but dense scene is in the clarity and resolve of the lords. Read the scene twice through.

On the second reading, ask students to highlight all the descriptions of Macbeth and his rule (e.g., 'disease,' 'weeds,' 'dwarfish thief'). Discuss how this collective portrait undermines his authority and justifies the rebellion. Compare this language with how Macbeth was described in Act One.

Big question

Why does Shakespeare show us the Scottish lords' perspective before the battle?

This scene provides political and moral framing for the climax. It explains the play's thematic shift from one man's internal tragedy to the national crisis his tyranny has caused. The thanes' unified, condemnatory perspective shows the audience that Macbeth's defeat is not just inevitable, but deserved. The scene also builds dramatic tension by contrasting the organised, purposeful advance of the rebels with the reports of Macbeth's frantic and isolated defence, making his final stand seem like the last gasp of a doomed regime. Finally, it re-establishes a moral order, suggesting that Malcolm represents a restoration of legitimate, healing kingship.

Themes

Appearance vs reality

In Acts One and Two, Macbeth and Lady Macbeth *constructed* false appearances to conceal reality: the 'innocent flower' masking the serpent, the 'false face' hiding the 'false heart'. In Act Five, the dynamic reverses. Reality now asserts itself through and against appearance. Macbeth's soldiers still obey, but their obedience is revealed as 'nothing in love': the appearance of loyalty persists, but the reality of hatred bleeds through. The secret murders 'sticking on his hands' are not a hallucination or a nightmare, but a public fact. Shakespeare shows that appearance cannot indefinitely obscure reality; eventually, the truth 'sticks' where it can be seen.

Disorder and the unnatural

The thanes' coordinated march towards Dunsinane represents the reassembly of a fractured society against the source of its disorder. This orderly scene symbolises the return of a unified, collective purpose that opposes Macbeth's chaotic and solitary reign.

Analysis

Motif: disease and medicine

This motif reaches its zenith here. Scotland itself is the 'sickly weal' (commonwealth), and Malcolm is to be its 'medicine.' Macbeth is the disease that must be purged. This collective, national imagery shows how the consequences of his actions have escalated from a personal 'mind diseased' to a plague upon the entire nation.

Motif: clothing

The clothing motif, which began with Macbeth feeling his new honours were like 'borrowed robes' but now they 'hang loose about him, like a giant's robe upon a dwarfish thief'. Angus implies that Macbeth's power never truly fit him; he was an unworthy thief who stole the crown. The metaphor reveals that his authority was always an ill-fitting disguise, and now it is being stripped away. Worse yet, Macbeth's 'distempered cause' is likened to a swollen belly, and the 'belt' of his rule can no longer be fastened around it. It is an almost comical image; Macbeth is not even in control of his clothing any more.

PAUSE POINT

S-T-R-E-T-C-H

Ask students to think-pair-share their knowledge of the motifs of clothing from earlier in the play. See Appendix B for a list of suggested quotations.

Text: iambic pentameter

Unlike the fractured prose of Lady Macbeth's sleepwalking (or the Witches' trochaic tetrameter), this scene is delivered in steady, collaborative iambic pentameter. The lords' lines are measured and rational, reflecting their unified purpose and the restoration of political and linguistic order.

Key quotation | 'Now does he feel / His secret murders sticking on his hands'

This image is an external confirmation of Macbeth's internal guilt. Shakespeare uses the adverb 'now' to signal a turning point; the hidden truth of Macbeth's crimes is becoming public knowledge. The verb 'sticking' directly echoes Lady Macbeth's 'damned spot', but instead of a hallucination, Macbeth now faces very real political disrespect in the eyes of his former supporters. This line bridges the private psychological torment of the previous scene with the public, political reckoning to come.

PAUSE POINT

CONSOLIDATION

Triplet discussion: To what extent does Shakespeare present the Scottish lords as heroic in this scene?

- Student A: Argue that Shakespeare presents the lords as heroes.
- Student B: Argues that the lords are opportunists, using Lennox as a key example of someone who switched sides once it was safe to do so.
- Student C: Summarise the discussion.

Model answer:

It could be argued that Shakespeare presents the Scottish lords as heroic in this scene, as they unite to overthrow the tyrant Macbeth. Menteith and Angus condemn Macbeth with scathing unanimity, calling him 'the tyrant' and a 'thief' while celebrating the 'good Macduff'. Caithness then speaks for the group when he announces that they intend to 'pour we [...] each drop of us' in their attempt to save Scotland; the image suggests complete dedication and heroic self-sacrifice.

Yet Lennox complicates this reading. In Act Three Scene Six, he privately condemned Macbeth as a 'tyrant' and acknowledged Scotland's suffering under his rule. He knew Macduff had gone to England to raise support. But in the very next scene, Lennox appears at Macbeth's side, calling him 'my good lord' and informing him of Macduff's departure – information that precipitates the slaughter of Lady Macduff and her children. He does not intervene when he hears Macbeth's plan. His appearance here beside Menteith and the other lords therefore feels convenient, even opportunistic. The contrast with Macduff's integrity is telling.

Upon the stage

This scene is often cut or shortened in performance, but when included, its tone is critical. It can be played as a grim, determined war council, highlighting the resolve of the rebels. Alternatively, a director might emphasise the lords' bitterness and anger, showing the personal cost of Macbeth's rule. Compare Nunn's intimate, immediate staging (1979) with Goold's film (2010), which highlights the lingering suspicion between the thanes, who do not yet seem resolved to fight for Scotland's future. Nunn's production emphasises the collective suffering of the country, while in Goold's Scotland every thane appears like a Macbeth in waiting, in need of a strong ruler to lead them back into collective unity.

Discuss what is gained by focusing on the collective national suffering versus the singular tragic hero.

CHAPTER 33

MY WAY OF LIFE / IS FALLEN INTO THE SERE

ACT FIVE SCENE THREE

At a glance

- **Plot and character development:** Macbeth, fortified in Dunsinane, oscillates between defiance and despair.
- **Social and historical context:** Renaissance medicine and purges
- **Vocabulary:** Nihilism
- **Big question:** Have the Witches betrayed Macbeth and 'won him to his harm'?
- **Themes:**
  - Tyranny
  - Appearance vs reality
  - Violence and masculinity
- **Analysis:**
  - Motif: disease and medicine
  - Image: white and red
  - Seyton
- **Key quotation:** 'my way of life / Is fallen into the sere'

PAUSE POINT

RETRIEVAL

Revisit the phrase emotional anguish. Signpost the difference between Macbeth's earlier turmoil and his growing nihilism in Act Five Scenes Three and Five.

Plot and character development

Macbeth dismisses reports of the advancing army, bullies a fearful servant and reflects on his empty life. His interaction with the Doctor reveals a disregard for Lady Macbeth's illness and his own delusional belief that Scotland's sickness can be cured like a physical disease.

Macbeth's development in this scene happens in three stages: arrogance bolstered by the Witches' prophecies, a moment of clear-eyed nihilistic despair and a delusional projection of his own sickness onto Scotland in his conversation with the Doctor. The formidable warrior-king is now a 'sick' heart, isolated and despised.

Social and historical context

Renaissance medicine and purges

Macbeth's command to 'purge' Scotland and his listing of 'rhubarb' and 'cyme' (senna) as 'purgative drugs' is grounded in the Renaissance theory of humours. Medicine sought to balance the body's four humours (blood, phlegm, black bile, yellow bile) by using emetics or laxatives to 'purge' excess or corrupt fluids. This makes Macbeth's plea a profound dramatic irony: he is attempting to apply a physical cure to a spiritual and political sickness. The true disease is his own tyrannical rule, a 'humour' of evil that has infected the body politic.

Vocabulary | Nihilism

Macbeth is not just guilty or afraid; he has reached a point of such existential exhaustion that he sees no meaning or value in anything, including his own life.

Definition:	**Characteristics:**
The belief that all values are baseless and that nothing can be known or communicated. It is often associated with extreme pessimism and a radical skepticism that condemns existence.	• Rejection of moral principles. • Belief in the meaninglessness of life. • Profound pessimism and despair. • Often follows a traumatic loss of faith or purpose.
Examples (from *Macbeth*):	**Non-examples (from *Macbeth*):**
Macbeth's speech about life being 'a tale / Told by an idiot, full of sound and fury, / Signifying nothing'.	Macduff's desire for revenge is driven by a firm belief in justice, family and moral order – the opposite of nihilism.

Reading the scene

As Macbeth reflects on his position, his emotions shift dramatically. Before reading the whole scene, ask students to rehearse these key lines in their triplets, using their voices to capture the range of emotions.

Line	Emotion
'Bring me no more reports. Let them fly all.'	Frustration
'What's the boy Malcolm? / Was he not born of woman?'	Disgust
'Where got thou that goose-look?'	Mocking
'I am sick at heart.'	Despair
'I'll fight till from my bones my flesh be hacked. / Give me mine amour.'	Angry, determined
'Canst thou not minister to a mind diseased?'	Curious

Then select your readers and read the scene. As you read, ask the listeners to highlight references to the Witches' prophecies.

PAUSE POINT

S-T-R-E-T-C-H

Shakespeare presents Macbeth as becoming increasingly nihilistic – declaring that he is 'sick at heart' – but he also insists that he will 'fight till from my bones my flesh be hacked'.

Triplet discussion: What motivates Macbeth to fight?

- Student A: Respond to the question by suggesting two reasons.
- Student B: Provide evidence or examples to support Student A's reasons.
- Student C: Summarise the discussion.

Model answer:

When Shakespeare first introduced Macbeth in Act One Scene Two, he was a respected military leader, defined by his unflinching courage and his successes on the battlefield. Yet, by Act Five, Macbeth has spent two acts within the castle walls, ordering murders from afar and becoming lost in his own thoughts. Now, Shakespeare shows Macbeth calling for his armour and announcing his desire to fight to the death; he is attempting to regain his former identity – and the admiration that accompanied it.

Big question

Have the Witches betrayed Macbeth and 'won him to his harm'?

Banquo's warning in Act One has proved prophetic. The Witches told a simple truth to gain Macbeth's trust, but that truth was a hook. Their 'honest trifles' were the prophecies of becoming Thane of Cawdor and King. The 'deepest consequence' is what we see now: a man so hollowed out by his own actions that he clings to their words not as a source of power, but as his only reason to keep breathing.

The Witches did not make Macbeth a murderer, but their manipulation gave him a specific, ambitious target. They then provided the deceptive security (the 'sweet bodements') that made him feel invincible long enough to destroy his own soul, isolate himself and become a monster. Now, in this scene, Macbeth seems entirely dependent on their final, equivocating promises. Shakespeare portrays him as their pawn, stripped of everything, fighting a battle he only thinks he can win because they told him a half-truth, making him the chief agent of his own destruction.

PAUSE POINT

WRITING

Build students' confidence in writing about Macbeth's soliloquies through this 'slow write' activity.

Read one phrase of the soliloquy at a time, asking students to write down their response in paragraph form.

> *This push*
> *Will cheer me ever, or disseat me now.*
> *I have lived long enough: my way of life*
> *Is fallen into the sere, the yellow leaf,*
> *And that which should accompany old age,*
> *As honour, love, obedience, troops of friends,*
> *I must not look to have; but in their stead,*
> *Curses not loud but deep, mouth-honour, breath*
> *Which the poor heart would fain deny, and dare not.*

If students require scaffolding, give them brief sentence starters:

- This line means...
- This phrase suggests...
- Macbeth is saying that...

Once you have finished the slow write, explore the meaning of the soliloquy through whole class discussion. Then ask students to redraft their ideas using your usual paragraph structure.

Themes

Tyranny

Shakespeare shows that Macbeth is utterly alone. His wife is 'infected,' his thanes have abandoned him, and he holds his remaining servants in contempt. The stage picture is of one man in a castle, surrounded by people who fear him but do not follow him out of love or duty. His isolation is the direct and inevitable consequence of his tyrannical rule.

Appearance vs reality

Macbeth's sense of security is a façade built on his literal interpretation of the Witches' words. He appears confident because 'none of woman born / Shall harm Macbeth' and Birnam Wood is unlikely to travel to Dunsinane. The audience, however, knows the reality: the prophecy is a deceptive trap.

Violence and masculinity

Does Shakespeare present Macbeth as courageous here? He arms himself and prepares to fight, but his motivation has dissipated. This is not the noble, principled valour of his past, but a desperate, nihilistic defiance. He fights not for a cause, but because he has nothing left to live for and nothing left to lose. The violence and masculinity so central to how he was first introduced are distant echoes now.

Analysis

Motif: disease and medicine

The motif culminates in a devastating inversion. Macbeth, who is the true disease of Scotland, wants The Doctor to 'purge' the land. He recognises the symptom but is blind to the cause: himself. His line 'Throw physic to the dogs; I'll none of it,' is a symbolic rejection of any cure for his own spiritual and moral sickness, resigning himself to his fate.

Image: white and red

Shakespeare uses a stark colour palette to undermine Macbeth's courage. He viciously attacks a servant's pallor ('cream-faced loon,' 'lily-liver'd boy,' 'whey-face') equating white with a cowardice he now derides in others. This is a stark reversal of his own 'white' and fearful heart after Duncan's murder. He commands his servant to 'prick thy face, and over-red thy fear'. The bloody valour we heard about in Act One feels very far away, and now blood appears only as a mask, or a nightmarish stain on Lady Macbeth's hands.

Seyton

Seyton's appearance serves as a powerful symbol of Macbeth's damnation and isolation. While he is technically Macbeth's armour-bearer, his function is thematic. The audible pun in his name ('Seyton' sounds like 'Satan') is almost certainly intentional, and transforms this mundane servant into a potent metaphor. We have not seen Macbeth since he consorted with the Witches in Act Four Scene One; now he appears to have co-opted this new servant, with this ominous name – could he even be read as Macbeth's familiar?

Key quotation | My way of life / Is fallen into the sere

In this line, Shakespeare creates a moment of devastating self-diagnosis. The word 'sere' means withered or dried up, and its pairing with the 'yellow leaf' creates a powerful metaphor of untimely decay. This is the bitter, ironic fulfilment of Duncan's promise to make him 'full of growing.' Shakespeare shows that Macbeth has indeed grown, but into a blighted, barren thing. His 'way of life' (his kingship, his identity) is now a wasteland. The image inverts the blood-soaked vibrancy of his crimes; where there was once the shocking red of ambition, there is now only the pale, desiccated yellow of decay. He has achieved power only to find himself spiritually dead, having destroyed the very soil in which he was meant to grow.

Upon the stage

This scene offers actors a choice: play Macbeth as a raging, cornered tyrant or as a deeply exhausted, hollowed-out man. Patrick Stewart (Goold, 2010)

PAUSE POINT

CONSOLIDATION

Triplet discussion: 'In Act Five Scene Three, Shakespeare presents Macbeth as more pitiable than hateful.' How far do you agree?

Remind students to balance tentative and assertive language in their discussion (see, p XIII).

- Student A: Argue that Macbeth is pitiable. Provide evidence for your ideas.
- Student B: Argue that Macbeth is hateful. Provide evidence for your ideas.
- Student C: Summarise the discussion.

Model answer:

Shakespeare here crafts a soliloquy that evokes profound pity for Macbeth, who seems crushed by weariness and despair. 'Sick at heart', he feels he has lost everything he aspired to achieve: 'honour, love, obedience, troops of friends'. His isolation is underscored by his physical solitude on stage, with only the ominously-named Seyton within calling distance. This isolation later deepens when he laments Lady Macbeth's illness and asks the Doctor to 'minister to a mind diseas'd'. The loss of her support further destabilises him, rendering Macbeth a deeply pitiable figure.

Yet Shakespeare is not interested in pity alone. Macbeth is more complicated: he may be diminished, and increasingly nihilistic, but he remains defiant. His arrogance flares as he mocks the 'false thanes' and 'English epicures' who stand against him, and his cruelty shows in his treatment of the servant who brings news of the ten thousand soldiers approaching. He clings to power, declaring he will 'fight till from my bones my flesh be hacked' and calling for armour—a symbolic echo of the masculine heroism that once defined him. Macbeth is hateful in both senses of the word: he is filled with hatred for his enemies, and he is himself increasingly hated for his callous tyranny.

PAUSE POINT

CONSOLIDATION

Shakespeare juxtaposes two key images in the scene: the 'yellow leaf' and Macbeth's armour.

Ask students to think-pair-share the symbolic meanings of these images.

- 'The yellow leaf': autumn, endings, decay, despair, death.
- Macbeth's armour: echo of Act One Scene Two, courage, heroism, masculinity, determination, strength.

played it with a quiet, terrifying stillness, his rage simmering beneath a surface of utter exhaustion. By contrast, David Tennant (Webster, 2023) portrayed a more volatile, feverish Macbeth, both frenetic and unstable. Rory Kinnear (Norris, 2018), by far the most sensitive of the Macbeths in our recommended productions, even seemed hopeful as he strategised.

Show your students these interpretations and challenge them to consider how they might approach this scene: which of these actors most powerfully conveys the 'sick heart' of the character?

CHAPTER 34
LET EVERY SOLDIER HEW HIM DOWN A BOUGH
ACT FIVE SCENE FOUR

At a glance

- **Plot and character development:** In the countryside near Dunsinane, Malcolm gives the strategic order for each soldier to cut down a bough from Birnam Wood to use as camouflage, unknowingly fulfilling the Witches' prophecy.
- **Themes:**
  - Appearance vs reality
  - Fate vs free will
  - Conflict
- **Analysis:** This short scene explains how Birnam Wood physically comes to Dunsinane; Shakespeare has to show us the pragmatic military decision because he cannot show an entire forest crossing the countryside. The themes of conflict, appearance vs reality and fate vs free will, present since the opening scenes, are all converging now as a final showdown looms.
- **Key quotation:** 'Let every soldier hew him down a bough / And bear't before him'

Upon the stage

Film adaptations, from Welles (1948) to Coen (2021), often rely on spectacular images to represent this scene. But Shakespeare wrote the scene for the stage, to show Malcolm emerging as a viable replacement for Macbeth. The scene's dramatic weight does not lie in the spectacle of moving trees, but in Malcolm's idea. We watch the future king *think* his way toward victory. Macbeth has spent the play asking the Witches what will happen, but here Malcolm asks himself what he can *make* happen. This suggests a clear difference between tyranny and legitimate rule. Branagh (2013) and Best (2014) understand this; they trust Malcolm's words and strategy to do the actual heavy lifting.

CHAPTER 35
SOUND AND FURY, / SIGNIFYING NOTHING
ACT FIVE SCENE FIVE

At a glance

- **Plot and character development:** Macbeth hears news of Lady Macbeth's death and that Birnam Wood appears to be moving toward his castle.
- **Social and historical context:** 'All the world's a stage'
- **Vocabulary:** Defiance and nihilism
- **Big question:** How does Shakespeare present the impact of Lady Macbeth's death on her husband?
- **Themes:**
    - Fate vs free will
    - Guilt and conscience
    - Appearance vs reality
- **Analysis:**
    - Macbeth's soliloquy
    - Motif: time
    - Motif: threes
    - Motif: darkness and light
- **Key quotation:** 'sound and fury, / Signifying nothing'
- **Handle with care:** This scene contains a profound expression of existential despair and the meaninglessness of life. Be mindful of students who may be sensitive to or struggling with these themes.

PAUSE POINT

KNOWLEDGE RETRIEVAL

Revisit key quotations describing Macbeth in Act One Scene Two. As you teach this scene, draw students' attention to the contrast between how Shakespeare presents Macbeth at the beginning and end of the play.

Plot and character development

This scene is the dramatic and philosophical climax of Macbeth's arc. He begins with the hollow, battle-hardened bravado of a tyrant, but the news of his wife's death and the moving of Birnam Wood destroy the two remaining pillars of his existence: his personal relationship and his supernatural security. His response is not rage, or even total surrender, but a compelling combination of nihilism and defiance.

Social and historical context

'All the world's a stage'

The notion that 'all the world's a stage' (*theatrum mundi*) was a familiar philosophical idea in Shakespeare's time, often used for moral reflection. However, Shakespeare's innovation was to internalise this concept to highlight Macbeth's profound nihilism. He transforms it from a general observation (made famous in his beloved comedy *As You Like It*) to a character's devastating personal revelation. By having Macbeth – a king and warrior – conclude that life is a 'tale told by an idiot,' Shakespeare transforms a common trope into a shattering, nihilistic climax.

Vocabulary | Defiance and nihilism

As we approach the end, Macbeth vacillates between defiance and nihilism: on the one hand he refuses to submit to his attackers, on the other he believes that his existence lacks value and direction.

Instead of using a traditional Frayer Model, give students the table below. This format helps students contrast the two attitudes tearing at Macbeth.

	Defiance	**Nihilism**
Definition	Refusing to follow the rules. Refusing to submit to authority.	The belief that all values are baseless and that nothing can be known or communicated.

Examples	A student might be defiant in school if they refuse to follow an instruction. Macbeth defies the Divine Right of Kings by committing regicide.	Macbeth's belief in Act Five Scene Five that nothing matters anymore, now that Lady Macbeth is dead.
Use it in a sentence	Shakespeare presents Macbeth as defiant when...	Shakespeare presents Macbeth as nihilistic when...

Reading the scene

Despite the apparent coldness of Macbeth's line 'she should have died hereafter', the death of Lady Macbeth seems to shake his determination and focus. Shakespeare highlights how Lady Macbeth provided an emotional foundation for her husband, spurred him to action and helped him to achieve the 'golden round'. Without her, Macbeth seems to lose direction.

Read the whole scene and then do a slow reading of Macbeth's soliloquy.

- Read the text through once so that students hear accurate pronunciation of the vocabulary.
- Prepare to read the text again. Ask students to highlight two details (words or images) they notice about the text during this second reading.
- Students then discuss their choices in triplets: what stood out to them and why? Did they like the sound of the word or phrase? Did they recognise an image you have explored before? Take feedback and annotate the scene.

Make sure you have discussed:

- Macbeth's reflections on time, which seems to be progressing at an excruciatingly slow pace – even as the play propels him toward his inevitable death. The triple repetition ('tomorrow and tomorrow and tomorrow') may link Macbeth's nihilism to the Witches, who do so much in threes. Their machinations have led to Macbeth's total despair.
- The image of 'dusty death'. This alludes to the burial service ('ashes to ashes, and dust to dust') and links with nihilism: Macbeth believes that all that will remain of a person is a pile of dust.
- The image of the candle being extinguished. The repetition of 'out' and the 'candle' echoes Lady Macbeth in Act Five Scene One ('out damned spot' and the light that she needs constantly by her side). This echo indicates that both husband and wife have been damned, plunged into torment and despair by their shared guilt. The 'brief' life of the candle indicates Macbeth's belief that any joy or hope in this short life is quickly extinguished.
- The final words – 'signifying nothing' – conclude the soliloquy with a profound feeling of nihilism.

Big question

How does Shakespeare present the impact of Lady Macbeth's death on her husband?

The news of Lady Macbeth's death produces not grief, but a kind of numbness that catalyses Macbeth's existential despair. His detached response, 'She should have died hereafter,' reveals a man beyond conventional emotion, generalising her end into a universal principle of futility in his soliloquy. Her death severs his last earthly tether, transforming his ambition into dust. Yet, this very nihilism becomes the foundation for his final defiance. Having concluded that life 'signifies nothing,' he is liberated from fear and hope alike. Regardless of what might happen in 'the life to come', Shakespeare indicates that Macbeth will perform his role to the end. When Macbeth chooses to 'die with harness on our back,' it is not for victory, but as a stark act of self-assertion against a meaningless universe.

PAUSE POINT

ORACY

Macbeth's statement that Lady Macbeth 'should have died hereafter' provides rich opportunities for analysis of language methods. Scaffold students' understanding of Shakespeare's choice of words by doing this substitution activity.

Tell students they are going to consider Macbeth's reaction to Lady Macbeth's death, and give students a copy of the table below.

Read the prompts below one by one, giving students time to build sentences using one phrase from each column.

Prompts:

- Macbeth's response to Lady Macbeth's death is loving and heartbroken (e.g. Students might construct the line: *My dearest love should never have perished at all*).
- Macbeth's response is cold and uncaring.
- Macbeth's response is formal.
- Macbeth's response is patronising and belittling.
- Macbeth's response is frustrated and annoyed.

Start of sentence	Modal verb	Verb	End of sentence
She	should	have died	hereafter.
The Queen	would	have perished	anyway.
My dearest partner of greatness	might	have passed away	later on.
My dearest love	could	have expired	whenever.
Our hostess	should never	have faded	at some point.
My dearest chuck	deserved to	succumbed	at all.

Remind students of the real quotation: 'she should have died hereafter'. Engage students in a whole-class discussion about Shakespeare's choice of words.

For example, why did Shakespeare choose the impersonal pronoun 'she' instead of repeating the earlier line 'my dearest partner of greatness'? This shift demonstrates the growing coldness between Macbeth and Lady Macbeth, as he emotionally isolated himself after the regicide.

Themes

Fate vs free will

Macbeth sees the moving wood and acknowledges his fate: 'I 'gin to be aweary of the sun, / And wish the estate o' the world were now undone.' What's worse, he begins 'to doubt the equivocation of the fiend': he no longer trusts the Witches' prophecies at all. However, he still exercises a final, defiant act of free will: he chooses to go out fighting, not because he believes in victory any more, but because it is the only action left to him. 'At least we'll die with harness on our back.'

Guilt and conscience

Macbeth receives news of his wife's death not with grief but with resignation: 'She should have died hereafter.' The line shows not coldness but exhaustion: his conscience has no energy left for remorse. Unlike his wife, whose guilt drove her to fevered sleepwalking, Macbeth's guilt has calcified into meaninglessness. Conscience, for Macbeth, does not arrive as a pang of regret; it arrives as the total extinction of all meaning. Lady Macbeth's guilt drove her to frantic motion, but Macbeth's drives him only to stillness. Shakespeare shows us, in this moment, that a guilty conscience need not punish with nightmares and visions; it can simply leave a man alone with what he has become.

Appearance vs reality

See 'Key quotation' section, page 218.

Analysis

Macbeth's soliloquy

Shakespeare uses this soliloquy as the nihilistic climax of his tragic arc, reducing his existence to a meaningless performance. He has sacrificed his humanity for a fruitless crown. Life, he concludes, is a mere 'walking shadow,' an actor strutting pointlessly on stage. The repetitive rhythm of 'Tomorrow, and tomorrow, and tomorrow' suggests the relentless tedium of a future stripped of purpose. This is not just despair, but a profound emptiness; his reign, his wife's death, and his own impending doom are all just a 'tale / Told by an idiot, full of sound and fury, signifying nothing.'

Motif: time

Time, which for Macbeth has been a chaotic force ('the future in the instant'), is now stripped of all meaning. The word 'tomorrow' is repeated to show its endless, monotonous and empty cycle. Time no longer leads to achievement or legacy; it merely stretches into a pointless succession of days, 'creep[ing] in this petty pace,' until death.

Motif: threes

The magical power of three, introduced so powerfully in the domain of the 'secret, black, and midnight hags,' is now drained of all excitement. The repetition of 'tomorrow' echoes the Witches' thrice-repeated charms, but for Macbeth it is a monotonous daytime rhythm under the wearying sun, leading to dusty death. All of the excitement of the prophecies has vanished into thin air; now Macbeth's wife, his security and his hope of survival are gone too.

Motif: darkness and light

Shakespeare directly contrasts 'brief candle' in Macbeth's soliloquy with the pervasive darkness of the play, serving as the motif's final, bleak summation. This fragile light recalls the literal candle Lady Macbeth requires to ward off her psychological darkness, yet Macbeth extends it into a universal metaphor. He concludes that life is not a triumphant dawn but a 'walking shadow,' a fleeting image projected by a feeble flame. The line 'Out, out, brief candle!' (also echoing Lady Macbeth) acknowledges her death and the darkness that will now overwhelm him.

Key quotation | 'sound and fury, / Signifying nothing'

If the *theatrum mundi* idea invited audiences to see the world as a stage and life as a play, *Macbeth* draws a darker conclusion. In this line, Shakespeare ties up a theme that has been at work since Act One: appearance vs reality. He has carefully avoided too much talk of Macbeth as an actor through the play, but here he allows the line between character and performer to blur, as Macbeth realises that all his lies and deceptions – all, in a sense, performances – have cost him dearly. Earlier, we saw Macbeth as the hesitant actor, coached by Lady Macbeth to 'look like the innocent flower, / But be the serpent under't.' Then came his histrionic, over-the-top performance upon Duncan's discovery in Act Two, Scene Three, played with enough passion to deflect suspicion of his guilt. Now the actor has seen behind the curtain. The 'poor player' of Macbeth's soliloquy is not just a metaphor he invents; it is also a profound self-indictment. He realises he was that player, strutting and fretting through his bloody reign. The 'sound and fury' of his earlier performances (the false grief, the feigned outrage, the declarations of power) all feel as hollow as his fruitless crown. This scene concludes the arc that began with conscious role-playing and ends with the nihilistic realisation that it was all just a performance, and that now his exit looms.

PAUSE POINT

CONSOLIDATION

Triplet discussion: 'Shakespeare presents Macbeth moving between defiance and nihilism in this scene.' Which attitude wins in the end?

- Student A: Argue that Macbeth is more defiant than nihilistic.
- Student B: Argue that Macbeth is more nihilistic than defiant.
- Student C: Summarise the discussion.

Model answer:

Throughout this scene, Macbeth's actions are more defined by defiance than despair. Lady Macbeth's death prompts a moment of reflection, but it does not paralyse him; immediately after the soliloquy, he calls for his armour and prepares for battle. When the messenger arrives with news of Birnam Wood moving, Macbeth's response is fury ('liar and slave!') and he threatens the messenger with death. This is not a man who has surrendered. He clings to the witches' remaining prophecy: 'Fear not, till Birnam Wood / Do come to Dunsinane.' Even as the world collapses around him, Macbeth searches for something to hold onto, some reason to keep fighting. His final command in the scene – 'Ring the alarum-bell! Blow, wind! come, wrack! / At least we'll die with harness on our back' – suggests that Macbeth is defiant to the last.

However, Macbeth's nihilism in this scene is profound and inescapable. His response to Lady Macbeth's death ('She should have died hereafter') is not coldness but exhaustion; grief itself has become meaningless. The 'Tomorrow' soliloquy articulates a universe stripped of purpose: life is a 'walking shadow', a 'tale told by an idiot, full of sound and fury, signifying nothing.' This is not momentary despair but a settled philosophy. The witches' equivocations have hollowed him out, leaving a man who no longer believes in honour, love or obedience. When the messenger brings news of Birnam Wood, Macbeth's fury is fleeting; beneath it lies the creeping realisation that the prophecies may have been deceptive. His final lines in the scene ('Blow, wind! come, wrack!') sound defiant, but they are the words of a man who has already concluded that life signifies nothing. He fights because there is nothing left to do but fight.

Ultimately, the two attitudes are intertwined. Nihilism has emptied the world of meaning, but defiance fills the space where meaning once was. Macbeth no longer believes in anything, but he will still fight. That paradox is what makes this scene so compelling: he is a man who has concluded that life signifies nothing, but cannot stop himself from acting as if it does. In the end, nihilism wins the argument, but defiance dictates Macbeth's final actions.

Upon the stage

The 'Tomorrow' soliloquy is one of the greatest challenges and opportunities for an actor playing Macbeth. Sir Ian McKellen (Nunn, 1979) delivered it with a quiet and introspective horror, making the audience lean in to witness his internal collapse. In contrast, Sir Patrick Stewart (Goold, 2010) spoke it over Lady Macbeth's corpse on a gurney, in a moment of calm before his towering rage at the messenger. Rory Kinnear (Norris, 2018) spoke the text cradling his Lady in his arms.

Encourage your students to debate which interpretation is more powerful: the despair of a man who has gone numb, or the rage of a man who realises his life has been a waste.

CHAPTER 36
CLAMOROUS HARBINGERS OF BLOOD AND DEATH
ACT FIVE SCENE SIX

At a glance

- **Plot and character development:** Outside Macbeth's castle and Dunsinane, Malcolm, Siward and Macduff give the battle cry. The men are to throw down their 'leafy screens' and show themselves.
- **Themes:**
  - Appearance vs reality
  - Conflict
- **Analysis:**
  - Language: corrupted speech
  - Image: trumpets as harbingers
- **Key quotation:** 'Make all our trumpets speak; give them all breath, / Those clamorous harbingers of blood and death.'

Analysis

Language: corrupted speech

This scene concludes Malcolm's journey from England to Macbeth's castle: it is finally time for battle. The 'leafy screens' that disguised the approaching army are thrown down, and in a final stripping away of pretence, directly after Macbeth's own realisations in the previous scene, appearance and reality become one. There is no more need for spies, prophecies, or equivocation. Macduff does not ask the trumpets to signal or summon; he asks them to speak. Throughout the play, speech has been corrupted: witches prevaricate, Macbeth lies, Lady Macbeth deceives. Now, at last, language abandons deception altogether.

Image: trumpets as harbingers

The trumpets announce only what is about to happen: blood and death. They are 'harbingers,' noisy messengers announcing a violence that no longer wears a mask. In this line, Shakespeare makes explicit what the entire play has been moving toward: a confrontation no longer mediated by pretence, only by violence.

Upon the stage

This scene is an opportunity for spectacle, as Malcolm's army enters disguised as Birnam Wood. Ninagawa's Japanese production (1980) was probably the most spectacular, since his production used images of cherry blossoms throughout and they appeared here as a very beautiful moving glade. The Japanese reading of cherry blossoms as a metaphor for life's transience permeated the entire show, but seeing soldiers wielding them as they marched into battle was a particularly evocative image. By contrast, Best's (2014) Globe production presented a handful of tall branches, more useful as percussion than disguise. Elegant, if perfunctory, they were swiftly discarded and added to the set design. Coen had an impressive forest – whose leaves fluttered constantly into Macbeth's castle – exemplifying the kinds of imagery possible on screen but not on stage. Findlay's stripped-down RSC production (2018) ignored the image entirely, resulting in a final showdown that was intensely personal and even private.

Ninagawa transformed the grove into a meditation on mortality; Findlay rejected the image altogether. Ask your students what a genuinely theatrical Birnam Wood would look like *to them* – and what might it argue?

CHAPTER 37
THEY HAVE TIED ME TO A STAKE; I CANNOT FLY
ACT FIVE SCENE SEVEN

At a glance

- **Plot and character development:** The battle rages and we get three glimpses into its progress; Macbeth fights Young Siward, Macduff searches for Macbeth and then Malcolm and Siward prepare to enter the castle.
- **Social and historical context:** Bear-baiting
- **Vocabulary:** Inevitable
- **Big question:** Why does Macbeth kill Young Siward?
- **Themes:**
  - Fate vs free will
  - Disorder and the unnatural
- **Analysis:**
  - Staging: battle scenes
  - Dramatic irony
- **Key quotation:** 'They have tied me to a stake; I cannot fly'

PAUSE POINT

RETRIEVAL

Young Siward here uses the word tyrant to insult Macbeth.

Remind students of the meaning of this word (see Chapter 20).

Challenge students to use the word in a range of sentences:

1. Shakespeare presents Macbeth as a tyrant when...
2. Shakespeare reveals Macduff's criticism of Macbeth's tyranny when...
3. Shakespeare warns his audience about the impact of tyranny by...

Plot and character development

The battle reaches its climax. Macbeth, isolated on the battlefield, boasts of his charmed life before slaying Young Siward. Macduff, alone, insists that he will only fight Macbeth and elsewhere Malcolm and Siward believe victory is imminent.

Social and historical context

Bear-baiting

In Shakespeare's London, bear-baiting was a savage public spectacle where a tethered bear was attacked by dogs for entertainment. This scene begins with Macbeth likening himself to such a bear; the image perfectly captures Macbeth's devolution in his final moments. Two scenes ago he saw himself as a tragic actor upon life's stage, but now he is reduced to a trapped animal, tied to his fate and fighting instinctively against the hounds that besiege him.

Vocabulary | Inevitable

Shakespeare may present Macbeth as still confident in his kingship, but the audience now realises that his death is inevitable.

Definition:	**Morphology:**
An event is certain to happen; it cannot be avoided.	Prefix: in = not e.g. inaccurate, incomplete, indecisive Root word: evitare = to avoid e.g. evade, evasive
Related words:	**Use it in a sentence:**
Definite, fatal, destiny, inescapable, unavoidable	Macbeth's fate is inevitable because... Macbeth's fate is inevitable, but...

PAUSE POINT

S-T-R-E-T-C-H

Triplet discussion: Why does Shakespeare present Macbeth as feeling overconfident?

- Student A: Respond to the question.
- Student B: Provide evidence or examples to support Student A's ideas.
- Student C: Summarise the discussion.

Model answer:

Shakespeare reveals that Macbeth's overconfidence stems firstly from his *hamartia* (fatal flaw): *hubris*. His prowess in battle at the start of the play, his successful accession to the throne and subsequent elimination of threats against his kingship mean he now feels secure. Macbeth's visit to the Witches have further strengthened his resolve: he believes he cannot be killed until seemingly impossible events happen. Yet Act Five Scene Two has hinted that the first of these (Birnam Wood walking to Dunsinane Hill) may be less impossible than it first appears.

Reading the scene

This scene includes three separate vignettes, reflecting the chaos and noise of battle.

First, Macbeth kills Young Siward. Then Macduff searches for Macbeth. Finally, Malcolm and Siward prepare to enter the castle.

Demonstrate this by choosing readers in three separate areas of the classroom.

Big question

Why does Macbeth kill Young Siward?

Macbeth kills Young Siward as a defiant affirmation of his 'charmed life,' clinging to the prophecy that none of woman born can harm him. This victory is thematically significant, because it is his last. Ever since he heard the Witches' first prophecy, that he would be king but that Banquo's children would be kings, Macbeth has attacked the children of his opponents; he forced Malcolm and Donalbain to flee, orchestrated the attempted murder of Banquo's son Fleance, slaughtered Macduff's children and now kills the son of Siward, the commander besieging his castle. Ever since Lady Macbeth's chilling line about dashing a baby's brains out, there has been a steady increase in violence against the young. Shakespeare shows how Macbeth attempts to eradicate the lineage of his enemies; Young Siward is the last of these killings. In shocking contrast with Duncan, who wanted to 'plant' his courtiers and see them 'full of growing', Macbeth systematically cuts down any hope of future generations.

PAUSE POINT

ORACY

In the second half of the play, many characters refer to Macbeth as a 'tyrant'. Sometimes, they add an adjective beforehand:

- Macduff (Act Four Scene Three): 'untitled tyrant'.
- Siward (Act Five Scene Four): 'confident tyrant'.
- Young Siward (Act Five Scene Seven): 'abhorred tyrant'.

Explore the meanings of each adjective with the class. Then ask students to work in triplets. Allocate one quotation to each student in the triplet. Give them two minutes to consider the connotations of the adjective in their quotation. Then ask students to feedback to their triplet, and finally to the whole class.

Themes

Fate vs free will

In this scene, Macbeth's belief in his 'charmed life' represents a final, fatal surrender of his free will to the concept of a pre-determined fate. Shakespeare presents him as no longer making choices based on ambition or strategy, but acting as a mere agent of the prophecies, believing his actions are consequence-free. This perceived invincibility is the ultimate trap set by fate, rendering him reckless and steering him directly towards the one man destined to destroy him.

Disorder and the unnatural

Macbeth's killing of Young Siward is the culmination of his war against the natural order, specifically the succession of generations. By destroying the son, he attacks the future itself. This act directly contrasts with the natural, generative authority of a true king like Duncan, who 'planted' his courtiers, and proves Macbeth's rule fundamentally sterile and destructive. He is not a king who nurtures his kingdom's future but a blight that cuts it down, an unnatural force that must be purged for Scotland to be healed.

Analysis

Staging: battle scenes

As mentioned in Act One Scene Two, Shakespeare was limited by the conventions of the Jacobean stage. He could not depict large-scale battles the way we might see in an epic movie. Instead, he creates the illusion of warfare through series of compressed, emblematic vignettes: the chaos of the final battle is conveyed through swift, brutal encounters: Macbeth's defiant skirmish with Young Siward, Macduff's frantic search for the tyrant and Malcolm and Siward's strategic advance. These provide a visceral sense of the conflict's scope and key personal stakes without a sprawling cast or set.

Dramatic irony

While today the phrase suggests a blessed, fortunate existence, Macbeth's declaration is steeped in tragic irony. His 'charm' is not a benign blessing but a supernatural curse woven by the 'juggling fiends.' He voices this twisted confidence just after slaying Young Siward, a deed that solidifies his belief in his own invincibility. However, this perceived immunity is the very trap that seals his fate; it is a 'charmed life' in the most literal and damning sense, a hex that makes him reckless and delivers him, unafraid, into the path of the one man not born of woman.

Key quotation | 'They have tied me a stake; I cannot fly'

This metaphor marks Macbeth's final, stark moment of self-awareness. Unlike his earlier grand soliloquies, this is a simple, brutal admission of his trapped state. He is no longer the 'player' on a stage but a beast condemned to a pit. The line reveals his acceptance of a grim new role: he cannot escape his fate, so he must turn and face it with pure, animalistic fury. This is the transition from the philosopher-king to cornered hell-hound.

PAUSE POINT

CONSOLIDATION

Ask students to re-read the scene independently and select one key moment.

Give them three minutes to write an explanation of why they have selected this moment, before taking verbal feedback from the class.

Students could consider how Shakespeare presents:

- The tyrant Macbeth in contrast to the honourable and courageous Young Siward.
- Macbeth's continued reliance on the prophecies.
- Macduff's desire for revenge.

Upon the stage

Eve Best's (2014) Globe production brilliantly captured the swift movement between the scenes of Act Five. Joseph Millson's Macbeth ran onstage through a crowd of exiting enemies and seemed every inch the trapped animal, tied to the stake. The struggle with Young Siward was startling, because Macbeth overcame the younger man and then killed him with his own sword. Comparably in Rufus Norris's (2018) National Theatre production, Rory Kinnear's Macbeth rejected his armour and stood roaring, bear-like, amid a forest of tall stakes in set designer Rae Smith's extraordinary set.

Ask your students to consider if Macbeth is still heroic in this scene: can a powerful actor make us sympathise with Macbeth even at the bitter end?

CHAPTER 38
DESPAIR THY CHARM
ACT FIVE SCENE EIGHT (LINES 1 TO 34)

At a glance

- **Plot and character development:** Macbeth and Macduff find each other and trade barbs before their decisive fight.
- **Social and historical context:** Childbirth
- **Vocabulary:** Anagnorisis
- **Big question:** Does Shakespeare present Macbeth's death as that of a tragic hero or a tyrant?
- **Themes:**
  - Appearance vs reality
  - Fate vs free will
  - Ambition and power
- **Analysis:**
  - Language: the naming of evil
  - Motif: public entertainment
- **Key quotation:** 'Despair thy charm'
- **Handle with care:** At the start of the scene, Macbeth refers to suicide.

Plot and character development

Macduff finally confronts Macbeth. Their showdown begins with Macbeth initially confident until Macduff reveals the crucial loophole in the prophecy: he was not 'of woman born' but was 'from his mother's womb / Untimely ripped'. Macbeth's spirit collapses and he refuses to fight. Macduff taunts him and Macbeth exits the stage, resolved to fight to the death but now devoid of all hope.

Social and historical context

Childbirth

In Jacobean England, childbirth was perilous, often fatal and shrouded in superstition. For a culture obsessed with lineage and inheritance, every birth was a negotiation with death. This context casts a dark shadow over the play, where the natural process of lineage and inheritance is systematically violated. Lady Macbeth's allusions to a baby whose brains she would have 'dashed out', the murder of Lady Macduff and her children and the Witches' gruesome, stolen ingredients all pervert the image of motherhood. Macduff's Caesarean birth is the most extreme example: he is a man defined by a birth that likely killed his mother, setting him in direct opposition to Macbeth, a man whose actions have killed the future itself. The play is haunted by the violence done to mothers and children, framing Macbeth's entire reign as a threat to nature's most fundamental order.

PAUSE POINT

RETRIEVAL

Shakespeare's emphasis on Macbeth's determination to fight mirrors the description of him as a respected warrior in Act One Scene Two.

Re-read the earlier scene and discuss how Shakespeare presented Macbeth's dauntless attitude to battle, his celebrated heroism and his patriotic decapitation of the traitor, Macdonwald.

As you read Act Five Scene Eight, support students in identifying similarities and differences between the scenes.

Vocabulary | Anagnorisis

As Macbeth faces Macduff, he has a moment of realisation: Macduff has not been born of woman and is therefore able to kill him.

Definition:	**Morphology:**
The protagonist has a moment of realisation or discovery.	Prefix: ana- = again or back Root word: gnōri- = knowledge

Examples:	**Non-examples (from *Macbeth*):**
Macbeth: when the tragic hero realises that the Witches have deceived him in relation to Birnam Wood, and Macduff not being of woman born.	Lady Macbeth dies without knowing the truth about the Witches' deception.
Oedipus Rex: when Oedipus realises that he himself is the murderer that has brought the plague upon Thebes.	Duncan is killed before he realises the truth about Macbeth's malevolence.

Reading the scene

Like many scenes in the play, there are several emotional shifts in this section.

Prepare students by asking them to rehearse key lines from the scene in their triplets:

Line	**Meaning**	**Emotion**
Macduff: 'turn, hell-hound, turn'	Macduff commands Macbeth to face him for battle.	Fury, rage, determination
Macbeth: 'my soul is too much charged / With blood of thine already'	Macbeth taunts Macduff by reminding him that he is responsible for the deaths of his family.	Mocking, taunting
Macbeth: 'I bear a charmed life, which must not yield / To one of woman born'.	Macbeth believes the Witches' prophecies completely and thinks he is invincible.	Confident, arrogant
Macduff: 'Macduff was from his mother's womb / Untimely ripped'	Macduff was born by Caesarean section and therefore technically was not 'of woman born'.	Triumphant
Macbeth: 'be these juggling fiends no more believed.'	Macbeth realises that the Witches (the 'juggling fiends') have been playing with him. He realises that he has been deceived.	Angry, defeated
Macbeth: 'I will not yield / To kiss the ground before young Malcolm's feet.'	Macbeth will not surrender, as he would have to accept Malcolm as king.	Defiant, determined to fight to the end

Then read the scene.

Big question

Does Shakespeare present Macbeth's death as that of a tragic hero or a tyrant?

Shakespeare presents Macbeth as both, and this is one reason for the play's enduring power. He is undoubtedly a tyrant in his actions: a regicidal usurper, a murderer of women and children and a blight upon Scotland. His death is a necessary and just purge. However, he meets that death with the consciousness of a tragic hero. He is not a mere monster like the 'hell-hound' Macduff names; he is a man who, in his final moments, fully comprehends the emptiness of his choices and the scale of his own damnation. His decision to 'try the last' is a final, flawed act of free will, a choice to face the consequences of his actions head-on. He dies not in ignorant defiance, but in clear-eyed despair, allowing the audience to witness the ruin of a great soul, thus fulfilling the tragic arc. He is a tyrant the world is right to destroy, but a hero whose internal ruin we are compelled to mourn.

PAUSE POINT

S-T-R-E-T-C-H

Macbeth insists that he will not 'yield / To kiss the ground beneath young Malcolm's feet'. He is aware that his defeat is inevitable, but insists that he will not submit to the rightful king.

Ask students to think-pair-share Shakespeare's presentation of the reasons for Macbeth's decision. Students could consider how Shakespeare presents:

- Macbeth's *hubris*.
- Macbeth's fear of public shame.
- Malcolm's relative lack of physical courage (compare the presentation of Malcolm and Macbeth in Act One Scene Two).
- Malcolm's youth.

Themes

Appearance vs reality

The apparent truth of the prophecy, that Macbeth was essentially invulnerable, is revealed to have been unequivocally false. The reality is that he was never protected; he was being herded toward this specific doom by the 'juggling fiends.' The 'hell-hound' is exposed as a mortal man; his 'charmed life' is shown to have come to naught.

Fate vs free will

The play's prophecies are fulfilled by fate, but Macbeth exercises a final, grim act of free will. He knows he will lose, and initially says he will not fight Macduff because he's already spilled enough of his family's blood. But finally he chooses to 'try the last,' raising his sword not to change his destiny, but to meet it with heroic defiance. His agency is stripped down to this one choice: how to face his inevitable end.

Ambition and power

Macbeth's ambition, which once promised him the world, has shrunk to this: all he has left is his grim survival instinct, devoid of purpose or legacy, facing single combat against a justified and motivated opponent. Macduff stands as Macbeth's antithesis. He seeks no crown, no title and no advancement. He has joined with Malcolm not to acquire power but to extinguish tyranny. He acts from duty alone, avenging his family and asking nothing for himself. Macbeth's ambition required continual feeding through bloodshed, but Macduff's resolve asks for no reward. Shakespeare concludes his examination of Macbeth's ambition not with its triumph, nor even its confession, but with its reduction to mere animal desperation.

Analysis

Language: the naming of evil

The Witches, first introduced as the mysterious 'Weird Sisters' whose prophecies seemed like fate, are now identified by Macbeth as 'juggling fiends'. Banquo knew from the start that they were 'instruments of darkness', but Macbeth was more seduced by them. This shift, from mystical to malevolent, reveals his belated understanding that they were never neutral arbiters of destiny but active deceivers 'palter[ing]' with him 'in a double sense.' This revelation is mirrored in his own trajectory. The play's first description of him as 'Valour's minion,' a heroic servant of bravery, has collapsed into Macduff's descriptive name: 'hell-hound.' He is no longer a man, but a panting minion of evil, a servant or an animal rather than a warrior. Together, these renamed identities strip away all ambiguity: the 'fiends' have manipulated the 'hell-hound,' and he must now face his final reckoning.

Motif: public entertainment

The idea of public entertainment traces Macbeth's catastrophic fall in terms of his public image, culminating in Macduff's ultimate threat. He began hailed as a hero, a role he embraced. He then saw himself as a tragic 'actor' upon life's stage, before being reduced to a baited 'bear', a spectacle of savage, trapped fury. Now, Macduff presents the final, degrading possibility: if he yields, he will become a passive object of ridicule ('the show and gaze o' th' time'), a painted joke on a pole for the masses to gawk at and jeer.

This descent, from hero to actor to beast to 'rarer monster', is too much for Macbeth. The threat of such an ending forces him to choose a warrior's death not for honour or victory, but to reject this final, emasculating role and reclaim his agency, even in defeat.

Key quotation | 'Despair thy charm'

Macduff's command is a devastating blow. He does not merely state a fact; he orders Macbeth to abandon the very core of his identity. Shakespeare uses the word 'despair' as an imperative verb here, as Macduff orders Macbeth to abandon whatever hope he may have left. The Witches 'wound up' their charm right before Macbeth's first entrance. He himself boasted about his 'charmed life': now the 'charm' that defined Macbeth's last acts is not just broken; it is revealed to have never existed, making his past confidence and violence seem not just wicked, but deluded.

PAUSE POINT

CONSOLIDATION

Ask students to compare and contrast Shakespeare's presentation of Macbeth in his first and last lines in the play. You could support students further by providing images of Macbeth in each scene:

- Act One Scene Three: 'So fair and foul a day I have not seen.'
- Act Five Scene Eight: 'Lay on, Macduff; / And damn'd be him that first cries, 'Hold, enough!'

Students could consider how Shakespeare presents:

- Macbeth as a warrior – returning from battle, or about to enter combat. Shakespeare presents Macbeth's military prowess as central to his identity. However, at the start of Act One Scene Three, he is loyal to Duncan, but at the denouement his only remaining loyalty is to himself and his reputation.
- Macbeth as being accompanied by his good friend Banquo in Act One Scene Three; by Act Five Scene Eight, Shakespeare reveals that Macbeth is isolated due to his own actions.
- A sense of ambiguity in Macbeth's first lines, while his final lines are focused and determined.

Upon the stage

The final encounter between Macbeth and Macduff is the face-off we have anticipated since their introduction as seeming equals in Act One. Their fight technically takes place offstage, but productions often find clever ways to show it. Welles (1948) brought back the crowned effigy molded by the Witches at the start of his film and knocked its head off, letting the smashed clay stand in for his own body. More gruesomely, both the Goold (2010) and Coen (2021) films had very realistic casts made of their respective star actors, brandished grimly in defeat. At the Globe, Best had Macbeth die centre-stage, before getting up and joining the full company in the theatre's customary jig.

Ask your students to consider what is ultimately more satisfying: dramatic symbolism, visceral horror or theatrical tradition? What does each staging choice reveal about how Macbeth should be remembered?

CHAPTER 39

THIS DEAD BUTCHER AND HIS FIEND-LIKE QUEEN

ACT FIVE SCENE EIGHT (LINES 35 TO END)

At a glance

- **Plot and character development:** Macduff re-enters with Macbeth's head, confirming the tyrant's death. Malcolm is hailed as king and, in a formal speech, establishes his rule, promising a return to peace, justice and natural order.
- **Social and historical context:** The Stone of Scone
- **Vocabulary:** Restoration of order
- **Big question:** Does the play have a hopeful ending?
- **Themes:**
  - Disorder and the unnatural
  - Kingship
  - The Divine Right of Kings
- **Analysis:**
  - The last prophecy
  - Image: the crown
- **Key quotation:** 'This dead butcher and his fiend-like queen'
- **Handle with care:** This scene deals with a decapitated head and political violence. Focus on the thematic resolution rather than the graphic detail.

PAUSE POINT

RETRIEVAL

Ask students to brain dump what they remember about Shakespeare's presentation of the killing of Macdonwald, which was reported in Act One Scene Two.

Students could consider how Shakespeare presents:

- Macdonwald as 'merciless'.
- Macbeth's initial loyalty and patriotism.
- The consequences of treachery.

Explain that in today's scene, Shakespeare shows that the action has come full cycle and now Macduff has decapitated Macbeth. The head that bore the 'golden round' has now been severed.

Plot and character development

The first section of the scene deals with Macbeth's killing of Young Siward. It picks up on the motif of masculine courage, as Siward asks whether his son died with his 'hurts before'. That is, Young Siward was wounded on the front, not the back, which demonstrates that he faced danger bravely.

The play then ends not with Macbeth's death, but with the restoration of political order. Macduff's entrance with Macbeth's head serves as a brutal but necessary indication that the threat has been eradicated. The focus then shifts entirely to Malcolm, who transforms from an awkward exile into a confident, gracious king. His exemplary speech shows sincere leadership: he dubs his supporters earls, calls home the exiles and vows to rule with 'grace' and 'measure, time, and place,' directly contrasting Macbeth's chaotic and murderous reign.

Social and historical context

The Stone of Scone

The Stone of Scone, also called the Stone of Destiny, is a powerful symbol of Scottish monarchy that Macbeth would have known well. Historically, it was used for centuries in the coronation of Scottish kings at Scone Palace. In 1296, it was captured by Edward I of England and placed in Westminster Abbey, where it resided for 700 years beneath the Coronation Chair to legitimise English, and later British, rule. Its recent return to Scotland, while still being loaned for future coronations, ensures this potent symbol of legacy and contested power, so central to Macbeth's themes, remains part of British royal ritual today. (See Rodell, *The Coronation Chair and Stone of Scone* (2013) for more detail.)

N.B. Scone is pronounced 'scoon' – (rhymes with spoon).

Vocabulary | Restoration of order

Ostensibly, the play concludes with the restoration of order; Malcolm takes the crown and establishes his authority within Scotland.

Definition:	**Characteristics:**
Chaos and violence are replaced by peace and harmony. The tyrannical usurper is succeeded by the rightful king.	• Violence is concluded. • Justice is enacted (Macbeth is killed). • The legitimate king takes the throne.
Examples:	**Non-examples:**
Othello (1603): There is some restoration of order as the murderer (Othello) is dead and Cassio becomes governor of Cyprus.	*Othello* (1603): Order is not completely restored because the play concludes in Cyprus, a place associated with chaos in the play. *An Inspector Calls* (1946): Order is not restored, as the final phonecall throws the family into disarray.

Reading the scene

This discussion is interrupted by Macduff bringing in Macbeth's head. The Rupert Goold production (2010) captures the shocking brutality of this moment, so you may wish to show a clip of this version.

Big question

Does the play have a hopeful ending?

The ending is ambiguous, balancing hard-won hope against profound loss. The hope lies in Malcolm's speech, which promises a new political system (the thanes are all made earls) and a return to the order that Macbeth shattered. But the cost has been catastrophic: a virtuous king (Duncan), a noble friend (Banquo), a mother and her children (the Macduffs) and Scotland itself have been brutalised. Siward's stoic reaction to his son's death ('He's worth more sorrow / And that I'll spend for him') reminds us of the personal toll. The peace is built on a foundation of graves, leaving the audience with a sober hope, not an untroubled celebration. Furthermore, Fleance's survival, while a victory over Macbeth's tyranny, also ensures that the Witches' prophecy of Banquo's lineage taking the throne still hangs over Malcolm's new reign like a shadow.

PAUSE POINT

S-T-R-E-T-C-H

Triplet discussion: 'Shakespeare ends chaos and restores order at the end of the play.' How far do you agree?

- Student A: Argue that order is restored.
- Student B: Argue that order is not restored.
- Student C: Summarise the discussion.

Model answer:

It could be argued that order is restored at the end of *Macbeth*, as the rightful heir is to become king of Scotland. Macduff has achieved his revenge and Macbeth's tyrannical reign has ended with his death. However, Shakespeare sows subtle seeds of doubt, as whilst Malcolm has the intelligence to lead (see his manipulation of Macduff in Act Four Scene Three), he is not presented as a strong military leader (see the reference to his rescue from enemy forces in Act One Scene Two). Additionally, his reaction to the news of Macduff's family reveals he lacks the empathy that an ideal leader would display. Furthermore, in Malcolm's final speech there is an uncanny echo of Duncan's lines in Act One: where Duncan said that he would make Macbeth 'full of growing', Malcolm also uses the imagery of 'plant[ing]'.

Shakespeare amplifies this unease by leaving two threads conspicuously unresolved. Fleance does not reappear, so the Witches' prophecy concerning Banquo's line remains unfulfilled. The Witches themselves are simply absent. Shakespeare does not defeat them or dismiss them. He lets them recede, which is more unsettling. Order may have been declared, but it has not quite been secured.

Themes

Disorder and the unnatural

The play concludes with order triumphing over chaos. Throughout, we have seen disorder and unnatural events, all set in motion by Duncan's murder, and these will be resolved by the killing of Macbeth. Malcolm's ascension ends the 'dead butcher's' reign of terror. His language is ordered, formal and public, signaling the return of law and stability after the feverish, internal soliloquies and supernatural chaos of Macbeth's rule. The crown, a symbol of divine order, is finally returned to its rightful head.

Kingship

Malcolm's speech provides the play's definitive model of good kingship. Unlike the paranoid, isolated Macbeth, Malcolm is inclusive, generous ('My thanes and kinsmen / Henceforth be earls'), and focused on the collective good of the nation. He embodies the qualities he and Macduff earlier tested: justice, temperance and piety.

The Divine Right of Kings

For a Jacobean audience, especially in the tense aftermath of the Gunpowder Plot, this conclusion was potentially reassuring. It dramatised the Divine Right of Kings, showing that a usurper could not prevail and that order would inevitably be restored. Malcolm's promise to rule by the 'grace of Grace' explicitly frames his kingship as divinely sanctioned. This would have deeply resonated with King James I, Shakespeare's patron, not only validating his philosophical beliefs but also offering a powerful piece of political propaganda: it reassured the king (and the nation) of his legitimate, God-ordained right to the throne, likening him to Malcolm as another king who saved his country from those who would destroy it.

Analysis

The last prophecy

The Witches' prophecy that Banquo's sons would be kings is the only one left intentionally unfulfilled on stage. By concluding with Malcolm's coronation, Shakespeare creates a moment of dramatic irony for his audience. King James I, who claimed descent from Banquo, was on the English throne. For them, the promise that Banquo's line would eventually reign was a historical fact, legitimising their own king as the ultimate, long-term victor in the play's conflict.

Image: the crown

The crown, which Macbeth seized through bloodshed, is now restored to its symbolic purpose. It is no longer an object of obsessive desire but a symbol of legitimate service and divine right. Its return to the rightful line through Malcolm's peaceful ascension represents the closing of a traumatic cycle and the healing of the 'disease' that had infected Scotland.

Key quotation | 'This dead butcher and his fiend-like queen'

Malcolm's epitaph for the Macbeths is a piece of public political rhetoric, not a nuanced character assessment. It brands the former rulers as monstrous and illegitimate, justifying his takeover. Reducing the complex, tormented Macbeth to a 'butcher' and Lady Macbeth to a 'fiend' is necessary for the state to move on, but this deliberately ignores the psychological tragedy the audience has witnessed. It shows the gap between how history remembers tyrants and the human complexity of their fall.

PAUSE POINT

CONSOLIDATION

Triplet discussion: Shakespeare presents Macbeth as transforming from a 'valiant' and respected warrior, to a maligned and 'dead butcher'. How does this transformation happen?

- Student A: Explain how the transformation happens.
- Student B: Provide evidence for this transformation.
- Student C: Summarise the discussion.

Model answer:

At the start of the play, Shakespeare establishes Macbeth's identity as a 'valiant' warrior, whose loyalty and violence are celebrated in the service of his king. However, Shakespeare also shows Macbeth's more personal ambitions through his immediate, 'rapt' reaction to the Witches' prophecy. This is not merely ambition enkindled, but a specific, dark potential within him being unlocked. The murder of Duncan is not a simple first step towards butchery, but the catastrophic moment where he consciously severs his public, loyal identity from his private, ambitious desires.

Yet, Shakespeare shows that the true mechanism of Macbeth's transformation is not the initial ambition, but the psychological aftermath of the regicide. The 'scorpions' in his mind are not just fear, but the manifestations of a profound and articulate guilt. This emotional anguish does not simply propel him to further murder; it systematically dismantles his ability to trust, to rest and to connect with others, including his wife. His subsequent violence against Banquo and Macduff's family is, therefore, a desperate and brutal attempt to build a wall of security around a self that is collapsing from within. He is not driven by fear alone, but by a tragic logic that tells him he is already so steeped in blood that turning back is impossible.

Shakespeare shows Macbeth's transformation through a chilling process of moral and psychological disintegration. Malcolm's label of 'dead butcher' is a necessary political simplification to secure his own reign, but it deliberately ignores the complex, imaginative life that makes Macbeth so tragically compelling. Macbeth falls not just because of ambition and fear, but because the act of murder shatters his very soul. He is left a hollowed-out man who can only navigate his self-made hell through further, increasingly nihilistic violence. His journey is not from hero to butcher, but from a man of multifaceted potential to a consciousness trapped in a nightmare of its own making.

Upon the stage

The play's ending – in which Malcolm delivers a politically shrewd but dramatically tepid final speech – often tempts directors to expand the final scene. Welles' film ends with the Witches still haunting the landscape, a choice also made in productions by Best (2014) and Findlay (2018). The Witches abandoned Patrick Stewart right before his final encounter with Macduff in the Goold film (2010) and did not appear at all at the optimistic, prayerful end of Branagh's production (2013). The question of Fleance is crucial. He reappeared very dramatically at the end of the Findlay production, armed with a sword and clearly gearing up to be the subject of the Witches' next enchantment. Coen (2021) showed Ross riding Fleance to safety in almost the final shot of the film.

Given how Holinshed traced a line from King James back to Banquo, it is understandable that productions might still explore ways to end the story with this connection, even if Shakespeare himself did not write it. Does Fleance's return represent hope and the restoration of the natural order, or does it suggest the cycle of violence and supernatural temptation is beginning anew? For a very rich discussion of Fleance, see the (2014) essay by William C. Carroll, 'Fleance in the Final Scene of Macbeth: The Return of the Repressed'.

By now your students should have a rich sense of the range of approaches this play can inspire and invite: ask them to debate what their ideal ending might communicate about the play's final attitude to the Macbeths.

CONCLUSION

Final reflections

As students reach the end of Macbeth, they may be left with a sense of profound unease; this is a play that moves with terrifying speed from prophecy to tyranny, while it lingers in the mind with its psychological depth and moral ambiguity. To help learners consolidate their understanding and engage with the play's enduring questions, invite them to reflect on the following:

Why does Shakespeare end with Malcolm's restoration, yet leave us with the memory of the Macbeths?

Shakespeare closes with the rightful king restored and order seemingly reclaimed. But the final image of Macbeth as a 'dead butcher' and Lady Macbeth as his 'fiend-like queen' feels reductive, almost like an attempt to tidy away the complex, tragic figures we have witnessed. Is this Shakespeare reassuring his Jacobean audience, or inviting us to question how history simplifies the messy truth of human ambition and fallibility?

Could Macbeth have stopped his descent at any point?

Learners might debate the moments where Macbeth's path might have diverged: after the prophecies? After Duncan's murder? Before Banquo's? Shakespeare meticulously dramatises each choice, but leaves us wondering: was this tragedy fated, or forged by Macbeth's own 'vaulting ambition'? When, if ever, was the point of no return?

Who is more responsible for the tragedy? Is it Macbeth, Lady Macbeth or the Witches?

The play refuses easy answers. The Witches prophesy but do not compel; Lady Macbeth orchestrates but does not wield the knife; Macbeth acts but is tormented by conscience. Is Shakespeare exploring how evil is a collaboration, between external temptation and internal ambition and corruption?

Is Macbeth a villain or a tragic hero?

By the end, Macbeth has become a tyrant who orders the murder of women and children. Yet Shakespeare gives him soliloquies of breathtaking poetry and psychological insight. Does the play ask us to condemn Macbeth, or to recognise in his downfall a warning about the seductive, corrupting nature of power?

PAUSE POINT

S-T-R-E-T-C-H

Deepen the debate further with these questions:

- **How does Shakespeare subvert expectations of gender and power?**
  Lady Macbeth's 'unsex me here' is one of the most radical speeches in literature. Her eventual breakdown, and Macbeth's descent into sterile tyranny, both suggest that violating 'natural' order comes at a terrible price. What is Shakespeare saying about masculinity, femininity and the sources of true power?
- **What does the play suggest about kingship and leadership?**
  Contrast Duncan's generous but naïve rule, Macbeth's paranoid tyranny, and Malcolm's calculated testing of Macduff. Does Shakespeare endorse the Divine Right of Kings, or show it as fragile, dependent on the morality of the individual?
- **Is *Macbeth* a play about fate or free will?**
  The Witches set the tragedy in motion, but Macbeth chooses to act. Does Shakespeare suggest our destinies are written, or that we write them ourselves through our choices?

Tracking themes

To help students see the play as a cohesive whole, return throughout your teaching to a central proposition, for example:

'Power corrupts, but conscience destroys.'

- Before reading: What do students understand by 'power' and 'conscience'?
- After Act Two: How has Macbeth's conscience responded to gaining power?
- After Act Four: How has his conscience changed as his power grows more brutal?
- After the play: To what extent does the ending support or challenge this idea?

Similarly, track the shifting sympathies of the audience:

- When do we pity Macbeth?
- Does he lose our sympathy? If so, when?
- How does Shakespeare make us feel about Lady Macbeth's madness?
- Does Macduff's vengeance feel like justice or further bloodshed?

Why teach Macbeth?

Not because it's on the exam. Not because it's a classic that must be taught. But because:

It is the most compressed psychological study Shakespeare ever wrote. In fewer than 2,500 lines, he charts a hero's descent into tyranny, a marriage's collapse and a nation's near-destruction, all driven by questions that still haunt us: What does ambition cost? Can guilt be outrun? Is evil something we choose, or something that chooses us?

It is a play about appearance and reality: about the 'false face' that must hide what the 'false heart' knows. About the roles we play and the selves we hide. About the moment the actor realises the performance has consumed the person.

It is a play about power: how it corrupts, how it isolates, how it makes monsters of those who grasp it and ghosts of those who do not. In an age of performative leadership and political crisis, *Macbeth* has never been more relevant.

Ultimately, *Macbeth* is a mirror. It shows us not just a medieval Scotland of witches and warfare, but the shadows within every society, and every self. To teach *Macbeth* is to give students a lens through which to examine the forces that drive history, politics and the human heart. It is, above all, a play that reminds us why Shakespeare remains not just relevant, but essential.

APPENDIX A: THEMES

Theme	Interpretation
Ambition and power	Shakespeare reveals the disastrous consequences of unchecked ambition and warns the audience about the damaging consequences of pursuing for power for its own sake. Unchecked ambition and lust for power are presented as corrupting forces.
Appearance vs reality	Shakespeare dramatises the disparity between deceptive appearances and hidden truths in the pursuit of power, ultimately revealing that façades of loyalty, masculinity or legitimacy cannot shield anyone from justice, fate or moral decay.
Conflict	From its very first scene, *Macbeth* establishes conflict as an inescapable and pervasive force, manifesting externally in war and rebellion and internally in the violent rupture between ambition and conscience, loyalty and treachery.
Disorder and the unnatural	The Macbeths' murder of Duncan is a catalyst, causing disorder both in the natural world (ominous weather, beasts behaving strangely, ghosts) and their own internal worlds (Macbeth's insomnia, Lady Macbeth's madness).
The Divine Right of Kings	The belief that royalty was anointed by God. James I was a fierce advocate for this doctrine.
Fate vs free will	Shakespeare poses an existential question: are our lives determined by fate, or do we have the free will to make autonomous choices?
Guilt and conscience	Shakespeare presents Macbeth as tormented by his deeds, revealing the psychological consequences of regicide.
Kingship	Shakespeare explores different models of kingship – from the benevolent but overly trusting Duncan, to the holy Edward the Confessor, to the tyrant Macbeth.
Loyalty vs treason	Shakespeare celebrates loyalty, while treason leads to duplicity and tyranny.
Tyranny	Tyranny is illegitimate power maintained by violence, which Shakespeare shows destroys the tyrant's humanity.
Violence and masculinity	Shakespeare binds violence and masculinity throughout: the same martial courage that makes Macbeth 'Valour's minion' leaves him defenceless when his wife weaponises that masculine ideal against him. Once legitimate bloodshed escalates to regicide, there is no braking mechanism: only the compulsive, isolating brutality of a man who must keep killing to remain, in his own eyes, a man.

APPENDIX B: MOTIFS

Motif	Quotations and interpretations
Birds	• I.ii: Macbeth and Banquo are compared to 'eagles' due to their courage in battle. • I.v: 'the raven' is an evil omen. • I.vi: Banquo notes the 'temple-haunting martlet' nesting in Macbeth's castle. He takes this as a good omen. • II.ii: Lady Macbeth hears an 'owl' shriek – an evil omen. • II.iv: The Old Man says that the 'mousing-owl' has killed a 'falcon'. This symbolises the killing of Duncan by Macbeth. • III.ii: Macbeth refers to the rook, which echoes Lady Macbeth's reference to the raven. • IV.ii and iii: Lady Macduff and her children are referred as the 'poor wren' and 'chickens', emphasising their vulnerability.
Blood and hands	• I.ii: Macbeth's sword 'smok'd with bloody execution' and he almost 'bathe[d] in reeking wounds.' Legitimate bloodshed is rewarded. • I.vii: Macbeth thinks that 'We but teach / Bloody instructions which... return to plague th' inventor'. He worries that he will set a precedent for regicide. • I.vii: Lady Macbeth evokes the horrific image of 'dash[ing] the brains out' of a child. She demonstrates an unparalleled capacity for violence. • II.ii: After the murder, Macbeth has 'hangman's hands' which Lady Macbeth says are a 'filthy witness' of the deed. • II.ii: As Macbeth laments 'Will all great Neptune's ocean wash this blood / Clean from my hand?', Lady Macbeth counters this with 'a little water clears us of this deed'. Macbeth is already haunted by guilt. • III.iv: Banquo's ghost has 'gory locks' that symbolise Macbeth's brutal betrayal of his friend. • III.iv: Macbeth recognises that 'Blood will have blood' – others will take their revenge on him. • III.iv: Macbeth is 'in blood stepped in so far'. The first murder has paved the way for others. • IV.i: Macbeth returns to the Witches, seeing the apparition of a 'bloody child'. • V.i: Lady Macbeth imagines blood on her hands: 'out damned spot'. 'All the perfumes of Arabia will not sweeten this little hand.' She is now haunted by guilt. • V.viii: Macbeth is reduced to a 'dead butcher', whose own blood is spilled.

Children	• I.iii: Shakespeare foregrounds the fact that Banquo has children ('your children shall be kings'). • I.vii: Lady Macbeth imagines committing an unspeakable act of violence against a baby ('dashed the brains out'). • III.i: Macbeth obsesses over his 'fruitless crown'. • III.iii: Macbeth orders the attempted murder of Fleance – a symbol of innocence who escapes the tyrant's grasp. • IV.i: The apparitions (a 'bloody child' and a 'child crowned') add to Macbeth's torment as he is unable to have children. • IV.ii: The 'savag[e] slaughter' of Macduff's children represents Macbeth's descent into tyranny and brutality.
Clothing	• I.iii: On becoming Thane of Cawdor, Macbeth is uncomfortable in his new identity: 'why do you dress me / In borrowed robes'. Banquo describes the title as 'strange garments'. • V.ii: Angus says that Macbeth's title 'hang[s] loose upon him, like a giant's robe / Upon a dwarfish thief'. Macbeth is a diminished figure, not fit to be king. • V.iii: Macbeth calls for his armour. He attempts to reclaim his old identity as a respected warrior.
Crown	• I.iii: Banquo says the prophecies might 'enkindle [Macbeth] to the crown'. The Witches have sparked Macbeth's ambition. • I.iii: Macbeth hopes that 'chance may crown me without my stir': he hopes to become king without committing murder. • I.v: Lady Macbeth wants to give Macbeth 'the golden round', which symbolises the allure of eternal power. • II.iv: Macduff says that Macbeth is 'gone to Scone / To be invested'. Macduff avoids the word crown, suggesting that Macbeth is not the rightful king. • III.i: Macbeth considers his 'fruitless crown'. • IV.i: The Witches taunt Macbeth with the image of a 'child crowned'. They show Banquo wearing a 'crown' that 'sears' Macbeth's 'eyeballs'. Macbeth is tormented by the thought that others will inherit the throne. • V.viii: Malcolm invites his followers to 'see us crowned at Scone'. The rightful heir has restored order and ended Macbeth's reign of terror.
Darkness and light	• I.iii: Banquo calls the Witches the 'instruments of darkness'. They are the epitome of evil. • I.iv: Duncan is connected to light and morality: he says 'signs of nobleness, like stars, shall shine / On all deservers'. • I.iv: Darkness invades Macbeth's mind. He says 'stars hide your fires' as he considers his 'black and deep desires'. • I.v: Lady Macbeth calls on 'thick night' to hide the murder from 'heaven'. • II.i: Just before the murder, Banquo comments on the unnatural darkness of the night: there's 'husbandry in heaven; / Their candles are all out'.

	• II.iii: After the murder, the Porter imagines that he is opening 'hell gate'. • II.iv: Ross says that 'dark night strangles the travelling lamp': it is unnaturally dark during the day. • III.iii: Banquo enters with a torch, but the murderers call for light, emphasising the contrast between good and evil. • III.iv: When Banquo appears at the banquet, Macbeth employs imagery of hell. • IV.i: The Witches convene in a 'dark cave', emblematic of their malevolence. • V.i: Lady Macbeth can almost see her future: 'hell is murky'. She carries a 'taper' (a candle) to ward off darkness. • V.v: Macbeth says 'out, brief candle'. Life and happiness can be quickly extinguished.
Disease and medicine	• IV.iii: King Edward is described as a good king, whose 'healing benediction' is good for the country, in contrast with the disease Macbeth brings to Scotland. • V.ii: The thanes discuss the disease infecting the body politic and how they must 'purge' Scotland to restore health to the 'sickly weal'. • V.iii: Macbeth asks the Doctor to 'cast the water' of the land and find her 'disease' – ironically wondering what medicine might help.
Imperative verbs	• I.iii: Macbeth attempts to command the Witches ('Speak, I charge you'). He believes he is in control. • I.v: Lady Macbeth uses imperatives to command the 'spirits' ('Unsex me here' 'fill me'). • I.v: Lady Macbeth commands her husband ('look like...'), demonstrating her dominance. • II.ii: Lady Macbeth remains in command ('Wash...', 'Carry...') • III.ii: Macbeth reverses roles with Lady Macbeth. He commands her ('Be innocent...') and calls on darkness ('Come...'). • IV.i: Macbeth again thinks he can command the Witches ('Call 'em...'), but he is actually ensnared by them. • V.i: Lady Macbeth recalls her early imperatives, but they hold no power ('Put...')
Milk	• I.v: Lady Macbeth says that Macbeth is 'too full o' the milk of human kindness / To catch the nearest way'. • I.v: Lady Macbeth calls on the spirits to 'take [her] milk for gall'. • I.vii: Lady Macbeth recalls 'how tender 'tis to love the babe that milks me'.

Names	• I.v: Macbeth refers to Lady Macbeth as his 'dearest partner of greatness', revealing his affection and dependence on her. • II.ii: Lady Macbeth refers to Macbeth for the first time as 'my husband' – he has become the man she wants him to be. • III.ii: Lady Macbeth calls Macbeth 'my lord', highlighting the growing distance between them. • III.ii: Macbeth diminishes Lady Macbeth with the phrase 'dearest chuck'. • V.v: On hearing of Lady Macbeth's death, Macbeth says 'she...', demonstrating the fracture of the relationship.
Nature and the unnatural	• I.iii: Banquo emphasises the Witches' unnatural appearance ('so withered and so wild...', 'beards...'). • I.iii: Thoughts of regicide cause Macbeth's heart to beat 'against the use of nature'. • I.v: Lady Macbeth desires to be filled with unnatural cruelty ('take my milk for gall'). • II.i: As Macbeth approaches Duncan's chamber, 'nature seems dead'. Goodness has been corrupted by his malevolent lust for power. • II.iii: Duncan's wounds look like a 'breach in nature', because the natural order has been destroyed. • II.iv: The Old Man notes unnatural happenings, which echo the unnatural 'deed'. • IV.ii: Macduff lacks the 'natural touch' as he has put his country above his family. • V.i: Lady Macbeth experiences a 'perturbation in nature' due to her unnatural deeds.
Sleep	• II.i: Banquo cannot find peace in 'repose' – the Witches have unsettled his mind. • II.ii: Macbeth has 'murder[ed] sleep' because he will be tormented by guilt. • III.ii: Macbeth is haunted by 'terrible dreams'. • III.iv: Lady Macbeth says Macbeth 'lack[s]...sleep'. They find no rest from the torment they have unleashed.

APPENDIX C: LIST OF PRODUCTIONS

All of these productions are available to stream or purchase online, as of early 2026. The majority are accessible via Drama Online, or NT Live at Home.

Certain productions (by Hynes, Boyd and Ninagawa) are mentioned for specific brilliant ideas, but may not be available online in their entirety.

This list is slightly biased towards UK stage productions, primarily because of their availability in the classroom. Of course we encourage teachers to explore further afield; Macbeth has inspired artists from all over the world, from Kurosawa's *Throne of Blood* to Vishal Bhardwaj's *Maqbool*. (Both of these make excellent viewing and could inspire a comparative study for an advanced class.) Be bold and resolute in your exploration!

1948: Dir. Orson Welles, Republic Pictures. M: Orson Welles, LM: Jeanette Nolan

1979: Dir. Sir Trevor Nunn, Royal Shakespeare Company. M: Sir Ian McKellen, LM: Dame Judi Dench

1980: Dir. Ninagawa Yukio, Toho. M: Hira Mikijiro, LM: Kurihara Komaki

2010: Dir. Rupert Goold, Chichester Festival Theatre, BBC. M: Sir Patrick Stewart, LM: Kate Fleetwood

2011: Dir. Michael Boyd, Royal Shakespeare Company. M: Jonathan Slinger, LM: Aislín McGuckin

2013: Dir. Sir Kenneth Branagh and Rob Ashford, Manchester International Festival. M: Sir Kenneth Branagh, LM: Alex Kingston

2014: Dir. Eve Best, Shakespeare's Globe. M: Joseph Millson, LM: Samantha Spiro

2018: Dir. Polly Findlay, Royal Shakespeare Company. M: Christopher Eccleston, LM: Niamh Cusack

2018: Dir. Sir Rufus Norris, National Theatre. M: Rory Kinnear, LM: Ann-Marie Duff

2021: Dir. Joel Coen, A24. M: Denzel Washington, LM: Frances McDormand

2023: Dir. Max Webster, Donmar Warehouse. M: David Tennant, LM: Cush Jumbo

2024: Dir. Simon Godwin, various co-producers. M: Ralph Fiennes, LM: Indira Varma

2025: Dir. Garry Hynes, Druid Theatre Company. M: Marty Rea, LM: Marie Mullen

REFERENCES

Bloch, M. (1973) *The Royal Touch: Sacred Monarchy and Scrofula in England and France.* London: Routledge.

Carroll, W. C. (2014) 'Fleance in the Final Scene of Macbeth: The Return of the Repressed'. in Hatchuel, Vienne-Guerrin and Bladen (eds) (2014). *Shakespeare on Screen: Macbeth* (pp. 263–280). [Ebook] Presses universitaires de Rouen et du Havre.

Curry, J. (2010) *Shakespeare on Stage.* London: Nick Hern Books.

Education Endowment Foundation (2021) 'Cognitive Science Approaches in the Classroom'. Available at: educationendowmentfoundation.org.uk/education-evidence/evidence-reviews/cognitive-science-approaches-in-the-classroom [Accessed: 7.3.26]

Hanratty, C. (2023) 'Episodes 43 and 44'. *The Hamlet Podcast.* Available at: www.thehamletpodcast.com/episodes-macbeth [Accessed: 7.3.26]

Hawkins, E. (1885) *Medallic Illustrations of the History of Great Britain and Ireland to the Death of George II* (p.196). London: British Museum.

Holinshed, R. et al (1587) *Chronicles of England, Scotland and Irelande.* London: J. Johnson.

Quigley, A. (2018) 'Vocabulary Knowledge and the "Frayer Model"'. Available at: alexquigley.co.uk/vocabulary-knowledge-and-the-frayer-model/ [Accessed: 7.3.26]

Rackin, P. (2005) *Shakespeare and Women.* Oxford: OUP.

Rodell, W. (2013) *The Coronation Chair and Stone of Scone - History, Archaeology and Conservation.* Oxford: Oxbow Books.

Shakespeare, W. (2008) *Macbeth.* New Cambridge Shakespeare updated edition. Edited by A. R. Braunmuller. Cambridge: CUP.

Shakespeare, W. (2015) *Macbeth.* Arden edition. Edited by S. Clark and P. Mason. London: Bloomsbury.

Watson, F. (2010) *Macbeth: A True Story.* London: Quercus.

Webb, J. (2025) 'What Should We Do For Our Disadvantaged Pupils?', Talk at Framwellgate School Durham, 21 February 2025.

FURTHER READING

Shakespeare

- Ackroyd, P. (2006) *Shakespeare: The Biography*. London: Vintage.
- Bryson, B. (2016) *Shakespeare*. London: HarperCollins.
- Dench, J. (2024) *Shakespeare: The Man Who Pays the Rent*. London: Penguin.
- O'Brien, P. (ed.) (2024) *Folger Guide to Teaching Macbeth*. London: Simon and Schuster.
- Hanratty, C. (2020) *Shakespeare in the Theatre: Yukio Ninagawa*. London: Bloomsbury.
- Greenblatt, S. (2004) *Will in the World: How Shakespeare Became Shakespeare*. London: Jonathan Cape.
- Pryke, S. and Staniforth, A. (2020) *Ready to Teach: Macbeth*. London: John Catt.
- Shapiro, J. (2015) *1606: Shakespeare and the Year of Lear*. London: Faber.
- Smith, E. (2020) *This is Shakespeare*. London: Penguin.

Online resources

- Conor Hanratty's Macbeth series of *The Hamlet Podcast* (2022-23) is available at www.thehamletpodcast.com/episodes-macbeth
- Amy Smith's teaching and revision resources are available on www.amysmithliterature.wordpress.com

Teaching and learning

- Davies, S. (2020) *Talking About Oracy*. London: John Catt.
- Fletcher-Wood, H. (2018) *Responsive Teaching*. Abingdon: Routledge.
- Gaunt, A. and Scott, A. (2019) *Transform Teaching and Learning Through Talk: The Oracy Imperative*. London: Rowman & Littlefield.
- Jones, K. (2019) *Retrieval Practice*. London: John Catt.
- Kolota, J. (2024) *Empowering EAL Learners in Secondary Schools*. Abingdon: Routledge.
- Quigley, A. (2020) *Closing the Reading Gap*. Abingdon: Routledge.
- Quigley, A. (2022) *Closing the Writing Gap*. Abingdon: Routledge.
- Sherrington, T. (2019) *Rosenshine's Principles in Action*. London: John Catt.
- Webb, J. (2021) *The Metacognition Handbook*. London: John Catt.

INDEX

A

B

C

D

E

S

T

U

V

W

Y